Essentials of Early English

'The author puts the essence of the History of English into the reader's hand. As the comprehensive histories bulk ever larger, the merits of a lean but not mean little digest like Smith's shine the brighter.'

Mary Blockley, *University of Texas at Austin*

Essentials of Early English is a practical and highly accessible introduction to the early stages of the English language: Old English, Middle English, and Early Modern English.

Designed specifically as a handbook for students beginning the study of early English language, whether for linguistic or literary purposes, it presumes little or no prior knowledge of the history of English.

Features include:

- numerous illustrative texts with accompanying notes
- an annotated bibliography to guide students towards further study
- thematic index of key terms used

A contextual introduction of the history of English is provided, which includes an outline of English in relation to its origins. A deeper analysis is then given on each of the three key stages of early English: Old, Middle and Early Modern English, using the language of King Alfred, Chaucer and Shakespeare respectively to illustrate points.

Each section follows a coherent structure with clear descriptions of spelling, pronunciation and main grammatical features. The essential characteristics of each stage of the language are provided to create the ideal coursebook for History of English courses and to give the student a firm foundation of basic linguistic knowledge which can be applied to further study.

Jeremy J. Smith is Reader in English Language at the University of Glasgow and has been actively teaching Early English for 20 years. He is the author of *An Historical Study of English* (1996).

LONDON AND NEW YORK

Essentials of
Early English

Jeremy J. Smith

ROUTLEDGE

First published 1999
by Routledge
11 New Fetter Lane, London EC4P 4EE

Simultaneously published in the USA
and Canada
by Routledge 29 West 35th Street,
New York, NY 10001

*Routledge is an imprint of the Taylor &
Francis Group*

© 1999 Jeremy J. Smith

Typeset in Times Ten by Keystroke,
Jacaranda Lodge, Wolverhampton

Printed and bound in Great Britain by
TJ International Ltd, Padstow, Cornwall

*British Library Cataloguing in
Publication Data*
A catalogue record for this book is
available from the British Library

*Library of Congress Cataloguing in
Publication Data*
Smith, J. J. (Jeremy J.)
  Essentials of Early English / by
Jeremy J. Smith.
    p.   cm.
    Includes index.
    1. English language—Grammar,
Historical—Handbooks, manuals, etc.
2. English language—Old English, ca.
450–1100—Grammar—Handbooks,
manuals, etc. 3. English language—
Middle English, 1100–1500—
Grammar—Handbooks, manuals, etc. 4.
English language—Early modern,
1500–1700—Grammar—Handbooks,
manuals, etc. I. Title.
PE1101.S58   1999
420′.9–dc21   98–48143
                                                CIP

ISBN 0–415–18743–5 (pbk)
ISBN 0–415–18742–7 (hbk)

For my parents

Contents

Section B Middle English texts 175

Section C Early Modern English texts 199

PART III BIBLIOGRAPHY, GLOSSARY AND THEMATIC INDEX 221

Preface

This book is designed as a practical handbook for students beginning the study of earlier stages of the English language, whose eventual aim is to proceed to more advanced work on the history of English, or on earlier English literature, or on both.

Although most courses in English studies offered by major universities include a component on the historical study of English, and on earlier states of the language, it is my impression that there is a paucity of clear descriptive accounts of the various stages of English for beginning students, laid out on modern lines and clarifying the connections between each stage. I believe that there is a need for what might be called, using a rather traditional term, a 'primer' in Early English, in which the essential characteristics of each stage of the language can be identified and the differences and similarities between the stages can be made explicit.

This book is designed to meet that need. Once a knowledge of the prototypical characteristics of Old, Middle and Early Modern English has been secured, it is hoped that students can then develop their knowledge of each stage of the language on a firm foundation. In short, I regard this book as a 'prequel' to more advanced books, enabling a swifter and more effective engagement with the materials there presented. It is for that reason that I have added an

Annotated Bibliography; it is hoped that this may act as a guide to the next stage in the sequential pattern of learning which this book promotes.

It is expected that students and their teachers will use this book in various ways appropriate to the conditions of the institution where they use it. However, it is envisaged that the most common approach to using the book will shift from text to discussion and then back to text again, concentrating on those passages in the grammars which are marked as of greatest importance. The trickiest material is obviously that to do with Old English, yet it is in my opinion essential that this material is not avoided; to discuss the history of English without reference to Old English, when the essential configuration of the language was established, seems to me misguided.

Any publication of the kind here presented must draw necessarily and heavily on the work of earlier scholars. In preparing this publication, I have found the following books, all of which are discussed in the Bibliography, of particular usefulness: Barber (1976), Burrow and Turville-Petre (1997 edn), Görlach (1991), Leech, Deuchar and Hoogenraad (1982), MacMahon (1997 edn), Mitchell and Robinson (1995 edn), Simpson (1985) and Sweet (rev. Davis, 1953).

Some may object that this book is focused on the emerging standard language and its predecessors. I would have much sympathy with such a criticism. Although it so happens that, for various reasons and at various times, standardised usages of diverse origins have been the only ones substantially recorded in the written mode, there is nevertheless an immense amount of evidence for the dialects and sociolects of English from the past – much of it still needing scholarly investigation. However, to have engaged with this material would have substantially lengthened the book and made it less suitable for the purposes for which it is designed. I have tried to hint at this diversity by means of appendices to the key descriptive chapters.

One variety not treated here in any detail, and which deserves greater attention, is Scots. Scots is, apart from English itself, the longest-attested variety derived from Old English; parallel introductory surveys, from different perspectives, are currently in preparation (G. Caie and J.J. Smith, *A Book of Older Scots*, forthcoming, and A. King, *An Introduction to Scots and Scottish English*, forthcoming), and a new major survey has just been published (C. Jones ed., *The Edinburgh History of the Scots Language*, Edinburgh: Edinburgh University Press, 1997).

Finally, I am sure that some teachers will complain about the normalisation of much of the Old English material on the basis of Early West Saxon, which is of course a somewhat (though not entirely) artificial variety. I make no apology for this. Early West Saxon was adopted by Henry Sweet in his great *Primer* of 1882, for excellent reasons to do with the study of the history of the language. I can think of no better forebear. As for normalisation itself: it may be noted that Old Icelandic, a cognate language frequently taught alongside OE, is generally taught in a normalised form without any complaint from scholars, and for an excellent reason: it is easier for beginners if they grasp prototypical usages at the outset of their study and *then* become aware of non-prototypical variations. The same, I believe, applies for Old English studies. Experience has taught me that students can easily despair if faced with what are really quite trivial variations at the very beginning of their studies.

Many people have helped in the preparation of this book, and in the various privately printed publications which have preceded it over the years. In particular, I should like to thank Jean Anderson, Merja Black, Mary Blockley, Graham Caie, Manfred Görlach, Richard Hamer, Ian Hamilton, Elaine Higgleton, Simon Horobin, Carole Hough, Christian Kay, Katie Lowe, Mike MacMahon, Jane Roberts, Michael Samuels, John Smith and Jane Stuart-Smith, all of whom have read and commented on part or on all of the book, or helped with advice or in other ways at one stage or another. I am also grateful for the comments of anonymous referees. My publishers have been, as ever, exceptionally encouraging, efficient and courteous, and I should like to thank in particular Jody Ball, Miranda Filbee, Beth Humphries and Louisa Semlyen. Above all, however, I should like to thank the many Glasgow colleagues and students who over the years have used, commented on and suffered from various versions of parts of this book. I should of course be very grateful for any further comments on the book, either from fellow-teachers or from students.

Students and teachers may be interested to know that a software package of interactive exercises to accompany the Old English component of this book has been produced. Enquiries should be addressed in the first instance to my co-author in that enterprise, Jean Anderson (Manager, STELLA Project, University of Glasgow,

GLASGOW G12 8QQ, Scotland; J.Anderson@arts.gla.ac.uk). Details are also available on the World Wide Web (http://www.gla.ac. uk/EngLang/).

Jeremy J. Smith
Glasgow 1998

Part one

Descriptive material

Introduction

1.1 About this book

This book has been planned as a practical, straightforward introduction for those beginning to study the early states of the English language, whether for linguistic or for literary purposes. It is divided into three Parts: Part I, consisting of descriptive material; Part II, consisting of illustrative texts with brief accompanying notes; and Part III, consisting of an Annotated Bibliography, an Old English glossary and a thematic index. Although it is designed to be self-standing, it is best used as an accompaniment to standard introductory histories of the language, and as a prequel to the more advanced books which currently serve as standard introductory surveys. All these works are described below in the Annotated Bibliography.

This book assumes little or no knowledge of the history of the language or even of the descriptive terminology needed to talk meaningfully about it. This contextualising Introduction, which includes a skeleton outline of the history of English in relation to its origins, is therefore followed in Chapter 2 by a short description of the linguistic terminology used elsewhere in the book. If readers are confident of their knowledge of phonetics, grammar, etc., they may, if they wish, skip this chapter.

This general sketch of linguistic terminology is followed by three descriptive chapters (3, 4 and 5) concerned with three stages in the history of English: Old English, Middle English and Early Modern English. The descriptions of these language-states provided here are focused on, although not restricted to, three usages which may be regarded as in some senses prototypical: the languages of King Alfred, of Chaucer and of Shakespeare respectively. Of these, Chapter 3 is the longest, since, although Old English is the most distant from present-day usage, the essential linguistic configuration of subsequent states of the language was established in Old English times. (It is for that reason that any student of the history of English needs at least a basic understanding of the structure of Old English – indeed, it may be argued that to study the history of English without a knowledge of Old English is to build on sand.) These descriptions make up the core of Part I of the book.

In Part II a set of illustrative and annotated texts is provided. These are designed simply as illustrations of the points made in Chapters 3, 4 and 5; it is expected that readers and teachers will want to supplement them with other material from other textbooks.

These descriptions are followed in Part III by suggestions for further reading and study. Although for simplicity's sake references in the body of the book have been avoided, this Annotated Bibliography has been provided so that students can pursue particular issues in greater depth than is possible here. Also included in Part III is a Glossary to the OE texts in Part II.

It is hoped that students who have worked their way through the book will have acquired a clear understanding of the structure of the various stages of early English. They should then be able to proceed to further study with a secure foundation of basic linguistic knowledge – essential whether the focus of their future work is to be philological/linguistic or more literary. It is held here that any philological work without such a foundation of core-knowledge is largely a waste of time. Moreover, any literary appreciation of stylistic choices made in earlier states of the language must surely be based on a secure grasp of what choices were available at the time.

1.2 A short history of English

English is now used as a first language by about 700 million speakers, and is a second language for many millions more. It appears in many guises, ranging from the 'new' Englishes of Africa and Asia, e.g. Indian English, through the usages of North America to the oldest established varieties (the English of England, Hiberno-English and Scots in Lowland Scotland). English is now the most widespread language in linguistic function and geographical extent that the world has ever seen.

The modern varieties of English have emerged over the last five or six centuries through contact with other languages and through dynamic interaction with each other. All, however, derive from one ultimate source: the Germanic language-variety which was brought to southern and eastern Britain from northern Germany by Anglo-Saxon invaders in the fifth century AD. The people who spoke this variety supplanted the Romano-British inhabitants, who gradually retreated to the northern and western parts of the island where, in North Wales and the Gaelic-speaking areas of Scotland, they remain. The invaders' language subsequently became a distinct language, English, which developed and spread within the British Isles up to the sixteenth century. English was taken beyond these islands with the imperial expansions of the seventeenth, eighteenth and nineteenth centuries.

During these centuries the structure of the English language changed radically. Our evidence for these changes comes, of course, not from the direct analysis of speech – for sound-recordings of English only began to be made at the end of the nineteenth century – but from comparative study of other languages, and through the painstaking analysis by scholars of the written records which have come down to us continuously from the seventh century onwards.

All Germanic languages derive from a common ancestor known as Proto-Germanic, which seems to have emerged during the third millennium BC as the language of a group of people living in what is now Denmark and southern Sweden. English is a member of the western branch of the Germanic languages, which also includes German, Dutch, Afrikaans, and (its closest Germanic relative) Frisian, this last being a language-variety spoken in what is now part of the Netherlands. Other branches of Germanic which are traditionally identified include North Germanic (Danish, Norwegian, Swedish, Faroese, Icelandic) and East Germanic (now extinct, and recorded for the most part in the fourth-century Gothic Bible translation of Bishop Ulfilas).

The Germanic languages are themselves part of a much larger language-family: the Indo-European group, which includes such diverse languages as Bengali and Brythonic, Russian and Romany, Sanskrit and Spanish. This group stems ultimately from Proto-Indo-European, which was probably originally spoken in what is now southern Russia many millennia ago. Scholars date this culture to anywhere between 7000 and 4000 BC.

English shares a number of characteristics with its Germanic relations. Probably the best-known of these is the Germanic modification of inherited consonantal sounds known as Grimm's Law, so-called after the philologist and folklorist J. Grimm (1785–1863). Grimm showed that there was a regular set of consonantal differences between the Germanic languages and the others of the

Indo-European family, which dated from the period of divergence of Proto-Germanic from the other Indo-European varieties. The effects of Grimm's Law in Old English can be seen through comparing groups of *cognates*, i.e. words in different languages with a common ancestor (cf. Latin *co* + *gnātus* 'born together'). Thus, for instance, *p* in other Indo-European languages corresponds to *f/v* in Germanic languages, e.g. FATHER (German *Vater*, but Latin *pater*, French *père*, Italian *padre*, Sanskrit *pitar-*), FOOT (Dutch *voet*, but Latin *pes*, *ped-*, French *pied*, Sanskrit *padám* FOOTSTEP), etc.

The discovery of such shared linguistic features has made it possible to reconstruct the relationships of the languages which derive from Proto-Indo-European. However, it is worth remembering that, just as children derive some of their linguistic behaviour from their parents but are also strongly influenced by their peer group, so language-varieties 'borrow' usages from those language-varieties with which they come into contact and transmit these acquired characteristics to future generations. Indeed, without such contacts the processes of linguistic change would have been much slower in operation: such a slow-moving pattern is observable in languages which have little contact with others (for instance Icelandic, which has been an isolated language for much of the last thousand years, has changed little compared with English during the same period). The history of English is not one of internal evolution, hermetically sealed from outside influences. Rather, its history is one of constant and dynamic interaction between inherited usage and the languages with which it has come into contact.

It is traditional to distinguish between **external history**, i.e. the changing functions of varieties of the vernacular in relation to other languages and to broader developments in society, and **internal history**, i.e. the changing forms of the language. This distinction has been adopted here for the sake of simplicity of organisation, although it is worth remembering that linguistic function and linguistic form are closely related over time and have affected each other very profoundly.

1.3 External history

The earliest forms of English were very different from those in present-day use, and the modern configuration has taken many centuries to emerge. The history of English is traditionally divided into a sequence of epochs distinguished by certain language-external events and characterised by language-internal differences.

When the Germanic invaders began to settle in what had been a province of the Roman Empire, Britannia, they developed there a distinct variety of Germanic which has become known as English. The following broad periods are generally recognised, although there is a good deal of scholarly debate about the precise boundaries between them.

Prehistoric Old English ('pre-Old English'): the period before written records, roughly 450–650/700 AD. During this period English diverged from the other members of the Germanic group to become a distinct language.

Old English, often referred to as Anglo-Saxon after the Germanic tribes who used it: the period from the appearance of written records in English to the Norman Conquest of 1066. During this period, English was used nationally for the documentary purposes of Anglo-Saxon government. It also had a literary function: the epic poem *Beowulf* was copied in a manuscript dating from *circa* 1000, and the end of the period saw the emergence of a formidable native prose tradition with the composition of the *Anglo-Saxon Chronicle* and the religious homilies of Ælfric and Wulfstan. Most Old English which has come down to us is written in the West Saxon dialect, since the national focus of power for much of the period lay in the south-western kingdom of Wessex. However, the Old English written record provides evidence for at least three other dialect-groupings: Old Mercian in the Midlands, Old Northumbrian in northern England and in what later became Lowland Scotland to the south of the Clyde–Forth line, and Kentish in south-east England.

Towards the end of the Anglo-Saxon period, large numbers of North Germanic (Scandinavian) peoples settled in northern England. Their language, in part because (so some scholars have argued) it seems to have been to a degree mutually intelligible with local varieties of Old English, had a profound effect on the subsequent history of English beyond the area of primary Scandinavian settlement. However, Scandinavian left little mark on the written record until after the Norman Conquest of 1066.

Middle English: the period from the Norman Conquest to the arrival of printing in Britain in 1476. The Conquest saw the large-scale replacement of the old Anglo-Saxon aristocracy with a French-speaking and European-centred elite. Although English remained in widespread use in speech, it lost in national status in writing; documentary functions were taken over by Latin, which was undergoing a revival in Western Europe, while many literary functions were taken over by varieties of French. The French-speaking elite seems to have shifted quite rapidly and generally to the use of the vernacular in speech, but French remained in prestigious use until at least the end of the fourteenth century. English, for much of the Middle Ages, was essentially of local significance, primarily used in its written form for initial education and for the production of texts with a local readership; it was thus strongly marked by dialectal variation in writing. This situation changed towards the end of the period. Geoffrey Chaucer's *Canterbury Tales*, written for an aristocratic and metropolitan audience *ca.* 1390–1400, marks one stage in the emergence of the vernacular as having a national significance, as does the translation of the Bible into English associated with the proto-Protestant Wycliffite movement at the end of the fourteenth century.

Towards the end of the Middle English period, distinct varieties of the language emerged outside England: **Older Scots** in Lowland Scotland, and **Hiberno-English** in eastern Ireland.

Early Modern English: the period from 1476 to the early eighteenth century. Caxton's introduction of printing to England at the end of the fifteenth century coincided with the elaboration of English as a vernacular capable of being used for all linguistic functions. The role of English was given impetus by the Protestant Reformation, which placed a religious duty of literacy on all, and provided national texts for the purpose: the vernacular Bible and Prayer Book. This national role coincided with the standardisation of written English and with the emergence during the sixteenth century of a prestigious form of pronunciation. Evolving class-structures in society, notably the rise of a powerful London bourgeoisie, provided audiences for sophisticated vernacular texts, such as the dramas of Elizabethan and Jacobean England, and the prestige of the vernacular was reinforced by the victories of the rising middle classes in the mid-seventeenth-century Civil War.

The foundation of the modern British state following the Act of Union between England, Wales and Scotland (1707) may be taken as an external marker of the end of the Early Modern period. Older Scots continued to be used up to this date, although it underwent severe competition from the forces of Anglicisation, particularly in

9

religious discourse. During the Early Modern period, new varieties of English/Scots appeared in overseas settlements such as the Plantations in Ulster from the end of the sixteenth century, and in the British Colonies in North America.

The Old, Middle and Early Modern English periods have sometimes been classed together as 'Early English'. This book is primarily concerned with this Early English period.

Later Modern English: the period from the early eighteenth century to the present day. Tendencies already prefigured in earlier centuries, such as the development of mass literacy and of urban varieties, came to fruition during this period. It is also the period when overt pride in the English language was most clearly signalled, notably with the arrival of large-scale codifications such as Samuel Johnson's *Dictionary* of 1755. Above all, the defining linguistic characteristic of this period is the spread of English beyond its place of origin, to the various parts of the Empire and later, with the cultural hegemony of the United States, to the new electronic media.

After 1707 Older Scots developed into Modern Scots, but became much more restricted in register, to non-prestigious speech and to specialised usages, e.g. in the verse of Robert Burns. Subsequent attempts to reinstate Scots as a national, i.e. Scottish, vernacular rather than as a collection of local varieties have met so far with mixed success. Other varieties within the English-language continuum have emerged as elaborated usages in their own right, e.g. Indian English, where a special variety with its own distinctive grammatical, lexical and accentual properties has emerged as a national prestigious usage. It is interesting that many of these varieties derive not from the prestigious usages of the British Isles but from non-standard ones.

1.4 Internal history

All of the developments in the social function of English described above left their mark on the internal evolution of the language, at every level: in pronunciation and spelling, in grammar and in vocabulary. The following is a brief sketch of material covered in greater detail later in this book; it is offered here as an outline only.

Spelling: Towards the end of the Old English period, spelling became standardised on the basis of West Saxon, for reasons already given above; but during the Middle English period it became usual for dialectal variation to be manifested in spelling. There are therefore, for instance, no fewer than 500 ways of spelling the simple word THROUGH in Middle English, ranging from fairly recognisable *thurgh, thorough* and *þorowe* to exotic-seeming *drowgȝ, yhurght, trghug* and *trowffe*. As long as English was used simply on a local basis this practice was comparatively unproblematic, since the phonic conventions of each locality could be accepted comparatively easily within that locality as an appropriate reflection of pronunciation. However, the inconvenience of not having a national system became much more apparent when English started to take on national functions once again. By the beginning of the fifteenth century the usage developed in London was starting to take on a national role, and London spelling of this period is in its essentials the basis of the present-day English pattern. During the sixteenth century, a parallel standardised Scottish system competed for a while with London spelling in Scotland, and a slightly modified form of the system appeared in the United States at the end of the eighteenth century (thus distinctions of the *coloured–colored* type) and has been subsequently sustained there and elsewhere.

Pronunciation: The reconstruction of pronunciation during the Old and Middle English periods is based upon a mixture of evidence of greater or lesser value: the interpretation of spellings, the analysis of rhyming practice in verse, comparison with other languages and with later states of the language. The major development in the history of English is a phenomenon called the Great Vowel Shift, which affected the 'long vowels' of later Middle English. This sound-change, which probably arose in London as a result of complex processes of social interaction, may be dated to the period between 1400 and 1600 by the evidence of words coming into the language. Thus *doubt* and *guile*, words derived from French which entered the language before 1400, were subjected to the diphthongisation processes of the Shift, while *soup* and *tureen*, later adoptions, were not so subjected.

The evidence for a standard form of pronunciation is uncertain until the sixteenth century. In 1589 the author of *The Arte of English Poesie*, almost certainly a writer called George Puttenham, advises the accomplished poet to adopt the accentual usage of *the better brought vp sort*.

ye shall therfore take the vsuall speach of the Court, and that of London and the shires lying about London within lx. myles, and not much aboue.

The history of standard pronunciation is a complex matter, and the evolution of present-day prestigious accents is a matter of inter-action of varieties rather than a simple process of descent. However, broadly speaking, Puttenham's description still holds for England at least, although other prestigious accents are found widely throughout the English-speaking world. Thus the accent-component of Scottish Standard English is prestigious in Scotland, and the accentual variety known as General American is prestigious in the United States.

Grammar: In grammar, the major change between Old and Present-Day English is the shift from **synthesis** to **analysis** in express-ing grammatical relations. Whereas the relationships within and between phrases in Present-Day English are largely expressed by word-order, in Old English these relationships are expressed to a much greater extent by special endings attached to words. These endings are called inflexions.

The Old English inflexional system means that Old English word-order can be much more flexible than that of its descendant. Thus, in Present-Day English

(1) The lord binds the servant
(2) The servant binds the lord

mean very different things. The word-order indicates the relative functions of the phrases *the lord* and *the servant*. This was not necessarily the case in Old English. Sentence (1) above can be trans-lated into Old English as

(3) *Se hlāford bint þone cnapan.*

NOTE: the letter *þ* corresponds to Present-Day English TH. See further Chapter 3 below.

However, it could also be translated as

(4) *þone cnapan bint se hlāford.*
(5) *Se hlāford þone cnapan bint.*

and so on. In sentences (3)–(5) above, the phrase *se hlāford*, because it is in the so-called nominative case, with a nominative form of the definite article 'the' (*se*) is always the subject of the clause in whatever position it appears. And, because it is in the so-called accusative case, with an accusative form of the definite article (*þone*) and an accusative inflexion on the accompanying noun (*-an*), *þone cnapan* is always the direct object of the clause. The cases, not the word-order, here determine the relationship between the two phrases. There were conventions in Old English that placed the subject in initial position, but these conventions could easily be departed from for stylistic effect.

NOTE: Some of the technical terms just used may be unfamiliar to some readers. They will be defined further in Chapters 2 and 3 below.

This system did not survive intact into the Middle English period; it appears that interaction with Scandinavian encouraged the loss of inflexions, and the conventions of word-order, whereby subject/object positioning had become stylistically formalised, became more fixed to take over the task originally performed by inflexions. The Present-Day English pattern resulted. However, it is wrong to describe Present-Day English as wholly uninflected: a few inflexions remain, even if we do not call them such (cf. *Tom, Tom's, pig, pig's, pigs*, etc.).

Lexicon: Perhaps most obviously, there have been changes in the lexicon between Old and Present-Day English, and these changes reflect the kinds of linguistic contacts which the language has under-gone. Although much of the core vocabulary of English is derived from Old English – e.g. *hand, head, wife, child, stone, name, man, fish, ride, choose, bind, love*, etc. – the lexicon in general has been greatly augmented by borrowings from other languages.

Scandinavian has affected some of the most basic features of the language, such as the pronoun system – *they, them* and *their* are all from Scandinavian – and the system of grammatical inflexion, e.g. the *-s* endings on some parts of the verb-paradigm in *loves*. Further, some items of core vocabulary are Scandinavian in origin, e.g. *take, ill, egg, skin*. More subtly, cognate forms in Scandinavian and English have developed distinct meanings, e.g. *skirt, shirt*, and many Scandinavian words are found only in some varieties, e.g. *kirk*.

French has had a massive effect on the range of vocabulary available in the language. To exemplify from the noun alone: words such as *action, bucket, calendar, courtesy, damage, envy, face, grief, honour, joy, labour, marriage, noise, opinion, people, quality, rage, reason, sound, spirit, task, use, vision, waste*, all of which are common in Present-Day English usage, are all derived from French. Many French words are found in high-register contexts, and this means that their meanings in English diverge from those in French, e.g. *commence, regard* which have high-register connotations in English not shared by French *commencer, regarder.*

Of course, numerous other languages have had an effect on English, reflecting various cultural and imperial developments. Latin learning, sometimes mediated through French, has given English words such as *arbiter, pollen, junior, vertigo* and *folio.* Contact with the world beyond Western Europe has given most of the European languages such words as *harem* (Arabic), *steppe* (Russian), *taboo* (Tongan), *chocolate* (Nahuatl/Aztec), and imperial expansion in India gave English such items as *thug, pyjama, gymkhana* and *mulligatawny.*

The hospitality of English to foreign words has often been commented on; indeed, borrowing is the characteristic method whereby English expands its vocabulary, something which marks English off from its near relatives such as German. Old English, like modern German, created new words through compounds, e.g. *sciprāp* (*cable*: lit. 'ship-rope'); cf. German *Fernseher* (*television*: lit. 'far-seer'). However, this is no longer a marked feature of Present-Day English. One reason for this change must be to do with the grammatical structure of the later states of the English language: there is no need to fit borrowed forms into a complex inflexional system. Another reason is probably to do with custom: the more English borrowed, the more borrowing became customary; the more borrowing became customary, the more English borrowed.

1.5 A preliminary illustration

The definitions given in the preceding paragraphs are based on external criteria of varying social/cultural significance, and on broad linguistic differences. It may reasonably be argued that such clear-cut criteria giving beginning and end-dates are fundamentally misleading: after all, English folk did not go to sleep on the day before the Battle of Hastings speaking Old English and awake the day after speaking Middle English. In subsequent chapters a more detailed set of language-internal criteria will be offered for prototypical examples of each of the stages of Early English distinguished above, accompanied by a preliminary annotated reader in Early English.

To conclude this introductory section, some examples of the various language-states described will be given, providing parallel versions of the same text. For cultural reasons, the text which is most easily found in parallel versions is the Lord's Prayer. No detailed analysis of these texts is offered here; it is enough at this stage to note that (1) the Old English passage looks to the untutored reader like a foreign language, emphasised by the appearance of unfamiliar letter-forms, (2) several later medieval versions are offered, of varying familiarity depending on the dialect represented, and (3) even the Alternative Service Book version offered as an example of Present-Day English has certain features which might be regarded as archaic. It is suggested that students return to these texts when they have completed the rest of the book, and carry out some analyses of their own.

Old English (West Saxon, late ninth century)
þū ūre fæder, þe eart on heofonum, sīe þīn nama gehālgod. Cume þīn rīce. Sīe þīn wylla on eorþan swā swā on heofonum. Syle ūs tōdæg ūrne dæghwāmlican hlāf. And forgief ūs ūre gyltas swā swā wē forgiefaþ þæm þe wið ūs āgyltaþ. And ne lǣd þū nā ūs on costnunge, ac ālīes ūs fram yfele.

Middle English (Kentish, 1340)
Vader oure þet art ine heuenes, yhalȝed by þin name. Cominde þi riche. Yworþe þi wil ase ine heuene and ine erþe. Bread oure echedayes yef ous today. And uorlet ous oure yeldinges ase and we uorleteþ oure yelderes. And ne ous led naȝt into uondinge, ac vri ous uram queade.

Middle English (Central Midlands, ca. 1380)
Oure fadir, þat art in heuenys, halewid be þi name. Þi kyngdom come to. Be þi wile don ase in heuene and in erþe. Ȝiue to us þis day oure breed ouer oþer substaunse. And forȝiue to us oure dettes, as and we forȝiuen to oure dettouris. And leede us not into temptaciouns, but delyuere us from yuel.

Older Scots (ca. 1520)
Our fader, that art in heuenis, hallewit be thi name. Thi kingdom cum to. Thi wil be done in erde as in heuen. Gefe to vs this day our breid ouer vthir substaunce. And forgif to vs our dettis, as we forgef to our dettouris. And leid vs nocht into temptacioun, bot deliuer vs fra euile.

Early Modern English (Book of Common Prayer, 1549)
Our Father, which art in heaven, Hallowed be thy Name. Thy kingdom come. Thy will be done, in earth as it is in heaven. Give us this day our daily bread. And forgive us our trespasses, As we forgive them that trespass against us. And lead us not into temptation; But deliver us from evil.

Present-Day English (Alternative Service Book)
Our Father in heaven, your name be hallowed; your kingdom come, your will be done, on earth as in heaven. Give us today our daily bread. Forgive us our sins, as we have forgiven those who have sinned against us. And do not bring us to the time of trial, but save us from evil.

Chapter 2

Describing language

2.1 Introduction

If we want to describe something, we need special terms to categorise its various parts. Thus, if we want to talk about, say, motor-cars or flowers, we need technical terms: *engine, tyre, exhaust, petal, stem, leaf.* The same goes for language and the academic discipline, **linguistics**, which seeks to understand it. To understand how language works, and how it is used, we need a special language for describing it. Without such a set of descriptive terms, any discussion about language is little more than vague generalisation. Thus the ability to describe language (the traditional term is **grammar**, though this term is used with a more restricted currency elsewhere in this chapter) can be regarded as an enabling skill. This point has to be made since for many folk (and, for many years, for many schoolteachers) 'grammar' means a set of prescriptive rules to be followed to accord with socially defined educational norms. In this book, grammar means description, not prescription.

The trouble is that many people find the special language generally used for talking about language rather tricky and, indeed, repellent. One reason may be that linguistic categorisation can seem unappealingly technical to those students of humanities who see their subject as opposed to rather than complementary with the so-called 'hard' sciences. Another reason may be because scholars in the field of linguistics have two habits which can seem annoying. One is the habit of using the terminology of language description in subtly different ways depending on which particular school of linguistics the scholar adheres to. Another is the habit of frequently developing new terminology to deal with the refinements of classification which the linguist seeks to make.

In this book, an attempt has been made to avoid using too many technical terms other than those in very common agreed use by linguists. Thus those already used (in Chapter 1 above) will not, it is hoped, have been too much of an obstacle. However, some terminology cannot be avoided, and this chapter introduces and defines some of the most important of those terms and notions which will regularly appear in the chapters that follow. Many, perhaps most, of these terms will be familiar to readers, and those who feel confident of their grasp of linguistic terminology are welcome to skip this chapter.

It is important to note that the account given here is only the very briefest sketch of linguistic categories. If students wish to study the subject further, they should consult some of the books referred to in the Annotated Bibliography in Part III; particularly recommended are MacMahon 1997 and Leech *et al.* 1982. You should also develop the habit, when puzzled by a technical term in later chapters, of consulting the Thematic Index in Part III, whereby (it is hoped) definitions of all terms used can be found easily.

2.2 The levels of language

To understand how language works, a model may be useful. Figure 2.1 is an attempt to schematise the way in which language is used to communicate ideas. The deepest level of language, in this diagram, is **semantics**, i.e. the level of meaning. Given that language is about the transmission of meaning from one person to another, it seems perverse to ignore it here. However, there are philosophical questions as to whether semantics can be deemed properly a part of the linguistic system, and semantics itself will not be a central part of the discussion in this book.

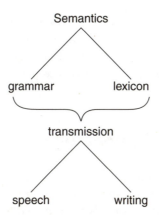

FIGURE 2.1 The levels of language

Meaning is expressed linguistically through the **grammar** and **lexicon** of a language. The lexicon of a language is its wordstock, whereas grammar is to do with the way in which words are put together to form sentences. Most readers are able to recognise **words** in English since they are clearly marked in our writing system, i.e. by spaces being left between them; and the same goes for **sentences**, which typically begin with a capital letter and end with a full stop. In turn, the grammar and lexicon of a language are **transmitted** to other language-users through **speech** or (a comparatively recent development in human history) through **writing**. The remainder of this chapter is divided into sections in accordance with this categorisation of the levels of language.

2.3 Speech and writing

The relationship between speech and writing is quite a complex one. Written English has throughout its history been an alphabetic language, and this means that there has been a broad correlation between individual speech-segments and written symbols. The term used for these written symbols, **letters**, does not need much definition here; the traditional method of teaching children to read, **phonics**, is based on the speech-segment/written-symbol correlation (e.g. 'C – A – T' says CAT'). However, this correlation has been at various times greatly obscured by various conventional usages, and by a temporal lag between writing and speech. Thus for instance, in Present-Day English, the letter *I* has various realisations in speech depending on its position in relation to other letters, cf. *ship*, *life*, *spaghetti*. The same goes for special clusters of letters such as *th* (cf. *thing*, *this*), or 'silent' groups such as *gh* in *night*, *through*. It is for this reason that modern teachers tend to accompany the phonic method of teaching reading in English with a shape-based approach called look-and-say.

2.4 Phonetics and phonology

With regard to speech, a distinction may be made between the linguistic sub-disciplines **phonology** and **phonetics**. Phonology is to do with the way in which sounds are grouped to produce a meaningful utterance; thus we distinguish the meaning of *pat* and *cat* because the replacement of the segment represented by the letter *p* with one represented by the letter *c* changes the meaning of the word. It is worth noting that phonologies are not necessarily the same for varieties of the same language. Thus Scots, for instance, makes a phonological distinction between the sounds represented by *w*, *wh* which Southern English speakers do not (cf. the pronunciation of *which*, *witch* in Scots and Southern English).

The science of phonetics, on the other hand, is to do with the way in which sounds are made, i.e. the whole process whereby air emitted from the lungs interacts with the various organs of the **vocal tract**. (The main part of the **vocal tract** appears as Figure 2.2.)

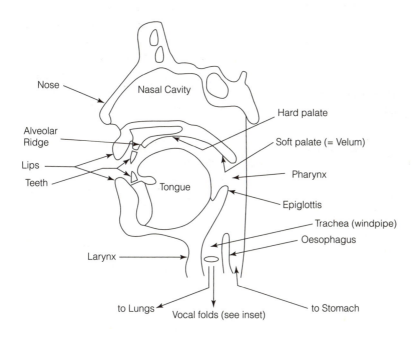

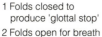

1 Folds closed to produce 'glottal stop'
2 Folds open for breath
3 Folds loosely together and vibrating to produce voiced sounds

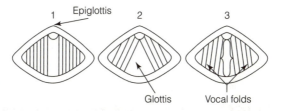

FIGURE 2.2 The vocal tract

To exemplify the concerns of phonetics, we might investigate the realisation of the sound represented by *rr* in *borrow*. Although I live in Scotland, I was brought up as a southern Englishman, and my pronunciation of this sound is what phoneticians call an 'approximant': as the air comes up from my lungs my tongue is curved up to approach the roof of my mouth, but it does not touch any part of it. However, many Scots realise the sound differently as 'taps' or 'trills', the tips of their tongues actually touching the roofs of their mouths. No meaning-change occurs – I can understand Scots speakers when they say *borrow*, and they seem to understand me – but the realisation of the *rr*-sound in the two varieties is very different.

Such distinctions, both in phonology and in phonetic realisation, are matters of **accent**. For various reasons it is extremely useful for scholars to have a set of conventional notations for reflecting pronunciation, supplementing the traditional letters. The best-known set of conventions is that developed by the **International Phonetic Association (IPA)**, whose chart (in simplified form, omitting symbols not generally used in varieties of English) appears as Figure 2.3; the

Place / Manner	Bilabial	Labio-dental	Dental	(Post-)Alveolar	Palato-Alveolar	Palatal	Velar	Labial-velar	Glottal
Nasal	m			n			ŋ		
Plosive	p, b			t, d			k, g		ʔ
Fricative		f, v	θ, ð	s, z	ʃ, ʒ		x, ɣ	ʍ	h
Approximant				ɹ		j		w	
Lateral				l					
Trill				r					
Tap				ɾ					

Consonants

Close

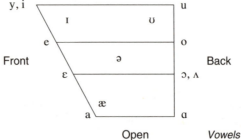

FIGURE 2.3 The phonetic alphabet (after the conventions of the International Phonetic Association)

meaning of the symbols is outlined in 2.4.1 and 2.4.2 below. When these symbols are being used to express phonological distinctions, it is conventional to place them in slash brackets, thus: / . . . /, e.g. /pat, pɪt/, where the change from /a/ to /ɪ/ changes the meaning of the word, i.e. *pat*, vs. *pit*. When a phonetic realisation is attempted, square brackets are used, [. . .]. Thus [pɪt, pɪt̪] are two different realisations of the word *pit* where the tongue is slightly differently placed in the mouth but where there is no resulting change of meaning.

2.4.1 Vowels

Sound-segments may be classified as **vowels** and **consonants**. Vowels may be defined as those sounds where the airstream from the lungs does not give rise to audible friction, or is not prevented from escaping through the mouth. All other sound-segments are consonants. Vowels may be defined as either monophthongs or diphthongs. The difference between diphthong and monophthong is as follows:

diphthongs are vowel-clusters with a glide from one vowel to another without any intervening consonant;
monophthongs are so-called 'pure' vowels without any real change in that vowel's quality in its duration.

Comparison of most Present-Day English pronunciations of *doubt* (with a diphthong) and *soup* (with a monophthong) will demonstrate the difference.

Different vowels are made by a combination of the following procedures: **raising and lowering the tongue**; **pushing the tongue forward or dragging it back**; **opening the mouth or making it less open** (on the scale open, mid-open, mid-close and close); **rounding or unrounding the lips**. It is usual to define a vowel with reference to the positioning of the highest point of the tongue combined with the presence or absence of lip-rounding. Thus for the sound represented by *ee* in *feed*, the highest point of the tongue is at the front of the mouth and the lips are unrounded, whereas for the sound represented by *oo* in *food* (RP accent) the highest point of the tongue is at the back of the mouth and the lips are rounded. Figure 2.4 shows the configuration of the tongue in relation to the lips when making the vowels in *feed*, *food*. Figure 2.3 might be compared here. It is a conventionalised diagram showing the rough location of each

23

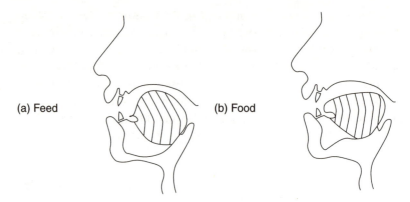

(a) Feed (b) Food

FIGURE 2.4 Tongue positions showing the front/back distinction in vowels

vowel-sound within the mouth; the positioning of vowels on this chart indicates the height of the highest point of the tongue when that sound is made.

The following list of phonetic symbols for vowels is derived from the notation of the IPA. Each symbol is accompanied by a **keyword**; the underlined letter in the keyword corresponds broadly to the sound symbolised. The pronunciations symbolised are for the most part those of a speaker of 'Received Pronunciation' (in Britain) or a speaker of so-called 'General American', but some other accents (and languages) are also referred to.

NOTE: Received Pronunciation, or RP, and General American, or GenAm, are what are sometimes referred to as 'reference accents', i.e. accents which are comparatively well described and generally taught to foreign learners of the language. Wells, in *Accents of English* (Cambridge, Cambridge University Press, 1982: 117–118) defines the two accents as follows:

> Geographically, RP is associated with England, though not with any particular locality within England. It is the most general type of educated British pronunciation (although there are many highly educated English people who do not use it). Socially, it is characteristic of the upper and middle class, insofar as members of the latter class, sociologically defined, speak with an accent not localizable within England.
>
> 'General American' is a term that has been applied to the two-thirds of the American population who do not have a recognizably local accent in the sense just mentioned. This is the type of American English pronunciation taught to learners of English as a foreign language ... 'General American' is by no means a uniform accent; and this is one of the reasons why the name 'General American' is nowadays looked at somewhat askance. ... [Nevertheless] it is convenient to use it as a basis for comparison.

The following are common monophthongs, i.e. 'pure' vowels, to be found in various states of the history of English, accompanied by a definition in terms of tongue- and lip-position.

* = as pronounced by an RP-speaker; + = as pronounced by a speaker of GenAm;
**= as pronounced by a Scots speaker; ++= French 'YOU' (sg.)

i	SEE*, +	front, close, unrounded
y	TU++	front, close, rounded
e	SAY**, DRESS*	front, mid-close, unrounded
ɛ	DRESS+	front, mid-open, unrounded
a	SAT**	front, open, unrounded
u	GOOSE*, +	back, close, rounded
o	GOAT+, **	back, mid-close, rounded
ɔ	THOUGHT*, +	back, mid-open, rounded
ʌ	STRUT*, +	back, mid-open, unrounded
ɑ	PALM*, +	back, open, unrounded

The following vowels are more centralised within the vowel-space:

ɪ	KIT*, +	centralised, mid-close, unrounded
u	FOOT*, +	centralised, mid-close, rounded

The following front, unrounded vowel is variously located by phoneticians, usually to midway between open and mid-open:

æ	SAT*, +	

The following unrounded vowel is central within the vowel-space:

ə	COMMA*, +	

NOTE: Most people find [y] the hardest vowel to pronounce. Try saying the vowel in *mean*, and then round your lips as you say it – without moving your tongue.

For the purposes of this book, diphthongs are probably best thought of as clusters of two monophthongs. The following keywords demonstrate the range of diphthongs in RP and GenAm:

eɪ	FACE*, +
əu	GOAT*
aɪ	PRICE*, +
ɔɪ	CHOICE*, +
au	MOUTH*, +
ɪə	NEAR*

ɛə SQUARE*

uə CURE*

2.4.2 Consonants

To help understand this section it may be useful to look again at Figure 2.2. Different consonants are made by a combination of the following procedures: bringing one of the organs of the vocal tract (e.g. teeth, lips, tongue) into contact or very near proximity with another; varying the nature of the contact between the organs of the vocal tract, such as allowing a small explosion of air to escape as the organs part (**plosive**, e.g. *b* in *bat*) or allowing a small quantity of air to pass between them, producing a hissing sound (**fricative**, e.g. *s* in *sat*); vibrating or opening the **vocal folds** or (an older term) **vocal cords**, a pair of membranes housed in the larynx between which passes the air on its way from the lungs to the mouth. (The larynx is an organ made of cartilage, a substance similar to bone but less hard. At the front it forms a marked point, and it is particularly prominent in slim males; it is thus referred to as the 'Adam's Apple'.)

Consonants may be defined therefore in threefold terms, with reference to:

the place of articulation,
the manner of articulation,
and the state of the vocal folds.

The most important **places of articulation** (leaving aside the tongue) are the lips, the teeth, the alveolar ridge (a prominent ridge of cartilage behind the top teeth), the hard palate and the soft palate (or velum). We can thus refer to consonants as being **bilabial** (made with the lips, e.g. *b* in *bat*), **labio-dental** (made with upper teeth and lower lip, e.g. *f* in *fat*), **dental** (made with tongue and teeth, e.g. *th* in *that*), **alveolar** (made with tongue and alveolar ridge, e.g. *d* in *dog*), **palatal** (made with tongue and hard palate, e.g. *y* in *yet*), **palato-alveolar** (made with tongue, hard palate and alveolar ridge, e.g. *sh* in *ship*), **velar** (made with tongue and velum, e.g. *k* in *kin*) and **labial-velar** (made with tongue and velum accompanied by lip-rounding, e.g. *w* in *wit*).

Most English consonants are produced as fricatives or plosives, but other **manners of articulation** include **nasal**, where the airstream is diverted to emerge through the nostrils (e.g. *m* in *mat*, *n* in *not*), **laterals**, where a partial closure is made in the mouth but air allowed to escape around it (e.g. *l* in *lap*), and **approximants** and **trills/taps**. **Affricates** are a special category, which may be defined for simplicity as units which begin as plosives and end as fricatives (e.g. *ch* in *chat*, *dg* in *judge*).

The **state of the vocal folds** also affects the nature of consonants. When the vocal folds are vibrating round the airflow, we refer to sounds as **voiced**; when the vocal folds are relaxed we refer to the sounds produced as **voiceless**. Thus, in most accents of English, the initial sound in

PAT is a voiceless plosive,
BAT is a voiced plosive,
SAP is a voiceless fricative,
ZAP is a voiced fricative.

As with the vowels, the following list of phonetic symbols for consonants is derived from the notation of the IPA. Again, each symbol is accompanied by a keyword. The pronunciations symbolised are for the most part those of a speaker of RP (in Britain) or a speaker of GenAm, but some other accents (and languages) are also referred to.

The following are common consonant sounds in varieties of English, accompanied by descriptions in terms of state of the vocal folds, place and manner of articulation.

b	BAT	voiced bilabial plosive
p	PAT	voiceless bilabial plosive
v	VAT	voiced labio-dental fricative
f	FAT	voiceless labio-dental fricative
θ	THIN	voiceless dental fricative
ð	THAT	voiced dental fricative
t	TIP	voiceless alveolar plosive
d	DIP	voiced alveolar plosive
s	SIP	voiceless alveolar fricative
z	ZIP	voiced alveolar fricative
ʃ	SHIP	voiceless palato-alveolar fricative
ʒ	TREASURE	voiced palato-alveolar fricative
r	RIP	voiced alveolar trill**/voiced post-alveolar approximant

l	LIP	voiced alveolar lateral
x	LOCH**	voiceless velar fricative
tʃ	CHILD	voiceless palato-alveolar affricate
dʒ	JAM	voiced palato-alveolar affricate
m	MAT	voiced bilabial nasal
n	NIP	voiced alveolar nasal
ŋ	SING	voiced velar nasal
w	WEB	voiced labial-velar approximant
ʍ	WHISKY**	voiceless labial-velar fricative
j	YARD	voiced palatal approximant

** = as pronounced by a Scots speaker

The consonant-systems of RP and GenAm are identical, but there are some differences of distribution of sounds within the lexicon. The most important of these is to do with the pronunciation of R; cf. RP [ʃaːp], General American [ʃarp] *sharp*.

2.4.3 Syllables

Groups of vowels and consonants make up **syllables**. A syllable in English consists of a vowel and any surrounding consonants; thus a word like *book* is made up of one syllable, and a word like *booklet* consists of two syllables.

Syllables may be **stressed** or **unstressed**; that is, they may be more or less prominent when pronounced. Thus, in the word *booklet*, the syllable represented in writing as *book* is more prominent than the syllable represented by *let*: *book* is stressed, *let* is unstressed.

NOTE: This is a very simplified account of stress. The student will quickly recognise that there are degrees of stress, most noticeably in polysyllabic words; and the manner in which prominence in syllables is achieved varies even between languages which are comparatively closely related, such as Italian and English. In the IPA, a stressed syllable is marked by a preceding ', e.g. [a'lɒŋ] ALONG.

2.5 Grammar and lexicon

Writing and pronunciation are fairly well-defined categories of linguistic analysis. Grammar, however, is a rather more nebulous category, and this has left its mark in the confusion which sometimes marks its definition in the literature. For some scholars, grammar refers to the whole range of linguistic activity, with the possible exception of lexicology; for others, it has a narrower meaning. In this book, the term is used comparatively narrowly, to refer to **syntax** and **morphology**. Syntax is concerned with the way in which words combine to form phrases, clauses and sentences; thus it deals with the relationships between words in such constructions as *Amy loves bananas*, *I love bananas*, where the choice of *loves* or *love* is determined by the relationship between this word and other words in the construction. Morphology is concerned with **word-form**, e.g. the kinds of ending which the form *love* can adopt (*love-ø* as opposed to *loves*). In short, grammar is to do with such matters as element-ordering and inflexional variation. It has a close connection with the **lexicon** or **vocabulary** of a language, indicated by the use of terms such as 'grammatical words'; this is not surprising, since both are ways of structuring meaning.

The grammatical structure of English has undergone a marked change during its history, and a number of categories of importance in earlier states of the language are no longer of great significance. This section simply presents a sketch of Present-Day English grammar, leaving room for further refinement and definition in later chapters. Since English grammar is an interconnected system, it is very hard in a small space to describe things without anticipating others not yet defined. Thus, to help the reader follow the discussion, cross-references are given throughout.

2.5.1 The hierarchy of grammatical units

The first thing to note about grammar is the hierarchy of grammatical units. **Sentences** are composed of one or more **clauses**; clauses are composed of one or more **phrases**; phrases are composed of one or more **words** (easy to distinguish in the writing-system commonly adopted for English); words are made up of **morphemes**. All units within the hierarchy have both form and function.

2.5.2 Morphemes

The morpheme is often defined as the minimal unit of grammatical analysis. For example, in the sentence

The papers reported the speech widely on their front pages

there are ten words (see 2.5.3 below), but fourteen morphemes. This can be demonstrated if we separate each morpheme with a hyphen (-):

The-paper-s-report-ed-the-speech-wide-ly-on-their-front-page-s

Thus the set of morphemes includes not only items which may form words on their own (e.g. *paper, on, their*), but also endings which do not have any meaning when separated from other morphemes (e.g. *-ed, -s, -ly*).

2.5.3 Words

Words have various forms: noun, adjective, verb, adverb, pronoun, etc. They function within phrases; thus a phrase can be composed of a noun with an accompanying adjective, e.g. *good women.*

In Present-Day English it is fairly easy to distinguish words since they are marked as such in our writing-system. However, it is worth noting that the concept 'word' is notoriously hard to define, and that the relationship between word and meaning raises a number of quite complex issues. A useful formal definition of the concept 'word' might be as follows: a grammatical unit, consisting of one or more morphemes, which is marked within the clause by positional mobility (i.e. it can be moved around within the clause), uninterruptability and internal stability. In the previous section, it was noted that there were fourteen morphemes, marked by hyphens in the sentence

The-paper-s-report-ed-the-speech-wide-ly-on-their-front-page-s.

However, these morphemes cannot be placed in any order to produce acceptable English sentences; some permutations are acceptable, e.g.:

The-speech-was-wide-ly-report-ed-in-the-paper-s-on-their-front-page-s.

but other combinations are not. Thus *speech, paper, page* etc. are potentially mobile or free, and can be employed in many positions, whereas *-s* and *-ed* above are immobile or bound morphemes, i.e. they must be attached to some other element to produce a 'block' within the sentence. Moreover, the ordering of elements within the block is stable, in the sense that *-s* and *-ed* have to follow, not precede, the element to which they are attached: thus *paper-s* and *report-ed* are acceptable, but not **s-paper* or **ed-report*. Finally, it is not acceptable to interrupt these blocks by interposing other elements, e.g. **paper-the-s*. These blocks may be termed words.

Of course, there are items which are conventionally called words which do not fulfil all three criteria, e.g. the article *the*, which may be interruptable (cf. *the page*, *the front page*) but is also stable and immobile, in the sense that it must always precede and accompany the noun which it modifies. Such items can be considered to be words since they fulfil one at least of the three criteria (positional mobility, uninterruptability, internal stability), but they are perhaps not so prototypical of the category as items which fulfil all three requirements.

The definition of 'word' offered above is a formal one, in that it is to do with the grammatical role of the category in question and its structural characteristics. However, another, older definition is that words map onto **concepts**, thus the word *table* maps onto the mental concept 'table'. There are several problems with this view – some of them a matter for philosophical debate since antiquity – but it has its uses. Lexicography would be hard pressed without the ability to map word onto definition; and children's language-learning would be impossible, for children build up their lexicons by isolating individual words and attaching them to individual concepts.

Words are traditionally classified into **parts of speech**. The parts of speech themselves fall into two classes: **open** and **closed**. The open-class set consists of:

Nouns (e.g. *girl, table, fire, thing, radiance, idea*). In traditional grammar, which depends on semantic definitions of grammatical categories, nouns are 'naming' words, i.e. words used as the name of a person, animal, place or thing. A sub-category, signalled in the English writing-system by the use of an initial capital letter, is made up of so-called 'proper' nouns which name particular places or persons (e.g. *Tom, Glasgow*). In English, all nouns can be modified in form depending on their role in the utterance, thus: *Tom, Tom's; pig, pig's, pigs*, etc. The sets of forms which individual nouns adopt in different grammatical situations are known as **paradigms**.

Lexical Verbs (e.g. *sing, drive, go, love*). The traditional definition of verbs is that they are 'doing' words, i.e. words expressing actions, processes, conditions. Of course this is, like all semantic definitions, a little problematic since a noun like *recitation* is surely to do with some kind of action. Thus it is usual for modern grammarians to classify verbs in terms of the job they do in the clause, or by the **paradigmatic patterns** in which they appear, e.g. *drink - drinks - drank - drunk, love - loves - loved, be - am - is - are*. Paradigmatic patterns of the *drink*-type, where the root-vowel changes within the paradigm, are referred to as **strong verbs**; those which add a suffix to create their past tense, such as *love*, are known traditionally as **weak verbs**; those like *be* are known as **irregular verbs**.

Adjectives (e.g. *good, bad, lovely, friendly*). Adjectives are often defined in traditional grammar as words which modify the noun; thus in a phrase such as *good men, good* is an adjective which gives more information about the *men*, e.g. distinguishing them from *bad men*. In Present-Day English, adjectives do not generally form paradigms although paradigmatic patterns are found in other languages (the English male/female distinction between *blond/blonde*, not always observed, is derived from French). Adjectives may be graded as **positive**, **comparative** and **superlative**, thus: *great, greater/more great, greatest/more great, good, better, best*, etc. This grading is known as **comparison of adjectives**.

Adverbs (e.g. *now, then, calmly, actually, today*). Adverbs are often defined as words which modify verbs, adjectives or indeed other adverbs. They do not form paradigmatic patterns. In the following examples, the italicised words are adverbs:

1 The little girl ran *quickly* into the room.
2 The woman was *very* beautiful.
3 She sang *very well*.

Open-class word-sets can be joined readily by new coinages, e.g. *scooter* (noun), *jive* (lexical verb), *hip* (adjective), *groovily* (adverb).

NOTE: A sub-category of the adjective is the **participle** or verbal adjective, a grammatical unit somewhere between the verb and the adjective and deriving characteristics from both. Thus, in *The ship was abandoned*, and *The abandoned ship*, *abandoned* is derived from the verb *abandon*; but the word *abandoned* occupies the same 'slot' as *beautiful*, an undoubted adjective, in *The ship was beautiful, the beautiful ship*. The *-ed* form of the verb here is described as the past participle. Another participle, the present participle, is similarly poised between categories; cf. *The cat was grinning, the grinning cat* beside *The cat was black, the black cat*.

The closed-class word-sets are:

Determiners (e.g. *the, a, this, that, some, any, all*) includes those words traditionally (and separately) defined as **articles** (*the =*

definite, *a(n)* = indefinite) and **demonstratives** (sometimes referred to, perhaps a little confusingly, as demonstrative pronouns: *this*, *these*, etc.). Determiners modify nouns. Most do not form paradigms in Present-Day English; *this* and *these*, *that* and *those* are exceptions.

    Pronouns (e.g. *I*, *me*, *you*, *they*). The traditional definition is that pronouns may 'replace' nouns; compare for instance,

4 *The good man* ate *the bananas*

with

4a *He* ate *them*.

There are sub-categories of pronoun, e.g. **relative** pronouns such as *who*, *whom*, *which* which connect a special kind of subordinate clause of the main clause, and **interrogative** pronouns, used in questions (e.g. <u>*Whom* did you mean?</u>). Pronouns have elaborate paradigms in Present-Day English, e.g. *she*, *her*, *hers*, although sometimes paradigmatic distinctions are not observed (thus the *who*, *whom* distinction is a feature of formal rather than informal discourse).

    Prepositions (e.g. *in*, *by*, *with*, *from*, *to*, *for*). Prepositions are traditionally defined as words placed in front of a noun or pronoun to show the relationship of that noun/pronoun to other elements in the sentence. In the following examples, the underlined words are prepositions: <u>*in*</u> *the car*, <u>*by*</u> *the brook*, <u>*on*</u> *the mountain*, <u>*with*</u> *the boy*, <u>*with*</u> *him*, <u>*by*</u> *her*, <u>*through*</u> *it*.

    Conjunctions (e.g. *and*, *but*, *that*, *if*, *when*, *because*). Conjunctions are traditionally defined as words which link other grammatical elements together, as in

5 Tom *and* Dick were walking along the road.
6 Virgil was a classical poet *but* Wordsworth was a Romantic poet.
7 Amy ate her food *because* she enjoyed spaghetti.

    Auxiliary verbs (e.g. *can*, *may*, *will*, *have*, *be*) are those verbs which modify the lexical verb in some way; thus in constructions such as

  8 The man *was* cooking sausages
  9 Amy *should* eat her breakfast
10 *Will* you eat your banana?
11 The dog *has* chewed the carpet

the *italicised* words are auxiliary verbs. Auxiliary verbs have quite elaborate paradigms: *am, is, are, be* etc.

Interjections (e.g. *oh, ah*) are fairly self-explanatory; they are usually defined as exclamatory words expressing emotion. In Present-Day English usage, *yes* and *no* may be placed in this category.

Numerals (e.g. *one, two, first, second*) are fairly easy to recognise. They fall into two categories in Present-Day English: **cardinal** and **ordinal**. Cardinal numbers are *one, two, three*, etc.; ordinal numbers are *first, second*, etc. The categorisation of numerals is somewhat complex; they seem, like participles, to be another category poised between larger sets, in this case between nouns and adjectives.

All these words function within the next element in the hierarchy: **phrases** (see 2.5.4 below). Prototypically, nouns function as the **headwords** (or the principal element) of **noun phrases** (e.g. <u>boy</u>, *good* <u>boys</u>, *the good* <u>boy</u>), and lexical verbs function as the headwords of **verb phrases** (e.g. <u>sings</u>, *was* <u>singing</u>). Adjectives prototypically function as **modifiers** (or the defining elements) of nouns within noun phrases (e.g. *the* <u>good</u> *boy*), although they can function as the headwords of **adjective phrases** (e.g. <u>good</u>, *very* <u>good</u> in *the boy is* <u>(very)</u> <u>good</u>). Adverbs can function as the headwords or modifiers of **adverb phrases** (e.g. <u>carefully</u>, <u>very</u> *carefully*), or as modifiers of adjectives within adjective phrases (e.g. <u>very</u> *good*).

Determiners always act as modifiers to nouns (e.g. <u>the</u> *man*), while auxiliary verbs act as modifiers to lexical verbs (e.g. <u>was</u> *singing*). Prepositions can be linked to noun phrases to produce **prepositional phrases** (<u>in</u> *the book*), while conjunctions prototypically link phrases or clauses together; for example:

12 The man *and* the woman;
13 *If* you eat that, you will be sick.

Pronouns function in place of nouns within noun phrases; cf.

14 The woman ate a banana.
14a *She* ate a banana.

Numerals prototypically act as modifiers within noun phrases (e.g. <u>two</u> *books*); interjections (e.g. *oh!, ah!*) form a special category with very special functions.

2.5.4 Phrases

Phrases can be defined as a unit intermediate between word and clause, consisting of one or more words which are linked together. They have various forms, depending on the principal element (or **headword**) within them: thus noun phrase, verb phrase etc.; for details of word-phrase relations, see the end of the previous section. They function within clauses: e.g. in *Good women eat bananas*, *good women* functions as the 'subject' of the sentence.

Phrases: Forms

There are six form-classes of phrase. **Noun phrases**, **adjective phrases**, **verb phrases** and **adverb phrases** all consist of a headword and can contain one or more modifiers, e.g. *good men*, *very good*, *was singing*, *very carefully*. In the clause

15 The good men were singing very sweetly

The good men is a noun phrase, *were singing* is a verb phrase and *very sweetly* is an adverb phrase. In the clause

16 The good men were very holy

The good men is a noun phrase, *were* is a verb phrase and *very holy* is an adjective phrase.

    Prepositional phrases and **genitive phrases** may be classed as special types of noun phrase, with special markers added to them. Prepositional phrases begin with a preposition; genitive phrases have the particle *'s* added to them. Thus *with a banana*, *of a book* are prepositional phrases, and *Tom's*, *the woman's* are genitive phrases. Genitive phrases almost always modify noun phrases, and typically denote possession or ownership; thus in *the boy's big book*, *the boy's* is a genitive phrase modifying *big book*.

Phrases: Functions

Phrases do not only have forms; they also have functions within a clause. Phrases can function as **subjects**, **predicators**, **objects**, **complements** and **adverbials**.

Verb phrases are always **predicators**, and, in most varieties of English, are required in any well-formed clause. A predicator is thus the 'doing' element within the clause; in the clauses

17 Amy loves porridge
18 Amy was eating her breakfast

loves and *was eating* are predicators.

Noun phrases can be subjects, objects and complements. **Subjects** prototypically denote the 'actor' of the action represented by the predicator, and therefore constrain the form of the predicator (i.e. there is 'agreement' between them); cf. *she loves, the man loves, they love*, where *she, the man* and *they* are subjects.

Objects prototypically denote the 'sufferer' of the action: *she loves bananas*. Most objects are of this kind, and are sometimes referred to as **direct objects**. **Indirect objects** also occasionally occur, e.g. in the sentence

19 She gave Elaine the banana

Elaine is the indirect object. Indirect objects are usually defined as the phrase denoting the 'recipient/beneficiary' in an action.

Complements prototypically refer back to the same entity as the subject, and are linked to the subject by a **copula verb** such as *become, be, seem*; they are sometimes called subject-complements. Thus, in the sentence

20 The woman was a princess

A princess is a complement and *was* is a copula verb. Noun phrases can also be object-complements, where the complement refers back to the same entity as the object; thus, in the sentence

21 The woman called Tom a fool

A fool is the object-complement.

Adjective phrases can be complements, e.g.:

22 The bananas were *very green* (subject-complement)
23 He called the bananas *very green* (object-complement)

It will be observed that again subject-complements 'refer back' to the subject, whereas object-complements 'refer back' to the object.

The function of **adverbials** within the clause is to add extra information about the circumstances of the clause, e.g. time, place, speaker's feelings. Because they are least closely integrated into the structure of the clause, they are mobile within the clause. Noun phrases, adverb phrases and prepositional phrases can all be adverbials, e.g.

24 Amy eats, *these days*, all her vegetables. (Noun phrase acting as adverbial)
25 *Really*, Amy likes all her vegetables. (Adverb phrase acting as an adverbial)
26 Amy eats all her vegetables *with great enthusiasm*. (Prepositional phrase acting as an adverbial)

In the above sentences, all the adverbials can be moved within the clause and meaningful sentences can still be produced, eg:

27 *These days* Amy eats all her vegetables.
28 Amy, *these days*, eats all her vegetables.
29 Amy eats all her vegetables *these days*.

But this mobility does not allow other phrases to be interrupted by the adverbial. Thus the following is not a well-formed sentence:

30 Amy eats all *these days* her vegetables.

Subordinate phrases

Phrases can also be **subordinate**, that is, forming part of another phrase. Thus, in the sentence

31 The men with red noses were drinking beer.

with red noses is a prepositional phrase, but not for once an adverbial. Rather, it is subordinate within the noun phrase *the men with red noses*.

NOTE: Confusion about prepositional phrases lies behind the old joke-advertisement: WANTED: PIANO FOR A LADY WITH SQUARE LEGS. Here, the prepositional phrase WITH SQUARE LEGS has been assigned its prototypical role as an adverbial, and thus given mobility within the utterance, whereas of course it should have been treated as an immobile subordinate phrase modifying *piano*.

2.5.5 Clauses

Clauses can be classified as **main** or **subordinate**, depending on their role in the sentence. Main clauses are capable of standing alone as sentences in their own right, e.g.:

32 The woman was eating the bananas.

When two or more main clauses are linked by a conjunction like *and* or *but*, which makes no causal link between them, then we refer to such clauses as **coordinated**.

Subordinate clauses typically function in positions where a phrase or even a word might be expected; thus, in the sentence

33 The woman was eating what she liked,

what she liked is a subordinate clause.

All clauses contain one predicator (i.e. verb phrase), and it is the presence of a predicator which indicates the presence of a clause.

Subordinate clauses have just been defined as prototypically functioning in positions where a phrase or even a word might be expected. That is, they can function as subjects, objects, complements and adverbials, and even as modifying elements within phrases. Here are some examples; the subordinate clause is in each case italicised. (34)–(36) are called **noun clauses**; (37) is an **adverb clause**; (38) is a **relative clause**; (39)–(40) are **comparative clauses**. It will be observed that relative and comparative clauses overlap in their functions; however, they differ a little in that comparative clauses can modify adjectives and adverbs as well as nouns. The main difference between relative and comparative constructions is that in the latter there is an element of comparison (either equating or differentiating) with the element being modified.

34 *What I want* is a banana. (Subordinate clause functioning as a subject = noun clause)
35 You should know *what we want*. (Subordinate clause functioning as an object = noun clause)
36 A banana is *what I want*. (Subordinate clause functioning as a complement = noun clause)
37 *Having eaten the banana*, Elaine left for work. (Subordinate clause functioning as an adverbial = adverb clause)
38 The man *who was eating bananas* was chosen to play for Scotland.

(Subordinate clause functioning as a modifying element within a noun phrase = relative clause)

39 The men eat more bananas *than we can grow.* (Subordinate clause functioning as a modifying element within a noun phrase = comparative clause)

40 The boys were eating the bananas more noisily *than seemed humanly possible.* (Subordinate clause functioning as a modifying element within an adverb phrase = comparative clause)

2.5.6 Some further grammatical categories

Noun phrase categories

The categories referred to here are to do with the form of the noun and pronoun: number, person, case and agreement.

Number is a very simple category. Nouns and pronouns have special forms depending on whether they are singular or plural, e.g. *pig: pigs, she: they.*

Person is particularly relevant to the pronoun. First person pronouns are *I, we, us* etc.; second person pronouns include Early Modern English *thou, ye* and Present-Day English *you;* third person pronouns are the equivalent of Present-Day English *he, she, it, they, him, them,* etc.

Case is functionally and formally more significant at earlier stages in the history of the language, and will be discussed in much greater detail in Chapter 3. It is relevant both to the noun and to the pronoun.

With regard to the singular noun, there are only two formal cases marked by the presence or absence of a special ending, which in writing is marked thus: *'s.* Forms marked by *'s* we describe as **genitive** or **possessive**. In the plural noun, genitive case is signalled by *s'.*

With regard to the pronoun, special forms are adopted depending on the function of the pronoun in the clause. If the pronoun is the subject of the clause, forms such as *he, she, I, you, we,* etc. are selected; if the pronoun is the object, then forms such as *him, her, us,* etc. are selected; if the pronoun is genitive or possessive, then forms such as *his, her, my,* etc. are selected. These various forms relate to the grammatical category 'case'. In the following examples, all these categories of pronoun are demonstrated:

41 *She* ate the banana. (Subject pronoun)
42 The elephant loved *her*. (Object pronoun)
43 The little girl loved *her* horse. (Genitive/possessive pronoun)

As with case, **agreement** is functionally and formally more significant in Old English than it is in Present-Day English. However, agreement within the noun phrase is demonstrated in Present-Day English when the form of the determiner is varied depending on the number of the noun being modified, e.g. *this book*, *these books*.

Verb phrase categories

As with the noun phrase, it is important when dealing with the verb phrase to be aware of a special set of grammatical categories: **agreement**, **finite-ness**, **simple** and **complex verb phrases**, **person**, **tense**, **mood**, **aspect**, **voice** and **transitivity**; **negation** may also be classed under this heading.

There is **agreement** in terms of number and person between the subject of a sentence/clause and the verb phrase which governs it.

In this context, the distinction **finite/non-finite** is also relevant. Finite verbs agree with their subject in number and person; non-finite verbs do not so agree. Finite verb phrases contain a finite verb plus one or more non-finite verbs; thus, in the clauses

44 He should eat
45 He has been eating
46 He has eaten

should, has are finite verbs and *eat, been eating, eaten* are non-finite. A main clause in Present-Day English has to contain one finite verb. The forms *eating* and *eaten* are known as **present** and **past participles**, respectively (see NOTE p. 32 above). The form *eat* in (44) is the base-form of the verb, usually referred to as the **infinitive**.

Verb phrases consisting of one finite verb may be called **simple verb phrases**, e.g.:

47 I *sing*.
48 She *loves* bananas.

Verb phrases consisting of more than one verbal element may be called **complex verb phrases**, e.g.:

49 I *am singing.*
50 She *had eaten* bananas.
51 The dog *was loved* by its owners.

In complex verb phrases, the first verb in the phrase is finite;
subsequent verbs are non-finite.

Finite verbs have two **numbers**: singular and plural. Which one
is used depends on whether the subject is singular or plural; cf.

52 He loves bananas.
53 They love_ bananas.

Finite verbs, like pronouns, have three **persons**: first, second and
third. First person is used when the subject governing the form of
the verb is a first person pronoun, i.e. *I, we;* second person is used
when the subject governing the verb is a second person pronoun, the
equivalent of Early Modern English *thou* and Present-Day English
you; third person is used when the subject governing the verb is a
noun, or a third person pronoun, i.e. *he, she, it* or *they.* Thus we
distinguish between

54 I love_ bananas
55 He loves bananas
56 Thou lovest bananas (archaic).

It will be observed that in Present-Day English no formal distinction
is made between plural verbs, whatever their person, e.g.:

57 We love_ bananas
58 They love_ bananas.

Finite verbs have special forms depending on whether they are
in the **present** or **preterite tense**, i.e. concerned with present or past
time respectively. Thus the forms *sing, love* in *I sing, I love* are
present tense verbs, whereas *sang, loved* in *I sang, I loved* are
preterite tense verbs.

In Present-Day English, there are three types of verb: **weak,
strong** and **irregular**. Weak verbs form their preterite tense generally
by adding *-(e)d* to the infinitive, e.g. *love : loved, laugh : laughed.*
Strong verbs form their preterite tense by changing the vowel of the
infinitive, e.g. *sing : sang, drive : drove, tread : trod.* Irregular verbs
have totally different forms for different parts of their paradigms, e.g.
be : was : were : am : is : are.

Mood may be defined as a category to do with different degrees of possibility with regard to the action referred to by the verb, including the speaker's attitude to the factuality or otherwise of that action. Three moods are traditionally distinguished: indicative, subjunctive and imperative.

Indicative mood verb forms are those where the form chosen indicates that the speaker regards the action referred to as a real action. This notion is expressed by means of verb phrases such as *I love*, *I am binding*. Thus in the sentence

59 Amy ate her breakfast this morning

ate is in the indicative mood, indicating that Amy *really* ate her breakfast.

Subjunctive mood causes most difficulty, because special forms for the subjunctive, which existed in Old English, Middle English and Early Modern English, have almost died out in Present-Day English, where auxiliary verbs within complex verb phrases are used instead. The subjunctive mood is used to suggest hypothesis, conjecture or volition; and we usually express it by means such as the following:

60 <u>May</u> God help us . . .
61 Even though it <u>may</u> happen . . .
62 If I <u>may</u> be so bold . . .
63 <u>Might</u> I suggest . . . ?

Thus in the sentence

59a   Amy might eat her breakfast tomorrow

might eat does not necessarily mean that Amy *will* eat her breakfast.

Earlier stages of English used special subjunctive forms of the verb rather than auxiliary verbs, as in this last example. Remnants of these forms still appear in Present-Day English, though their use is now considered by many people to be over-proper or formulaic:

64 If I *were* you . . .
65 So *be* it then . . .
66 We insist that he *come* . . .
67 God *help* us . . .
68 Long *live* the Queen.

Imperative mood is used for commands; in Present-Day English, the 'base-forms' of the verb are adopted: *go! come!*, etc. For example:

69 Eat your breakfast!

Aspect is a special grammatical category to do with such things as whether the action is completed or not. In some languages, such as Present-Day Russian, aspect is expressed by special forms of the verb; in Present-Day English it is expressed by means of contrasting simple and complex verb phrases. The easiest way of understanding Aspect is by means of examples. Thus, in Present-Day English, we distinguish between two kinds of aspect:

Progressive/non-progressive, where progressive aspect is marked by *-ing* and non-progressive by the use of simple present or preterite forms, e.g.:

70   *I am singing* a song
70a *I was singing* a song

beside

71   I *sing* a song
71a I *sang* a song

Perfect/non-perfect, where the perfect aspect is marked by *-ed*, *-en* or a vowel-change in the verb, e.g.:

72   I *have composed* a song
72a I *have written* a song
72b I *sang* a song

beside

72c I *sing* a song

Voice is a category which indicates whether the subject governing the form of the verb is the agent or the target of the action, **active** or **passive** voice respectively, e.g.:

73   I *love* the girl.
73a I *am loved* by the girl.

The **passive progressive** and **passive perfect** constructions are common in Present-Day English, e.g.:

74   He is being loved.
74a He has been loved.

Transitivity is an important notion in the categorisation of verbs. **Transitive** verbs and verb phrases are those capable of governing ('taking') a direct object, e.g.:

75   I *love* bananas.
75a I *hate* carrots.

Intransitive verbs and verb phrases are verbs not capable of governing a direct object, e.g.:

76   I *have arrived.*
76a I *am coming.*

Finally, **negation** is to do with whether a statement is negative, e.g. *I don't know* rather than positive, e.g. *I (do) know.* In Present-Day English, negation is expressed through the negative particles *not, -(n)'t,* and is only possible (in most varieties of Present-Day English, including standard varieties) in complex verb phrases. Thus the 'dummy' auxiliary verbs *don't* etc. are common in negative verb phrases. Examples in Present-Day English are

77 Amy *won't eat* her breakfast.
78 She *doesn't like* carrots.

Constructions such as *I know not* are archaic; see p. 141 below.

There are of course many other terms and notions necessary for full linguistic description. These will be discussed as they arise in the following chapters, where the linguistic terminology described here will be used to discuss early states of the language.

Chapter 3

Old English

3.1 Introduction

The oldest recorded stage of the English language is Old English (OE), sometimes called Anglo-Saxon. Manuscript records in OE begin in the sixth century AD, and continue until the Norman Conquest of 1066; OE shades into Middle English (ME) after 1100–1150. Several dialects of OE are recorded, but one variety, Late West Saxon, seems to have achieved the status of a standardised written language in the years before the Norman Conquest. In origin, West Saxon was the language of the Kingdom of Wessex, in the south-west of England; Wessex had achieved political and cultural hegemony in England by the end of the Anglo-Saxon period. The texts in this book have been normalised into Early West Saxon, the form of this dialect current in the time of King Alfred (849–899 AD), since this provides the most useful basis for subsequent study. However, students will quickly become aware that West Saxon is not a fixed variety, and at the end of this chapter a short Appendix I has been included on the main differences between Early and Late West Saxon. Appendix II contains a very brief discussion of the dialects of OE.

NOTE: The normalisation of the OE material in this chapter, and in some texts in Part II, has been undertaken for the same reason as it is usually undertaken in Old Icelandic studies, i.e. to make OE easier for beginners. For further discussion, see the Preface.

Although OE looks very different from Present-Day English (PDE) – so much so that there was a tendency at one time in some parts of the wider discipline 'English Studies' to exclude OE from the curriculum – the grammatical configuration established in Anglo-Saxon times is of crucial importance for the subsequent history of the language. It is for this reason that this chapter is the longest of those offered in this book, and later chapters constantly refer back to structures defined and described here.

This chapter is divided into four main parts: Spelling and Pronunciation, Syntax, Paradigms and Lexicon. This division is for ease of reference, and it is not intended that the sections should necessarily be read straight through in the order given here. There should be an iterative relationship between the Old English texts in Part II, which are organised in ascending order of difficulty, and the discussion presented here. I have taken examples from the texts in Part II, but I have drawn upon other texts where illustration of some common point is required. Cross-references are given throughout.

An attempt has been made to distinguish between features of less and greater importance for beginners' understanding of OE. Phenomena of major significance appear in paragraphs marked at the beginning and end with an arrow icon ➔ . . ←. This does not mean that the other paragraphs can be ignored. Their significance will become apparent later in students' encounters with OE texts.

3.2 Spelling and pronunciation

3.2.1 The alphabet

➔ Most OE letters are the same as those used in Present-Day English, being derived from the Latin alphabet. However, Anglo-Saxon scribes also used three letters not in the PDE alphabet:

Æ, æ ('ash')
Þ, þ ('thorn')
Ð, ð ('eth')

In the Glossary, *æ* follows *ad-* and *þ-* follows *t-*. *Æ* seems to have been an open, unrounded front vowel, in quality like the pronunciation of A in RP and GenAm, e.g. *trap*, i.e. [æ]. In late OE times, *þ* and *ð* were largely interchangeable, both representing either [θ] or [ð]. *ð* is not used in the present chapter, but it occurs in a few of the texts in Part II. The scribes also used 'wynn' (not to be confused with *þ* or *p*) for *w*, and *ʒ* (so-called 'insular g'; not to be confused with the phonetic symbol [ʒ]) for *g*. In accordance with modern conventions, only *w* and *g* are used here. Several OE letters had a different significance when pronounced from the usual symbol–phoneme correspondences in PDE (see pp. 48–49).←

NOTE: Not discussed here is the alternative OE script known as **runes**. Runes form an alphabetic system used particularly in carving on wood or stone; they are found used throughout the Germanic world. They survived longest in Scandinavia, but were used in Britain as well; several English inscriptions survive. The letters þ 'thorn' and ᵖ 'wynn' are runic letters which were transferred to the Latin-derived alphabet used for writing OE during the course of the Anglo-Saxon period. For a discussion of the runes, see R.I. Page, *An Introduction to English Runes* (London: Methuen, 1973).

3.2.2 Diacritics

In OE words and texts in this book, a diacritic is sometimes used, viz. the macron or length-mark over certain vowels, e.g. $\bar{e}$ or $\bar{o}$. The significance of this will be described and discussed on p. 49. These diacritics are a modern convention, and have a useful function for students of the history of English. They have been included in this book since they are important in more advanced work, and because they can help with word-recognition.

3.2.3 Pronunciation

There is still much scholarly dispute about the details of OE pronunciation, although there is general agreement on the main characteristics. Our knowledge of OE usage derives from the analysis of spelling, and from comparative and reconstructive work with other related languages and later states of English. These notes are offered as a brief guide only. It is important for beginners not to worry too much about the precise pronunciation of OE; there are (of course) no tape-recordings from Anglo-Saxon times, and our current ideas are based on the work of researchers over the last century or so. There is still a good deal of uncertainty about the various details of OE pronunciation, and different accounts have been published. The phonetic symbols used here are those of the International Phonetic Association; for details, see Chapter 2, p. 22.

➔ In general, all **vowels** should be pronounced in OE. Most scholars agree that there were almost no 'silent' vowels, like *e* in PDE *life*. (An exception is the optional *e* in spellings such as *sceolde* SHOULD, *hycgean* THINK common in late West Saxon beside *scolde*, *hycgan*, where the *e* seems to be a kind of diacritic indicating the quality of the preceding consonant cluster.) Vowels in unstressed syllables were generally pronounced more distinctively than they are in varieties of PDE; thus the endings *-an/-en/-on* were all distinguished. ⬅

To understand the OE vowel system it is important to note quantitative and qualitative distinctions. **Quantity** is to do with whether a vowel is long or short; **quality** is to do with the location of the vowel in question with regard to place of articulation (e.g. 'close', 'open', 'mid-close', etc.) and to the roundedness or unroundedness of the lips.

The OE vowel system carefully distinguishes between **long** and **short** vowels. A macron (⁻) has been placed above all long vowels in OE words, e.g. *ē*. Distinguishing between long and short vowels can be difficult at first. Scottish speakers will notice a quantitative distinction in their pronunciations of the stressed vowels in *greed* and *agreed*; many English speakers might compare their pronunciation of *grid* with *greed* (although the quality as well as the quantity of these latter vowels differ). Some examples of the difference of meaning length of vowels can make in OE are indicated by the following pairs of words: *God* GOD and *gōd* GOOD, *wendon* TURNED and *wēndon* BELIEVED, *āwacian* TO AWAKEN and *āwācian* TO GROW WEAK.

The symbols for **monophthong vowels** in OE were *y, i, e, æ, a, o* and *u*; all could be pronounced either long or short, and there seem to have been no qualitative distinctions between long and short vowels until well after the end of the OE period. These symbols largely correspond with those of the IPA, except that *a, ā* were probably pronounced [ɑ], [ɑː] respectively, as in modern German *Mann* MAN, RP/ GenAm *palm*. The vowel inventory of OE therefore consisted of something like the following: [y(ː), i(ː), e(ː), æ(ː), ɑ(ː), o(ː), u(ː)]. There were also three sets of **diphthongs**: *ea, ēa, eo, ēo, ie, īe*. There is much controversy about the exact pronunciation of these diphthongs; indeed, some scholars consider that they were not diphthongs at all. It is probably simplest for beginners to consider them as combinations of monophthongs.

NOTE: No qualitative distinction between long and short vowels is made in OE; cf. the PDE difference in quality between the vowels in *pit, peat*. This failure to make a qualititative distinction is a controversial matter which will not be pursued in this book.

➔ All **consonants** must be pronounced in OE, e.g. *c* in *cnapa* SERVANT, *r* in *gēar* YEAR, *w* in *wrītan* WRITE, *g* in *þing* THING. Most OE consonant-symbols are pronounced in the same way as in PDE, with a few exceptions. The chief of these are as follows:

(a) Sometimes, *c* is pronounced [tʃ] and *g* is pronounced [j]; this often (but not always) happens when these letters precede *e* or *i*, e.g.

cēosan CHOOSE, *gēar* YEAR; otherwise they are generally pronounced [k] and [g] respectively.

(b) *f*, *s* and *þ* are pronounced voiced between vowels, i.e. [v, z, ð]: a
useful thing to remember, since it makes forms like *yfel* more easily
recognisable as EVIL. Elsewhere they are voiceless.

(c) Doubled consonants are distinct from single ones; thus the *dd* in
biddan ASK (FOR), *bid* is pronounced like the -*d d*- in the phrase *bad
debt*.

(d) The combinations *sc*, *cg* are usually pronounced [ʃ], [dʒ] respectively; thus *scip* SHIP and *ecg* EDGE are pronounced the same in both
OE and PDE. ←

→ The above account must be taken as only a rough scheme.
The important thing is not to worry too much. Students should try
to develop fluency in reading OE and understanding what they
read rather than worrying about the correct pronunciation of every
letter. ←

3.3 Syntax

This component of the grammar is divided into three fundamental
areas of syntax: the **noun phrase**, the **verb phrase** and **sentence
structure**. This section is to do with the various functions performed
by the various forms; for details of forms, constant reference should
be made to section 3.4. For the grammatical terminology used, see
Chapter 2.

The principal difference between OE and PDE is that OE is, to
a much greater degree than PDE, an **inflected** language. Whereas the
relationships between words in PDE are largely expressed by word-
order, in OE these relationships are expressed to a much greater
extent by special endings attached to words. These endings are called
inflexions. OE and PDE are not so very different in this respect; we
still use a number of inflexions today, even if we do not call them
such. Thus, in the sequences *Tom* : *Tom's*, *pig* : *pig's* : *pigs*, *run* : *runs*,
the -*s* endings could be referred to as inflexions. However, it is true
to say that OE has many more inflexions than PDE has. It can be
compared in this respect with other languages, such as Present-Day
German, or Classical Latin.

3.3.1 The noun phrase

→ It is important when dealing with the inflexions of the Noun Phrase to grasp four key concepts: **case**, **agreement**, **number**, **gender**. ←

Case and the noun phrase

→ The notion **case** is a category with much greater formal significance in OE than in PDE. In OE, nouns, pronouns, determiners and adjectives vary in form according to the functions they have in a clause or phrase. These various forms are called cases. ←

→ There are four cases in OE: **nominative**, **accusative**, **genitive** and **dative**. The correlation between case and function raises some theoretical problems (which need not concern the beginner), but, very roughly, the following correspondences can be noted. The most common use of each case appears in bold type in the following list.

Nominative   **Subject**
Subject complement

Accusative   **Direct object**
Object complement
within some prepositional phrases (i.e. nouns or noun phrases preceded by a preposition), especially after prepositions involving motion.

Genitive   **In Genitive Phrases** (i.e. nouns or noun phrases denoting possession by means of '*s, s'* etc.) occasionally, within some prepositional phrases rarely, after certain verbs, direct object

Dative   **Within many prepositional phrases**
indirect object
after certain verbs, direct object ←

For details of the various inflexional forms of noun in accordance with case, see pp. 67–71. Those verbs which cause objects to 'take' cases other than accusative are listed accordingly in the Glossary. The reason why some verbs cause their objects to behave in this way relates to semantics, and is not pursued further in this handbook.

NOTE: There are vestigial remnants of a fifth case in OE: **instrumental**. The instrumental was sometimes used to signal means, manner or time. Formally it is generally identical to the dative and is merged with that case. The most common exceptions are found in the determiners; thus expressions appear such as *þȳ ilcan dæge* ON THE SAME DAY. For details of the instrumental paradigm in determiners, see NOTE, p. 74.

Agreement and the noun phrase

➜ **Agreement** (sometimes called **concord**) is functionally and formally much more important in OE than in PDE. Agreement is demonstrated when a **noun**, along with the modifier applying to it, will be assigned the appropriate case ending required by its function in the sentence. Thus, in the sentence

1 *Se hlāford bindeþ þone cnapan*
   THE LORD BINDS THE SERVANT

Se hlāford is the subject and thus is in the nominative case, while *þone cnapan* is the direct object and thus in the accusative case. The form of the word THE (*se, þone*) varies according to the case of the noun which it modifies; and this marking for the same case of words within the same phrase is known as agreement. ←

Number, gender and the noun phrase

➜ In OE, modifiers (determiners, adjectives) agree with the **nouns** to which they apply not only in case, but also in number and gender. ←
   ➜ **Number** is for our purposes a very simple concept; it refers to whether a word is singular or plural. There are special inflexions to indicate this in OE, not only on nouns and pronouns (as in PDE) but also on the determiners and adjectives which modify nouns. ←
   ➜ **Gender** is a little more complex for PDE speakers to understand, since it has no real equivalent in PDE grammar. Nouns and pronouns in OE belong to one of three types, and this categorisation affects the endings they have, and the endings that any of their modifiers have. Traditionally the three types are called masculine, feminine and neuter genders. Sometimes this 'grammatical' gender corresponds to biological ('natural') gender, but sometimes it does not. For instance, the word for STONE in OE is a masculine noun

(*stān*), the word for WOMAN is neuter (*wīf*), and the word for GIFT is feminine (*giefu*). A pronoun referring to any of these nouns should be in the same gender as the noun; however, towards the end of the OE period, this rule begins to be ignored and natural gender starts to determine the choice of *hē*, *hēo*. OE grammatical gender is comparable with Present-Day French, where all nouns, however sexless they might be, are either masculine or feminine (e.g. *la table* THE TABLE is feminine in Present-Day French), or Present-Day German, where, for example, 'female' nouns can have 'neuter' grammatical gender, as in *das Weib* THE WOMAN). ←

The noun phrase: Pronouns

→ As in PDE, OE **pronouns** are categorised by **person**. First person pronouns are the equivalent of PDE *I*, *we*; second person pronouns are the equivalent of Early Modern English *thou* and PDE *you*; third person pronouns are the equivalent of PDE *he*, *she*, *it*, *they*. Third person singular pronouns are usually selected on the basis of the grammatical gender of the noun to which they refer, although *hēo* (SHE), etc. can sometimes be used to refer to nouns referring to female persons (e.g. *wīf* WOMAN), whatever the grammatical gender of the noun adopted. Pronouns are also inflected to signal case, as in PDE; cf. PDE *he*, *his*, *him*. The indefinite pronoun *man* ONE is treated as a third person pronoun. For details of the various inflexional forms of pronoun in OE, see pp. 71–3 below. ←

The noun phrase: Adjectives

→ Because of agreement, the form of the **adjective** depends on the number, gender and case of the noun which it modifies, and OE adjectives can take several distinct inflexional endings because of this rule. However, this is not the only complexity; for there are in OE two adjectival paradigms, called **strong** and **weak**. Determining which paradigm to use depends on the relationship between the adjective and other words. If the adjective is preceded by the determiners equivalent to PDE *the*, *that*, *this*, *those*, *these*, then the weak form is used. Elsewhere, the strong paradigm is generally used. Thus there is a formal distinction between *Se gōda wer* THE GOOD MAN, with a weak adjective ending in -a, and *Se wer wæs gōd* THE MAN WAS GOOD, where the adjective is strong and is here endingless. For details of the various inflexional forms of adjective, see pp. 74–5. ←

NOTE: The weak form of the adjective is also, but not always, used after possessive pronouns and the genitive of pronouns, and in 'vocative' constructions where persons are addressed directly, e.g. *þū yfla cnapa* YOU BAD SERVANT.

The noun phrase: Determiners

→ As with the adjective, the form of the **determiner** is in OE conditioned by agreement with the noun which it modifies. Determiners agree with the noun they modify in gender, number and case; cf. *Se hlāford* THE LORD, *þæt wīf* THE WOMAN, etc. For details of the various inflexional forms of determiners, see pp. 73–4. Of course, some PDE determiners still agree with the noun they modify, e.g. THIS BOOK, THESE BOOKS. ←

The noun phrase: Numerals

In PDE, as in OE, **numerals** fall into two groups: **cardinal** (*one, two*, etc.) and **ordinal** (*first, second*, etc.). Of the OE cardinal numerals, *ān*, *twā* and *þrēo* inflect in the same way as adjectives, in agreement with the noun they modify; thus *ān wer* ONE MAN, *mid twæm cnapum* WITH TWO SERVANTS. Cardinal numerals from *fēower* are generally undeclined, and cause the noun they modify to appear in the genitive case, e.g. *hund wera* 100 MEN (literally 100 of men), *twentig scipa* TWENTY SHIPS. This peculiarity is shared by the adjective *fela* MANY, e.g. *fela wera* MANY MEN. Ordinal numbers (*forma, ōþer, þridda*, etc.) agree with the adjectives they modify and are always declined in accordance with the weak adjective paradigm, except for *ōþer*, which is always declined strong, e.g. *se forma wer* THE FIRST MAN, *on þone þriddan dæg* ON THE THIRD DAY. For details of the various inflexional forms of Numerals, see pp. 84–5.

The noun phrase: A note about genitive phrases

Genitive (or possessive) phrases of the type *John's book, the woman's coat* may be considered a special kind of noun phrase. **Subordinated Genitive Phrases** often cause problems for students of OE, notably in the agreement of determiners and adjectives. Since determiners inflect in OE, there are problems with expressions like *the good man's book*; does *the* modify *good man* or *book*? The evidence is that *the* in such constructions was considered to modify *good man*, and was part of the genitive phrase. Thus *the good man's book* in OE is *þæs gōdan weres bōc*, where the adjective is in agreement with *weres* MAN'S rather than *bōc* BOOK.

The noun phrase: A note about prepositional phrases

Prepositional phrases, i.e. noun phrases including a preposition and frequently functioning as adverbials or modifiers, form a distinct category of phrase. Prepositions cause the phrase in which they appear to inflect, generally in the dative, but sometimes in the accusative and (rarely) in the genitive, e.g. *tō þǣre stōwe* TO THE PLACE, *on þone þriddan dæg* ON THE THIRD DAY. Common OE prepositions, with an indication of the cases they govern, are given in the Glossary in Part III. Prepositions are usually placed at the beginning of the prepositional phrase they are attached to, but sometimes fall at the end, especially when the rest of the phrase consists of a single pronoun, e.g. *him tō* TO HIM.

3.3.2 The verb phrase

➔ As with the OE noun phrase, it is important when dealing with the OE **verb phrase** to be aware of a special set of grammatical categories: agreement, finite-ness, simple and complex verb phrases, person, tense, mood, aspect, voice, transitivity, negation. For definitions of these categories, all of which are relevant to PDE grammar as well, see pp. 40–4. For details of the inflexional forms of the verb reflecting all these categories, see pp. 76–84. ⬅

Agreement and the verb phrase

➔ **Agreement** with regard to the noun phrase was defined on p. 52. As in PDE, in OE it is also relevant to the verb phrase, in that there is agreement in number and person between the subject of a sentence/clause and the verb phrase which governs it, e.g. *ic lufige* I LOVE, *hē lufaþ* HE LOVES, *hīe lufiaþ* THEY LOVE. ⬅

Finite and non-finite verbs and the verb phrase

➔ In this context, the distinction **finite/non-finite**, as defined in Chapter 2, is also relevant. Finite verbs in OE agree with their subject in number and person, e.g. *ic lufige* I LOVE, *hē lufaþ* HE LOVES. Of the non-finite verbs, the infinitive (i.e. base-form) and present participle do not agree with the subject in OE, but the OE past participle, which is a kind of verbal adjective, can; see p. 57. ⬅

NOTE: The usual form of the **infinitive**, ending in -*an*, may be regarded as the base-form. However, there is also the **inflected infinitive**, e.g. *tō āhreddenne* TO RESCUE (*āhreddan* RESCUE). The inflected infinitive has various functions. Perhaps the most important is to express purpose; thus the sentence

2   *God self wāt þæt wē winnaþ rihtlīce tō āhreddenne ūre folc*
2a God himself knows that we fight justly in order to rescue our people.

Simple and complex verb phrases

➔ Simple and complex verb phrases are both characteristic of PDE, and both may also be distinguished in OE. **Simple verb phrases**, i.e. those containing one verbal element, are rather more commonly used in OE than they are in PDE; thus *hē lufaþ* would typically be used not only where PDE would use HE LOVES, but also where PDE typically uses constructions such as HE IS LOVING. However, **complex verb phrases**, i.e. those containing more than one verbal element, may also be distinguished in OE, e.g.:

3   *Hē sceal bindan*
     HE OUGHT TO BIND

4   *Hē hæfde hine gebundenne*
     HE HAD BOUND HIM

5   *Hē is gecumen*
    HE HAS (lit. IS) COME. ←

NOTE: There are some theoretical problems about categorising *sceal bindan, hæfde
... gebundenne* and *is gecumen* simply as complex verb phrases, signalled for example
by the fact that the past participle in *hæfde ... gebundenne* agrees with the object of
the clause; *-ne* is an adjectival inflexion (see the adjective paradigm on p. 75). However,
for the sake of simplicity it is perhaps acceptable to consider these constructions to be
complex verb phrases on the PDE pattern.

Number and the simple verb phrase

→ Finite verbs in OE have two **numbers**: singular and plural, as in
PDE; thus there is a distinction between, e.g. *hē lufaþ* HE LOVES and
hīe lufiaþ THEY LOVE. ←

Person and the simple verb phrase

→ Finite verbs in OE, as in PDE, have three **persons**: first, second
and third. First person is used when the subject governing the form
of the verb is a first person pronoun, i.e. *ic* I, *wē* WE; second person
is used when the subject governing the verb is a second person
pronoun, i.e. *þū* (cf. Early Modern English *thou*), *gē* YOU (cf.
EModE *ye*); third person is used when the subject governing the verb
is a noun, or a third person pronoun, i.e. *hē* HE, *hēo* SHE, *hit* IT, *hīe*
THEY. ←

Tense and the simple verb phrase

→ Finite verbs in OE, as in PDE, have special forms depending on
whether they are in the **present** or **preterite tense**, e.g. *ic binde*
I BIND, *ic band* I BOUND; *ic lufige* I LOVE, *ic lufode* I LOVED. ←

Mood and the verb phrase

→ OE has special forms of the finite verb to express indicative,
subjunctive and imperative **moods** within simple verb phrases. Mood
may be defined as a category to do with different degrees of possibility

with regard to the action referred to by the verb, including the speaker's attitude to the factuality or otherwise of that action. The PDE configuration differs somewhat; see Chapter 2 for details.

Indicative mood verb forms are those where the form chosen indicates that the speaker regards the action referred to as a real action. These forms may be regarded as the 'normal' forms of the verb, e.g. *hē lufaþ* HE LOVES, *hīe bundon* THEY BOUND.

Subjunctive mood causes most difficulty, because special forms for the subjunctive have almost died out in PDE; instead, auxiliary verbs within complex verb phrases are used, e.g. <u>may</u> *God help us*. OE, however, uses special subjunctive forms of the verb, e.g. *hē binde* HE MAY BIND. Remnants of these forms still appear in PDE, e.g. IF I <u>WERE</u> YOU (cf. OE *gif ic wǣre . . .*).

Imperative mood is still found in PDE. Special forms of the verb are used for commands in OE, e.g. *Bind!* BIND! ⬅

Complex verb phrase constructions

So far we have been concerned with simple verb phrases. The most important **complex** verb phrase constructions were: (1) *wesan + present participle*; (2) *habban/wesan/weorþan + past participle*; (3) *willan/sculan + infinitive*. By these means, OE could express further verbal categories beyond simple present and preterite: **aspect**, **voice** and **future time/ volition/ obligation**.

Aspect is a category to do with such things as whether the action is completed or not. In PDE, aspectual choices depend on distinguishing between certain kinds of complex and simple verb phrase.

Voice is a category which indicates whether the subject governing the form of the verb is the agent or the target of the action, active or passive voice respectively. As with aspect, the distinction between active and passive voice involves distinguishing certain kinds of simple and complex verb phrases. Aspect and voice produce various verb phrase constructions in PDE.

In OE, *wesan/bēon + present participle* is occasionally used to express PDE **progressive aspect**, e.g. *ic eom singende* I AM SINGING. However, the non-progressive forms (e.g. *ic singe*) were much more commonly used in OE than in PDE, and such progressive constructions are rare.

In OE, as in PDE, **perfect aspect** and **passive voice** are expressed by means of complex verb phrases, where the lexical verbs were formally past participles. The auxiliary verbs in such phrases can be *habban* TO HAVE, *wesan/bēon* TO BE or *weorþan* TO BECOME. When the auxiliary verb is *wesan* or *weorþan* then the past participle agrees in case, number and gender with the subject of the sentence; when the auxiliary verb is *habban*, the past participle agrees with the direct object. The past participle is declined like a strong adjective (see p. 75); thus in OE, it is hard to decide whether the past participle is a 'verby' adjective or an 'adjectival' verb. Cf.

6   *Hīe wurdon gebundene*
    THEY WERE (lit. BECAME) BOUND

7   *Hīe hæfdon hine gebundenne*
    THEY HAD BOUND HIM.

Wesan/bēon TO BE + *past participle* is often used to express perfect aspect of **intransitive** verbs (i.e. verbs which do not take direct objects), e.g.:

8   *Hīe sind gecumene*
    THEY HAVE COME (lit. THEY ARE COME);

with **transitive** verbs (i.e. verbs taking direct objects), it can be used to express passive voice. *Weorþan* TO BECOME + *past participle* is however much more commonly used to express passive voice, e.g.:

9   *hē wearþ geslægen*
    HE WAS (lit. BECAME) STRUCK

It is also common to use the *man*-construction where PDE uses BE + past participle, e.g.:

10 *man Horsan ofslōg*
    (lit. ONE SLEW HORSA) HORSA WAS SLAIN.

The auxiliary verb + lexical verb constructions described just above are not as common in OE as in PDE. Not only do simple verb phrase constructions appear more frequently than they do in PDE, but adverbs were employed where distinct kinds of verb phrase would appear in PDE, e.g.:

11 *ic lufode ǣr*
    (lit. I LOVED FORMERLY) I HAD LOVED.

Future time (cf. PDE I SHALL GO, SHE WILL GO, WE'LL GO) was generally expressed in OE by means of the simple present tense, and futurity was inferred from the context of the phrase, e.g.

12 *On morgenne, gā ic tō þæm dūnum*
IN THE MORNING, I (SHALL) GO TO THE HILLS.

If the verb TO BE is used in this way, the *bēon* forms tend to be used instead of *eom*, *is*, etc. The verbs *willan* and *sculan*, whose PDE reflexes WILL, SHALL are used to express futurity, are used differently in OE.

Willan + *infinitive*, to express future time, seems to have been used towards the end of the OE period. However, *willan* normally has a **volitional** meaning; thus, for example, *ic wille gān* usually means I WANT TO GO.

Sculan + *infinitive* is used to express **obligation** in OE; thus *hēo sceal gān* means SHE MUST GO.

Negation and the verb phrase

➔ **Negation** in OE is expressed by the negative particle *ne*, frequently assimilated to the words it precedes (e.g. *nis* = *ne* + *is*). Double or multiple negation (cf. PDE stigmatised I AIN'T GOT NOTHING) was entirely acceptable, and frequent, in OE, e.g. *Hit nā ne fēoll* IT DID NOT FALL. ⬅

3.3.3 Sentence structure

Word-order

➔ The OE inflexional system, with more distinctive forms than those of PDE, means that OE **word-order** can be much more flexible than that of its descendant. Thus, in PDE,

13 The lord binds the servant
14 The servant binds the lord

mean very different things. The word-order indicates the relative functions of the phrases *the lord* and *the servant*. This was not necessarily the case in OE. Sentence (13) above can be translated into OE as

15 *Se hlāford bindeþ þone cnapan.*

However, it can also be translated as

16 *þone cnapan bindeþ se hlāford*

or

17 *Se hlāford þone cnapan bindeþ.*

In the three sentences above, the phrase *se hlāford*, because it is in the nominative case, is always the subject of the clause in whatever position it appears; because it is in the accusative case, *þone cnapan* is always the direct object of the clause. The cases, not the word-order, here determine the relationship between the two noun phrases.

This does not mean, however, that OE word-order is entirely arbitrary. In a sentence like

18 *þæt wīf bindeþ hit*
   THE WOMAN BINDS IT,

for instance, there are no inflexional means of determining that *þæt wīf* is the subject and *hit* the direct object, for the nominative and accusative forms of these words are not differentiated. Although OE allowed more variation in word-order than PDE does, nevertheless there were norms of word-order in OE.

Three types of OE phrase-order may be identified in clauses:

(a) SP: the predicator (= verb phrase) immediately follows the subject;
(b) S ... P: other elements of the clause come between subject and predicator;
(c) PS: the subject follows the predicator.

SP is the usual order in main clauses; S ... P is most commonly found in subordinate clauses; and PS occurs most commonly in questions, and in main clauses introduced by certain adverbials (notably *þā* THEN). Here are some examples of prototypical usages:

19 *Se wer lufode þone gōdan engel*
   THE MAN LOVED THE GOOD ANGEL (SP).

20 *For þǣm þe se wer þone Ælmihtigan lufode, hē fērde tō þǣm dūnum*
   BECAUSE THE MAN LOVED THE ALMIGHTY (S ... P), HE TRAVELLED TO THE HILLS.

21 *þā band hē his sunu*
THEN HE BOUND HIS SON (PS).

However, OE writers frequently departed from these norms for stylistic effect. ←

When the predicator consists of a complex verb phrase, the ordering of elements is a little different. For instance, in subordinate clauses, the two parts of the predicator are usually separated; the auxiliary verb follows directly after the subject, and the lexical verb is left to the end of the clause. This can also happen in main clauses. Here are some examples (the illustrating verb phrases are underlined):

22 (Subordinate clause) *þā se wer <u>wæs</u> tō þære stōwe <u>gecumen</u>, þā band hē his sunu*
WHEN THE MAN HAD (LIT. WAS) COME TO THE PLACE, THEN HE BOUND HIS SON.

23 (Main clause) *Sē yfla wer <u>hæfde</u> þone gōdan hlāford <u>gebundenne</u>*
THE EVIL MAN HAD BOUND THE GOOD LORD.

Sentence Structure: Clauses

➔ **Clauses** in OE, as in PDE, can be both **coordinated** and **subordinated** within sentences; and these relationships are often signalled by conjunctions:

Coordinating conjunctions in OE include: *and* AND, *ac* BUT, etc., e.g.:

24 *Se hlāford fērde tō þæm dūnum, ac sēo hlǣfdīge tō þæm tūne fērde*
THE LORD TRAVELLED TO THE HILLS, BUT THE LADY TRAVELLED TO THE SETTLEMENT.

NOTE: the element-order in linked coordinated clauses is sometimes that more characteristic of subordinate clauses, with the lexical verb in final position. This fact suggests that the Anglo-Saxons did not draw as clear a distinction between subordinated and coordinated clauses as is done in PDE.

Subordinating conjunctions in OE include: *forþon, for þǣm, for þǣm þe* BECAUSE; *oþ, oþ þæt* UNTIL; *gif*** IF; *þā, þā þā* WHEN; *þæt* (SO) THAT; *þēah, þēah þe*** ALTHOUGH; *þonne* THAN; *swā swā*** LIKE; *ǣr, ǣr þan þe*** BEFORE; *æfter, æfter þan/þǣm þe* AFTER; *þȳ lǣs, þȳ lǣs þe*** LEST. ←

Several of the subordinating conjunctions are or can be composed of a number of words; however, for practical purposes, they can be analysed as single units. Some imply the use of the subjunctive mood in the subordinate clause involved; conjunctions which are normally associated with verbs in the subjunctive are marked with a double asterisk ** in the list above.

Here are two examples of sentences containing subordinate clauses:

25 *For þæm þe hē wīs wer wæs, hē weorþode þone Ælmihtigan Hlāford*
BECAUSE HE WAS A WISE MAN, HE HONOURED THE ALMIGHTY LORD.

26 *Se gōda cyning lufode þæt folc swā swā se Ælmihtiga Hlāford ealle weras lufaþ*
THE GOOD KING LOVED THAT PEOPLE JUST AS THE ALMIGHTY LORD LOVES ALL MEN.

The finite verb in a subordinate clause can be either subjunctive or indicative. The indicative is generally used when the event in the subordinate clause is complete or certain; the subjunctive is often used when some doubt is involved, or when the event in question has not yet happened or is hypothetical. Thus *æfter þan þe* AFTER 'takes' the indicative, whereas *ǣr þan þe* BEFORE 'takes' the subjunctive, e.g.:

27 *Æfter þan þe hīe þone wer bundon, hīe ofslōgon hine*
AFTER THEY BOUND THE MAN, THEY SLEW HIM.

28 *Ǣr þan þe hīe þone wer ofslōgen, hīe bundon hine*
BEFORE THEY SLEW THE MAN, THEY BOUND HIM.

There are also **correlative** words, e.g. *þā...þā, forþon... forþon*, whereby two elements are linked together in parallel correspondence or contrast. In these pairs, one may be classed as an adverb, the other as a subordinating conjunction. The most common involves the use of *þā...þā...*, where *þā* can mean either THEN or WHEN. The meaning of *þā* in such sentences can be deduced from the word-order of the rest of the sentence; when *þā* is a subordinating conjunction (= WHEN), the lexical verb in the subordinate clause goes to the end of the clause; when *þā* is an adverb (= THEN), the finite verb follows immediately after. Thus the sentence

29 *þā hēo þone wer geseah, þā lufode hēo hine*
can be translated <u>WHEN</u> SHE SAW THE MAN, <u>THEN</u> SHE LOVED HIM.

Subordinate clauses fall into various categories, as in PDE. **Noun clauses** are subordinate clauses which function as the subject, object or complement of a main clause. The most common are introduced in OE by the conjunction *þæt*, e.g.:

30 *Hē bæd þæt hīe þone gōdan cyning binden*
HE COMMANDED THAT THEY BIND THE GOOD KING.

Another kind of noun clause involves the so-called **accusative and infinitive construction**. This construction is frequently used after 'verbs of saying and thinking' (KNOW, ORDER, TELL etc.), e.g.:

31 *Hē hēt þone wer hine bindan*
HE COMMANDED THE MAN TO BIND HIM.

It may be noted that here the subject (THE MAN) of the subordinate clause is in the accusative case in OE, and that the predicator (TO BIND) of the subordinate clause is in the infinitive in OE as well as in PDE; this is why the construction is so named.

Gif, meaning IF or WHETHER, can be used to introduce a noun clause (cf. PDE WHETHER SHE DOES THIS IS UP TO HER), but it is generally used (meaning IF) to introduce a conditional **adverb clause**, e.g.:

32 *Gif þū þone wer binde, se hlāford lufige þē*
IF YOU BIND THE MAN, THE LORD (WILL) LOVE YOU.

Relative clauses (i.e. clauses which function as subordinated modifiers within noun phrases) are constructed distinctively in OE. The relative particle *þe*, which is indeclinable, is frequently used on its own to introduce a relative clause, e.g.:

33 *Se wer þe man Ælfred nemneþ*
THE MAN WHOM ONE NAMES ALFRED.

However, *þe* is often further defined by the determiner *sē, sēo, þæt*, etc., which is declined according to its function within the relative clause. We could rephrase the preceding sentence thus:

34 *Se wer þone þe man Ælfred nemneþ.*

Sometimes the determiner takes over from *þe* altogether:

35 *Se wer þone man Ælfred nemneþ.*

Sometimes no relative marker is employed at all:

36 *Se wer, man Ælfred nemneþ.*

Sometimes personal pronouns are used instead of determiners:

37 *Se wer þe hine man Ælfred nemneþ.*

The verb in the relative clause is generally in the indicative mood.

Comparative clauses are clauses which function as modifiers not only within noun phrases but also within adjective and adverb phrases. In OE they are introduced by such conjunctions as *þonne* THAN or *swā (swā)* (JUST) AS, e.g.:

38 *Sēo cwēn dēmde hine rihtlicor þonne dyde se cyning*
THE QUEEN JUDGED HIM MORE JUSTLY THAN THE KING DID.

Adverb clauses are subordinate clauses which function as adverbials. They fall into two groups: (a) those where the predicator consists of a non-finite verb, not liable to inflexion in relation to the subject, e.g.:

39 *Singende þus, hē fērde tō þǣre stōwe*
SINGING THUS, HE TRAVELLED TO THAT PLACE

and (b) those introduced by a conjunction. For examples of (b), see sentences on pp. 63–64.

Sentence Structure: Some special features

Mitchell and Robinson (1995) note three characteristic features of OE sentence-structure which differ markedly from PDE usage: parataxis, recapitulation and anticipation and the splitting of heavy groups. It will be noticed in subsequent chapters that these special features recur, albeit with modifications, in later stages of Early English.

Parataxis, more common in OE than in PDE, means the juxtaposition of two or more simple clauses rather than the subordination of one clause to another (which is called **hypotaxis**). Parataxis can be of two kinds: syndetic (with coordinating conjunctions, such as *and* or *but*) or asyndetic (without such conjunctions). Mitchell and Robinson (1995) give the following PDE examples:

40 'Hypotaxis': When I came, I saw. When I saw, I conquered.
41 'Asyndetic parataxis': I came, I saw, I conquered.
42 'Syndetic parataxis': I came and I saw and I conquered, e.g.:

43 *And þā gefeaht Æþered cyning and Ælfred his brōþor wiþ þone here æt Meretūne, and hīe wæron on twæm gefierdum, and þær wearþ micel wælsliht on gehwæþere hond, and þær wearþ Hēahmund biscoþ ofslægen.*
AND THEN KING ÆTHERED, AND HIS BROTHER ALFRED, FOUGHT AGAINST THE ARMY AT 'MERETOWN', AND THEY WERE IN TWO ARMIES, AND THERE WAS GREAT SLAUGHTER ON EITHER SIDE, AND THERE BISHOP HEAHMUND WAS KILLED.

Recapitulation and anticipation. Expressions such as *the people who lived here, they loved wisdom* and *they learned that thing, that they were foolish* strike us as clumsy; in formal PDE, we would omit the commas and the words underlined. Such expressions were entirely acceptable in OE, e.g.:

44 *Ūre ieldran, þā þe þās stōwa ær hēoldon, hīe lufodon wīsdōm.*
(lit.) OUR FOREFATHERS, THOSE WHO FORMERLY HELD THESE PLACES, THEY LOVED WISDOM.

The splitting of heavy groups. It is characteristic of OE to 'split' long phrases and modifiers, which were apparently regarded as clumsy. Thus, where we would say TOM AND DICK WERE WALKING ALONG THE ROAD or SHE WAS A GOOD AND BEAUTIFUL WOMAN, a common OE arrangement was TOM WAS WALKING ALONG THE ROAD, AND DICK or SHE WAS A GOOD WOMAN, AND BEAUTIFUL, e.g.:

45 *Hē fērde mid twæm cnapum tō þæm dūnum, and Isaāc samod*
(lit.) HE TRAVELLED WITH TWO SERVANTS TO THE HILLS, AND ISAAC AS WELL.

Such usages are of course found in PDE, but they may be regarded as stylistically salient, e.g. IT WAS COLD IN THE CAR, AND UNCOMFORTABLE; INSPIRED BY BRITISH CHEERS AND LOUD/ PROCEEDING FROM THE FRENZIED CROWD (Hilaire Belloc).

3.4 Paradigms

➔ Paradigms are model patterns for the various word-classes. It is recommended that students should try to learn the OE paradigms in the paragraphs marked by arrow-icons ➔ .. ←. The paradigms given here are *not* exhaustive, and the Glossary in Part III should also be referred to for further information.

Since in OE paradigmatic choice depends to such a large extent on syntactic function, reference should be made to the Syntax section on pp. 50–66 throughout, using the Thematic Index in Part III. ←

3.4.1 Nouns

➔ Most PDE **nouns** have a very simple paradigm, taking account of number and genitive (i.e. possessive) case: *pig* : *pig's* : *pigs* : *pigs'*. OE nouns are similar, but have to take account not only of a more complex case-system but also of 'grammatical' gender. Moreover, there are several irregular sequences in PDE: *child* : *child's* : *children* : *children's, mouse* : *mouse's* : *mice* : *mice's*. These irregularities go back to OE times, and were rather more widespread then. ←

➔ OE nouns can be classified into five groups, or **declensions**. In decreasing order of frequency of occurrence in OE, these declensions are:

(1) General Masculine Declension
(2) General Feminine Declension
(3) General Neuter Declension
(4) the -*an* Declension
(5) Irregular Declensions

Declensions (1)–(3) are often referred to as **strong declensions**, whereas declension (4) is often called the **weak declension**. ←

NOTE: The terms 'strong' and 'weak' are unfortunate, given their different use with reference to adjectives and verbs; they are used here because they will be encountered in more advanced books.

The following are some typical paradigms for these declensions. Most nouns decline in accordance with these paradigms; however, there are a number of nouns which deviate a little from these models.

→ The noun: General Masculine Declension

Case	Singular	Plural
Nom.	*stān* STONE	*stānas*
Acc.	*stān*	*stānas*
Gen.	*stānes*	*stāna*
Dat.	*stāne*	*stānum*

Many masculine nouns are declined on this pattern, e.g. *cyning* KING, *bāt* BOAT, *hlāf* LOAF, *hlāford* LORD. ←

Many other masculine nouns are declined in almost the same way as Declension (1), but with minor modifications. *Dæg* DAY has the same inflexions as *stān*, but in the plural the part of the word to which inflexions are added (the **stem**) appears thus: *dagas, dagas, daga, dagum*. Sometimes, in disyllabic words, the unstressed vowel of the second syllable is lost when the word is inflected (= 'syncopation'), e.g. *engel* ANGEL becomes *engles, engle*, etc. There are also a few nouns which end in *-e* in the nominative and accusative singular but otherwise decline like *stan*, e.g. *here* RAIDING ARMY, *bæcere* BAKER, *wine* FRIEND.

→ The noun: General Feminine Declension

Case	Singular	Plural
Nom.	*lār* TEACHING	*lāra, -e*
Acc.	*lāre*	*lāra, -e*
Gen.	*lāre*	*lāra, -ena*
Dat.	*lāre*	*lārum*

Many feminine nouns are declined on this pattern, e.g. *ecg* EDGE, *hwīl* SPACE OF TIME, *glōf* GLOVE. ←

Many other feminine nouns are declined in almost the same way as this declension, but with minor modifications. A large group has *-u* in the nominative singular, but is otherwise identical to *lār*, e.g. *giefu* GIFT, *talu* TALE, *andswaru* ANSWER. As with Declension 1, syncopated forms are found: *sāwol* SOUL, *sāwle*, etc. Another large group has accusative singular the same as the nominative singular, and *-e* regularly in nominative and accusative plural; all have long root syllables (i.e. the 'rhyming' element of the word before an inflexion is added consists of a long vowel plus a single consonant, or a short vowel plus two consonants), e.g. *dǣd* DEED, *miht* POWER, *wynn* JOY.

→ The noun: General Neuter Declension

Case	Singular	Plural
Nom.	*scip* SHIP	*scipu*
Acc.	*scip*	*scipu*
Gen.	*scipes*	*scipa*
Dat.	*scipe*	*scipum*

It will be observed that, with the exception of the nominative and accusative plural, the endings of the General Neuter Declension are identical with those of the General Masculine Declension. Many neuter nouns are declined on this pattern, e.g. *bod* COMMAND, *gewrit* WRITING. ←

Many other neuter nouns are declined in almost the same way as the General Neuter Declension, but with minor modifications. The most common variant group simply omits -*u* in the nominative and accusative plural, e.g. *hūs* HOUSE, *bān* BONE, *gear* YEAR, *þing* THING, *wīf* WOMAN, *scēap* SHEEP (cf. PDE plural SHEEP). *Cild* CHILD, *cealf* CALF and *lomb* LAMB are declined as *hūs*, except that they have a variant nominative/accusative plural in -*ru* and genitive plural in -*ra*. Many nouns with nominative/accusative singular in -*e* otherwise decline as *scip*, e.g. *wīte* PUNISHMENT, *rīce* KINGDOM. Syncopated forms are sometimes found, e.g. *wǣpen* WEAPON, *wǣpnes*.

→ The noun: The -*an* Declension

This declension includes masculine, feminine and neuter nouns. The feminine nominative singular ends in -*e*, the neuter nominative and accusative singular end in -*e*; otherwise they do not differ from the masculine paradigm.

Case	Singular	Plural
Nom.	*nama* NAME	*naman*
Acc.	*naman*	*naman*
Gen.	*naman*	*namena*
Dat.	*naman*	*namum*

Like *nama* are *guma* MAN, *cnapa* BOY/SERVANT, and many others. Feminines include *heorte* HEART, *tunge* TONGUE, *hlǣfdīge* LADY, etc. There are only two neuter nouns in this declension: *ēage* EYE and *ēare* EAR. ←

A few nouns are declined in almost the same way but with minor modifications. Some ending in a long vowel or diphthong omit -*a*-, -*e*-, -*u*- in inflexions, e.g. *frēa* LORD, *frēan*, *frēana*, *frēam*, *lēo* LION, *lēon*, *lēona*, *lēom* (although *lēo* is sometimes declined regularly with the addition of an intrusive -*n*-, e.g. *lēonan*, *lēonum*).

The noun: Irregular declensions

These minor declensions can be subdivided into three groups, classified by their way of forming the plural: (a) -*a* plurals, (b) uninflected plurals, (c) 'mutation' plurals.

(a) The -*a* plural declension includes the masculines sunu son, wudu wood, and the feminines duru door, nosu nose and hond hand. Hond declines like the others, except that it has an endingless nominative and accusative singular.

Case	Singular	Plural
Nom.	*sunu* SON	*suna*
Acc.	*sunu*	*suna*
Gen.	*suna*	*suna*
Dat.	*suna*	*sunum*

(b) In general, **uninflected plurals** decline like the General Masculine, Feminine and Neuter Declensions above, except that the nominative and accusative plural is the same as the nominative and accusative singular. Of importance here are 'relationship' nouns: *fæder* FATHER belongs to the General Masculine Declension (except that the dative singular and, sometimes, the genitive singular are endingless), but masculine *brōþor* BROTHER and feminine *mōdor* MOTHER, *dohtor* DAUGHTER decline according to the following paradigm:

Case	Singular	Plural
Nom.	*dohtor* DAUGHTER	*dohtor*
Acc.	*dohtor*	*dohtor*

Gen.	*dohtor*	*dohtra*
Dat.	*dehter*	*dohtrum*

Sweostor SISTER follows the same paradigm, except that the dative singular is identical to the nominative/accusative/genitive singular.

(c) **'Mutation' plurals** are so-called because the dative singular and some of the plural forms change the stressed vowel of the singular form; this reflects a prehistoric OE sound-change, known as '*i*-mutation' or '*i*-umlaut'. The details of this sound-change need not concern us here, although something similar happens in PD German in the alternation between *Apfel* APPLE and *Äpfel* APPLES. A number of these nouns remain irregular in PDE, e.g. *fōt* FOOT, *gōs* GOOSE, *mūs* MOUSE, but others, e.g. *bōc* BOOK, *frēond* FRIEND, have become regular. *Fōt* provides a useful model paradigm, although other nouns show minor deviations from this model.

Case	Singular	Plural
Nom.	*fōt* FOOT	*fēt*
Acc.	*fōt*	*fēt*
Gen.	*fōtes*	*fōta*
Dat.	*fēt*	*fōtum*

Fēond ENEMY (cf. PDE FIEND) and *frēond* FRIEND are similar to *fōt*, except that they have medial *-īe* in the dative singular and nominative/accusative plural. Feminine nouns, with genitive singular ending in *-e* rather than *-es*, include *gōs* GOOSE, *bōc* BOOK. Other common feminine nouns of this declension include *burg* FORTRESS (dative singular, nominative/accusative plural *byr(i)g)*, *lūs* LOUSE and *mūs* MOUSE (dative singular, nominative/accusative plural *lȳs*, *mȳs*). There are other minor variations.

3.4.2 Pronouns

➔ OE **pronouns**, like nouns, have number and case, and, in the third person, gender. Like nouns, they decline. It is important to learn them all (save the duals). ⬅

   ➔ It may be helpful to note that some of the equivalent forms in OE (though not all) resemble in form those used in PDE, e.g. *mē* ME, *hē* HE, *wē* WE, *ūs* US. ⬅

The OE **pronoun-paradigms** are as follows:

→ First person

Case	Singular	Plural
Nom.	*ic*	*wē*
Acc.	*mē*	*ūs*
Gen.	*mīn*	*ūre*
Dat.	*mē*	*ūs* ←

→ Second person

Case	Singular	Plural
Nom.	*þū*	*gē*
Acc.	*þē*	*ēow*
Gen.	*þīn*	*ēower*
Dat.	*þē*	*ēow* ←

→ Third person

Third person pronouns are distinguished not only by number and case, but also by gender.

Case	Singular Masc.	Fem.	Neut.	Plural All genders
Nom.	*hē*	*hēo*	*hit*	*hīe*
Acc.	*hine*	*hīe*	*hit*	*hīe*
Gen.	*his*	*hiere*	*his*	*hiera*
Dat.	*him*	*hiere*	*him*	*him*

Mīn, þīn, ūre, ēower may be declined like strong adjectives; *his, hiere, hiera* are indeclinable. ←

In OE there are also **dual** forms of the first and second person pronouns:

Person:	First	Second
Nom.	*wit* WE TWO	*git* YOU TWO
Acc.	*unc*	*inc*

Gen.	uncer	incer
Dat.	unc	inc

The dual pronouns are comparatively rare in OE, and died out entirely early in the ME period.

An **indefinite pronoun** *man* ONE is often used, often where a passive construction would be used in PDE, e.g. <u>Man</u> *Horsan ofslōg* HORSA WAS SLAIN (lit. ONE SLEW HORSA).

➜ The relative particle *þe* WHO, WHICH, THAT, etc. may be considered a **relative pronoun**. It is indeclinable, but is sometimes used in conjunction with the definite article; see p. 64 above. It is to be distinguished from the **interrogative pronouns** used in questions, i.e. *hwā* WHO, *hwelc* WHICH. *Hwelc* is declined like a strong adjective; the paradigm of *hwā* (singular only) is as follows:

Case	Masc./Fem.	Neut.
Nom.	*hwā*	*hwæt*
Acc.	*hwone*	*hwæt*
Gen.	*hwæs*	*hwæs*
Dat.	*hwǣm*	*hwǣm* ←

NOTE: There are also separate instrumental forms in the neuter: *hwȳ, hwon*.

3.4.3 Determiners

➜ In PDE, determiners include the **articles** (**definite** and **indefinite**, i.e. THE, A(N) respectively, and **demonstratives**. Strictly speaking, OE has no indefinite article as such; *sum* A CERTAIN and *ān* ONE fulfil some of the functions of the PDE indefinite article A(N). The demonstrative determiner equivalent to PDE THAT also functions as the definite article with the meaning THE. This determiner agrees with the noun which it modifies in gender, number and case. It is essential to know determiners well, since very often they provide the only sure clue to the grammatical structure of an OE clause. The paradigm is as follows:

	Singular			Plural
Case	Masc.	Fem.	Neut.	All genders
Nom.	*se*	*sēo*	*þæt*	*þā*
Acc.	*þone*	*þā*	*þæt*	*þā*

Gen.	þæs	þǣre	þæs	þāra
Dat.	þǣm	þǣre	þǣm	þǣm

Se etc. can also be used as a pronoun (as *sē*), and often appears with the relative particle *þe*. ←

NOTE: A distinct **instrumental** form is occasionally found in the singular: *þȳ* (Masc), *þȳ/þon* (Neut), *þǣre* (Fem).

→ The paradigm of the **demonstrative determiner** equivalent to PDE THIS, THESE is as follows:

Case	Singular Masc.	Fem.	Neut.	Plural All genders
Nom.	þes	þēos	þis	þās
Acc.	þisne	þās	þis	þās
Gen.	þisses	þisse	þisses	þissa
Dat.	þissum	þisse	þissum	þissum ←

3.4.4 Adjectives

→ OE **adjectives**, like nouns, have inflexions to indicate gender, number and case. Because of agreement, the form of the adjective depends on the form of the noun which it modifies; see p. 52 above. ←

→ There are two major adjectival paradigms, strong and weak. Determining which paradigm to use depends on the sequential relationship between the adjective and other words; see pp. 53–4 above. ←

→ Two paradigms for a model adjective, *gōd/gōda* GOOD, follow here. Many of the endings of the strong and weak adjectives are identical with those of the strong and weak nouns; however, a few (e.g. *-um*) do indicate different functions from those which might be expected in noun paradigms.

(a) **Weak paradigm**
   gōda GOOD

Case	Singular Masc.	Fem.	Neut.	Plural All genders
Nom.	gōda	gōde	gōde	gōdan
Acc.	gōdan	gōdan	gōde	gōdan
Gen.	gōdan	gōdan	gōdan	gōdra/gōdena
Dat.	gōdan	gōdan	gōdan	gōdum

(b) **Strong paradigm**

gōd GOOD

	Singular			Plural		
Case	Masc.	Fem.	Neut.	Masc.	Fem.	Neut.
Nom.	*gōd*	*gōd*	*gōd*	*gōde*	*gōde*	*gōd*
Acc.	*gōdne*	*gōde*	*gōd*	*gōde*	*gōde*	*gōd*
Gen.	*gōdes*	*gōdre*	*gōdes*	*gōdra*	*gōdra*	*gōdra*
Dat.	*gōdum*	*gōdre*	*gōdum*	*gōdum*	*gōdum*	*gōdum*

Most adjectives behave like *gōd*. The main group of exceptions consist of adjectives such as *cwic* ALIVE, which differ from *gōd* in the strong nominative singular and plural, thus:

Sg: Masc *cwic*, Fem *cwicu*, Neut *cwic*
Pl: Masc *cwice*, Fem *cwice/-a*, Neut *cwicu*

The *cwic*-group of adjectives are those whose rhyming element when no inflexion is suffixed consists of a short vowel plus a single consonant (i.e. they contain 'short' root-syllables). ←

Comparison of adjectives is generally straightforward. Just as in PDE -ER and -EST are added to the stem of the adjective (e.g. DEAR, DEARER, DEAREST), so in OE *-ra* and *-ost* are added to the stem (e.g. *lēof* DEAR, *lēofra*, *lēofost*). However, in OE the *-ra* and *-ost* forms (known traditionally as **comparative** and **superlative**) do decline. Comparatives always decline in the weak paradigm whether or not preceded by a determiner; superlatives decline according to weak or strong paradigm, the selection being determined according to the same criteria as for the simple adjective. As in PDE, there are some irregular comparative and superlative forms (cf. PDE GOOD, BETTER (vs. *GOODER), BEST (vs. *GOODEST)). The most important are:

eald OLD	*ieldra*	*ieldest*
geong YOUNG	*gingra*	*gingest*
lang LONG	*lengra*	*lengest*
strang STRONG	*strengra*	*strengest*
hēah HIGH	*hīerra*	*hīehst*
gōd GOOD	*betera, betra, sēlra*	*betst, sēlest*
yfel EVIL	*wiersa*	*wier(re)st*
micel BIG	*māra*	*mǣst*
lȳtel LITTLE	*lǣssa*	*lǣst*

3.4.5 Adverbs

In general, OE adverbs end in -e or in -lice, and are indeclinable. For comparative and superlative forms, -or and -ost are added to the stem or -līc-.

3.4.6 Verbs

→ In PDE, there are three types of verb: **weak**, **strong** and **irregular** (see p. 41). OE similarly distinguishes between strong, weak and irregular verbs, e.g. hē band HE BOUND (strong; cf. hē bindeþ/bint HE BINDS), hē lufode HE LOVED (weak; cf. hē lufaþ HE LOVES). ←

→ All OE verb paradigms take account of person, number, tense and mood. For details, see pp. 55–60. ←

→ Both strong and weak verbs follow regular patterns or paradigms. These paradigms are called **conjugations**. ←

→ Here are four **model conjugations**: bindan TO BIND, a typical strong verb; fremman TO PERFORM and lufian TO LOVE, typical weak verbs which follow slightly different paradigmatic patterns; and the most important irregular verb, wesan/bēon TO BE. ←

→ (1) bindan TO BIND

	Indicative	Subjunctive
Present		
1st person sg	binde	binde
2nd person sg	bindest, bintst	binde
3rd person sg	bindeþ, bint	binde
All persons pl	bindaþ	binden
Preterite		
1st person sg	band	bunde
2nd person sg	bunde	bunde
3rd person sg	band	bunde
All persons pl	bundon	bunden
Imperative		
2nd person sg	bind (one person is commanded)	
2nd person pl	bindaþ (more than one person is commanded)	

Participles
Present   *bindende*
Past   *(ge)bunden*

Note the different stem-vowel in the present and preterite tenses, the defining characteristic of a strong verb. Just as in PDE, there are many other kinds of strong verb, with different vowel-alternations. All OE forms used in this book are recorded in the Glossary in Part III. ←

→ (2) *fremman* TO PERFORM

	Indicative	Subjunctive
Present		
1st person sg	*fremme*	*fremme*
2nd person sg	*fremest*	*fremme*
3rd person sg	*fremeþ*	*fremme*
All persons pl	*fremmaþ*	*fremmen*
Preterite		
1st person sg	*fremede*	*fremede*
2nd person sg	*fremedest*	*fremede*
3rd person sg	*fremede*	*fremede*
All persons pl	*fremedon*	*fremeden*

Imperative
2nd person sg   *freme* (one person is commanded)
2nd person pl   *fremmaþ* (more than one person is commanded)

Participles
Present: *fremmende*
Past: *(ge)fremed*

Note the addition of a medial *-ed-* in the preterite forms of the verb. This indicates that *fremman* is a weak verb. ←

→ (3) *lufian* TO LOVE

	Indicative	Subjunctive
Present		
1st person sg	*lufi(g)e*	*lufi(g)e*
2nd person sg	*lufast*	*lufi(g)e*
3rd person sg	*lufaþ*	*lufi(g)e*
All persons pl	*lufiaþ*	*lufi(g)en*
Preterite		
1st person sg	*lufode*	*lufode*
2nd person sg	*lufodest*	*lufode*
3rd person sg	*lufode*	*lufode*
All persons pl	*lufodon*	*lufoden*

Imperative
2nd person sg   *lufa* (one person is commanded)
2nd person pl   *lufiaþ* (more than one person is commanded)

Participles
Present: *lufiende*
Past: *(ge)lufod*

Note the addition of a medial *-od-* in the preterite forms of the verb. This indicates that *lufian* is a weak verb. ←

→ (4) *wesan, bēon* TO BE

	Indicative	Subjunctive
Present		
1st person sg	*eom/bēo*	*sīe/bēo*
2nd person sg	*eart/bist*	*sīe/bēo*
3rd person sg	*is/biþ*	*sīe/bēo*
All persons pl	*sind/sindon/bēoþ*	*sien/bēon*
Preterite		
1st person sg	*wæs*	*wǣre*
2nd person sg	*wǣre*	*wǣre*
3rd person sg	*wæs*	*wǣre*
All persons pl	*wǣron*	*wǣren*

Imperative
2nd person sg   *wes/bēo* (one person is commanded)
2nd person pl   *wesaþ/bēoþ* (more than one person is
                        commanded)

Participles
Present: *wesende*

Note that there are no forms derived from *bēon* in the preterite.
Instead, the forms of *wesan* are used. This replacement of one form
by another within the same paradigm is called **suppletion**. ←

NOTE: A minor form of the paradigms above is the so-called **inflected infinitive**, e.g. *tō
bindenne* TO BIND. The functions of this particular form are discussed on p. 56.

The *ge-* prefix seems to have originated as a marker of perfect aspect, although
it had lost much of this function by the time of recorded OE. It is common in past
participles.

More about strong verbs

→ *Bindan* can act as the general model for all strong verbs, since the
same inflexions appear in all of them. However, you will be aware of
the existence of varying patterns of alternation in stem vowels, as in
PDE; cf. RISE : ROSE : RISEN, CHOOSE : CHOSE : CHOSEN, DRINK :
DRANK : DRUNK, COME : CAME, SHAKE : SHOOK : SHAKEN etc. A
similarly varying set of patterns is to be found in OE. ←

This alternation in the strong verb paradigms of OE derives
from a Proto-Indo-European phenomenon usually referred to by the
German term *Ablaut* (often translated as *gradation*). It is a feature
not only of the strong verb system, but has also left its mark in such
pairs as PDE HOT, HEAT.

The range of alternations in any strong verb paradigm is
indicated by the form of (1) the infinitive, (2) the third person present
sg indicative, (3) the first person preterite indicative, (4) the preterite
plural, (5) the past participle. These forms are traditionally known as
the **principal parts** of the strong verb, since from them a complete
paradigm of the verb can be generated.

NOTE: Strictly speaking, (2) in the above paragraph is not a principal part of the
strong verb paradigm, since it is produced not by ablaut but by a later Germanic
phenomenon, **mutation** or **Umlaut**; see also p. 71 above for a similar phenomenon in
the noun-system.

Here are some examples of the seven classes of strong verb distinguished by their principal parts. Classes of strong verb can generally be recognised by their infinitive form (e.g. Class I verbs have *ī* as the stressed vowel followed by a single consonant), but Classes III and VII present special difficulties, and there are some exceptions elsewhere in the system.

Class I

    SHINE *scīnan scīnþ scān scinon (ge)scinen*

Other verbs belonging to this class include: *bītan* BITE, *drīfan* DRIVE, *(ā)rīsan* RISE, *snīþan* CUT, *stīgan* ASCEND, *rīdan* RIDE, *(ge)wītan* DEPART.

Class II

    CREEP *crēopan crīepþ crēap crupon (ge)cropen*

A variant paradigm for this class is represented by

    ENJOY *brūcan brȳcþ brēac brucon (ge)brocen*

Other verbs belonging to this class include *bēodan* OFFER, *flēogan* FLY, *scēotan* SHOOT, *būgan* BOW, *scūfan* PUSH. Some verbs of this class change the medial *-s-* to *-r-* in parts of their paradigm ('rhotacism'), e.g.:

    CHOOSE *cēosan cīest cēas curon (ge)coren*

Like *cēosan* are *hrēosan* FALL, *(for)lēosan* LOSE. Another variation appears in

    BOIL *sēoþan sīeþþ sēaþ sudon soden*

Class III

In prehistoric times, these verbs followed the same pattern. However, subsequent sound-changes have obscured this similarity, and the resulting forms are very various. Typical paradigms are:

PULL	bregdan	brītt	brægd	brugdon	(ge)brogden
BIND	bindan	bint	band	bundon	(ge)bunden
PAY	gieldan	gielt	geald	guldon	(ge)golden
HELP	helpan	hilpþ	healp	hulpon	(ge)holpen
FIGHT	feohtan	fieht	feaht	fuhton	(ge)fohten
BURN	biernan	bi(e)rnþ	barn	burnon	(ge)burnen
BECOME	weorþan	wierþ	wearþ	wurdon	(ge)worden

The paradigm of *bregdan* is comparatively near to the original pattern; the other paradigms have deviated from this, for various reasons. A common feature is that the stressed syllable of the infinitive *generally* consists of a vowel (monophthong or diphthong) followed by two consonants. This class of verbs also includes *berstan* BURST, *drincan* DRINK, *delfan* DIG, *weorpan* THROW.

Class IV

BEAR *beran bi(e)rþ bær bǣron (ge)boren*

Beran is typical, and this class also includes *brecan* BREAK, *stelan* STEAL, *teran* TEAR. Also of this class, but with a different paradigm resulting from subsequent sound-changes, is

CUT *scieran scierþ scear scēaron scoren*

The verbs *niman* TAKE and *cuman* COME, with irregular paradigms, also belong to this class:

TAKE *niman nimþ nōm, nām nōmon, nāmon (ge)numen*
COME *cuman cymþ cōm cōmon (ge) cumen*

Class V

TREAD *tredan tritt træd trǣdon (ge)treden*

Similar are *etan* EAT, *sprecan* SPEAK, *wrecan* AVENGE. A few verbs of this class have different stem-vowels in the infinitive, e.g. *sittan* SIT, *licgan* LIE, *biddan* PRAY, but are otherwise the same. *Giefan* GIVE belongs to this class, but its paradigm is

GIVE *giefan giefþ geaf geafon (ge)giefen*

Class VI

GO *faran fǣrþ fōr fōron (ge)faren*

is typical; others are *scacan* SHAKE, *sacan* QUARREL. *Standan* follows the same pattern, except that it drops *-n-* in the preterite tense (*stōd, stōdon*). The following have weak presents, but otherwise follow this pattern: *hebban* LIFT, *scieppan* CREATE, *swerian* SWEAR.

Class VII

A very complex class, with various vowels in the infinitive. Some common verbs of this class are:

HOLD	*healdan*	*hielt*	*hēold*	*hēoldon*	*(ge)healden*
FALL	*feallan*	*fielþ*	*fēoll*	*fēollon*	*(ge)feallen*
KNOW	*cnāwan*	*cnǣwþ*	*cnēow*	*cnēowon*	*(ge)cnāwen*
WEEP	*wēpan*	*wēpþ*	*wēop*	*wēopon*	*(ge)wōpen*
SLEEP	*slǣpan*	*slǣpþ*	*slēp*	*slēpon*	*(ge)slǣpen*
CALL	*hātan*	*hǣtt*	*hēt*	*hēton*	*hāten*

An important subset of strong verbs are known as **contracted verbs**. These are verbs whose infinitives, in prehistoric times, ended in *-han*, but *-h-* was lost before the time of written records and irregular infinitives resulted. They are found in several classes of strong verb. The following are probably the most important of the group:

I:	COVER	*wrēon*	*wrīhþ*	*wrāh*	*wrigon*	*(ge)wrigen*
II:	DRAW	*tēon*	*tīehþ*	*tēah*	*tugon*	*(ge)togen*
V:	SEE	*sēon*	*si(e)hþ*	*seah*	*sāwon*	*(ge)sewen*
VI:	STRIKE	*slēan*	*slīehþ*	*slōg*	*slōgon*	*(ge)slǣgen*
VII:	SEIZE	*fōn*	*fēhþ*	*fēng*	*fēngon*	*(ge)fangen*

More about weak verbs

As well as variations in the conjugation of strong verbs, there were alternations in the conjugation of weak verbs. Weak verbs fall into three classes: Class I, which conjugates like *fremman*, Class II, which conjugates like *lufian*, and Class III, consisting of the verbs *habban* HAVE, *libban* LIVE, *secgan* SAY and *hycgan* THINK.

Weak **Class II** verbs can be recognised by their ending in *-ian* in the infinitive after consonants other than *r*. *Werian* DEFEND, *herian* PRAISE, etc. are, therefore, Class I verbs. *Andswarian* ANSWER, *gaderian* GATHER and *timbrian* BUILD are exceptions to this rule; they belong to Class II.

The forms of weak **Class III** verbs are much like those in Classes I and II, but they also show certain variations in the stressed vowels which can lead the beginner to suppose them to be strong verbs. Their principal parts are as follows:

HAVE	*habban*	*hæfþ*	*hæfde*	*hæfdon*	*(ge)hæfd*
LIVE	*libban*	*leofaþ*	*leofode, lifde*	*leofodon, lifdon*
			(ge)leofod/-lifd		
SAY	*secgan*	*sægþ*	*sægde*	*sægdon*	*(ge)sægd*
THINK	*hycgan*	*hogaþ*	*hog(o)de*	*hog(o)don*	*(ge)hogod*

More about irregular verbs

Irregular verbs fall into two groups: (I) **preterite-present verbs**, whose present tense is formed from an old preterite paradigm and whose new preterite is formed on the weak model; and (II) so-called **anomalous verbs**. Common Group (I) verbs are: *witan* KNOW, *āgan* OWN, *cunnan* KNOW, *magan* BE ABLE TO, *sculan* BE OBLIGED TO, HAVE TO, *mōtan* BE ALLOWED, *þurfan* NEED; common Group (2) verbs are *wesan/bēon* BE, *willan* WANT TO, *nyllan* NOT WANT TO, *dōn* DO and *gān* GO. These verbs are very common in OE. The full paradigm of *wesan/bēon* is given on pp. 78–9. Here are the principal parts of other common irregular verbs (nb. 'no pp.' = no recorded past participle):

Group I

KNOW	*witan wāt wiste wiston (ge)witen*
OWN	*āgan āh āhte āhton ǣgen*
KNOW	*cunnan can(n) cūþe cūþon (ge)cunnen*
BE ABLE TO	*magan mæg meahte/mihte meahton/mihton*
	no pp.

BE OBLIGED TO	*sculan*	*sceal*	*sc(e)olde*	*sc(e)oldon*	no pp.
BE ALLOWED	*mōtan*	*mōt*	*mōste*	*mōston*	no pp.
NEED	*þurfan*	*þearf*	*þorfte*	*þorfton*	no pp.

Group II

WANT TO	*willan*	*wil(l)e*	*wolde*	*woldon*	no pp.
NOT WANT TO	*nyllan*	*nyle*	*nolde*	*noldon*	no pp.
DO	*dōn*	*dēþ*	*dyde*	*dydon*	*(ge)dōn*
GO	*gān*	*gāþ*	*ēode*	*ēodon*	*(ge)gān*

3.4.7 Numerals

➔ Numerals are divided into **cardinal** (ONE, TWO, etc.) and **ordinal** (FIRST, SECOND, etc.) types. The following are the OE cardinal numbers 1–10, 100 and 1000, and equivalent ordinal numbers for 1–10.

	Cardinal	Ordinal
1	*ān*	*forma*
2	*twā*	*ōþer*
3	*þrēo*	*þridda*
4	*fēower*	*fēorþa*
5	*fīf*	*fīfta*
6	*siex*	*siexta*
7	*seofon*	*seofoþa*
8	*eahta*	*eahtoþa*
9	*nigon*	*nigoþa*
10	*tīen*	*tēoþa*
100	*hund, hundred, hundtēontig*	
1000	*þūsend*	

Ān ONE is declined like the adjectives, both strong and weak (weak forms are usually used in the sense ALONE). *Twā* TWO declines thus: Nom/Acc *twēgen* (Masc), *twā* (Fem), *twā/tū* (Neut); Gen *twēgra/ twēg(e)a* (all genders); Dat *twǣm* (all genders). *þrēo* THREE declines thus: Nom/Acc *þrīe* (Masc), *þrēo* (Fem/Neut); Gen *þrēora* (all genders); Dat *þrim* (all genders). All other cardinal numbers are generally indeclinable. ←

Ordinal numbers are always declined weak, except for *ōþer* SECOND, which is always declined strong.

3.5 Lexicon

➔ The OE **lexicon** consists of a mixture of forms inherited from its Germanic ancestor and forms 'borrowed' from languages with which OE had come into contact. New forms were also derived from processes of word-formation: compounding and affixation. The details of OE lexical development are complex, and are probably best studied as part of a general historical survey; see further Barber (1993), Baugh and Cable (1993) and Mitchell and Robinson (1995: esp. chapter 4), and also Smith (1996: chapter 6). These notes are designed to give a very basic outline of the principal characteristics of OE vocabulary. ⬅

3.5.1 Inheritance and borrowing

The bulk of the OE lexicon was inherited from Proto-Germanic. This component included words which have no cognate in the other Indo-European languages, and which presumably either entered Germanic through early contact with non-Indo-European languages now extinct, or are forms whose cognates have simply not survived in those languages, e.g. *wīf* WOMAN, *drincan* DRINK; cf. Present-Day French *la femme* WOMAN, *boire* DRINK, Present-Day German *Weib* WOMAN, *trinken* DRINK.

Some elements of OE vocabulary, however, did derive from contact with other Indo-European languages, whereby a foreign word would be adopted and modified to comply with OE structures. This process is traditionally termed borrowing.

NOTE: The term 'borrowing' is in a sense not particularly apt since the word usually remains in the parent language; however, it does draw a metaphorical parallel between the development of vocabulary and monetary exchange, which is quite a useful one.

OE, for a mixture of extra- and intralinguistic reasons, seems to have been relatively inhospitable to words from other languages. Nevertheless, a number of languages did leave their mark on the OE lexicon: Greek, Latin, Celtic, Scandinavian and French.

A few **Greek** words are found in all the Germanic languages, and may have come into Germanic directly through contact between Greek and Proto-Germanic. However, all such words were also borrowed into Latin, so it is quite possible that these words entered Germanic through contact with Latin. Examples of such words in their OE forms are *dēofol* DEVIL, *engel* ANGEL, *cirice* CHURCH.

Latin borrowings fall into two sets: (1) words borrowed at an early date, mostly in the Proto-Germanic period, and (2) learned words borrowed after the Anglo-Saxons came to Britain. Examples of (1) are: *draca* DRAGON, *ceaster* CITY, *disc* DISH, *strǣt* ROAD, *pīnung* TORTURE; examples of (2) are: *gīgant* GIANT, *cleric* CLERIC, *dēmon* DEMON. Unsurprisingly, many Latin loanwords are to do with Roman technology or with the spread of the Christian religion.

There are very few **Celtic** loanwords in OE, other than those in place-names (a category with a distinct function); these borrowings are generally specialised ones, e.g. *drȳ* MAGICIAN, *torr* ROCK.

Scandinavian and **French** loanwords are rarely reflected in the OE written record; they will be discussed further in Chapter 4.

3.5.2 Word-formation

Much more than by borrowing, OE increases its wordstock through word-formation, rather as Present-Day German does (cf. Present-Day German *Fernsprecher* TELEPHONE, lit. 'distant-talker'). Two principal methods are used: **compounding** of words already existing in the language, and **affixation**. Such phenomena are attested in PDE, but they seem to be particularly common in OE.

Examples of compounding are: *sciprāp* SHIPROPE, CABLE; *wīdsǣ* WIDE/OPEN SEA, *ǣrdæg* EARLY DAY/FIRST LIGHT (all nouns); *lofgeorn* EAGER FOR PRAISE, *wīdcūþ* WIDELY KNOWN, *blīþemōd* HAPPY IN SPIRIT. Examples of affixation are: *bedǣlan* DEPRIVE (*be + dǣlan* = FROM + SHARE), *unfriþ* STRIFE (*un + friþ* = UN + PEACE), *cildhād* CHILDHOOD (*cild + hād* = CHILD + -HOOD/STATE).

3.6 Appendix I: From Early to Late West Saxon

As indicated in 3.1 above, the variety of Old English (OE) with which the body of this chapter is concerned is a regularised form of Early West Saxon, a written dialect current in Wessex at the time of King Alfred (AD 849–899). An understanding of this variety remains the most useful basis for those pursuing subsequent philological work. However, most of the OE texts which survive from the Anglo-Saxon period were written in Late West Saxon, which seems, through being copied outside its area of origin, to have achieved the status of a written standard language in the late tenth and eleventh centuries. Like other medieval 'standard' languages – and unlike PDE standard written languages – this Late West Saxon standard admitted of a fair degree of minor variation, some of which signals an incipient collapse of earlier inflexional distinctions. Since most modern editors of OE texts do not normalise their texts, texts you encounter may differ slightly in forms from those you are used to.

Of course, any normalised version of OE is artificial, and thus open to scholarly criticism. But the variation of 'real' OE is unhelpful for the beginning student of the language for whom this book is designed, so a normalised variety has been adopted for most texts in Part II, and for the examples demonstrating grammatical form in this chapter. However, since the serious student will soon encounter non-normalised texts, it may be helpful to have an account here of the most common differences between Early and Late West Saxon, to accompany the 'bridge' passages from one of Ælfric's homilies and from *Beowulf* (Texts A, (7) and (8)).

The differences between Early and Late West Saxon, and the types of variation in the latter, can be divided for convenience into two groups: **spellings** and **inflexions**. The second group is more important.

3.6.1 Spellings

(1) Compensatory lengthening. Early West Saxon *g* between a short vowel and *d, n* disappeared, and the vowel was lengthened, e.g. *sægde > sǣde* SAID.

(2) Early West Saxon *ie, īe* were replaced by *i, ī, y, ȳ* in Late West Saxon, e.g. *Scieppend > Scyppend* CREATOR.

(3) Early West Saxon (-)*weor-*, (-)*wier-* appear as (-)*wur-*, e.g. *sweord > swurd* SWORD.

(4) When followed by *ht, hs* at the end of a word, Early West Saxon *eo, io* became *i;* hence *cniht* BOY, but *cneohtas* (pl.).

(5) Other frequent variations in spelling include *a ~ o* before nasal consonants (e.g. *hand ~ hond* HAND), *æ ~ a* in words like *þǣm ~ þām*.

3.6.2 Inflexions

Towards the end of the OE period, unstressed vowels seem to have become indistinct in pronunciation. This may have been part of a trend in the history of English away from inflexions towards the use of prepositions, and a more fixed word-order, to express the relationship between words. This spoken-language development is reflected in the written mode by the interchangeability of endings such as *-an, -on, -en*, etc. For instance, the ending *-an* on verbs, classically an infinitive inflexion, could function as a preterite plural indicative marker, and *-en* could function as an indicative as well as a subjunctive inflexion.

3.7 Appendix II: On OE dialects

The study of OE dialects is a somewhat complex matter; and, since most OE which students will regularly encounter is written in West Saxon, very little discussion of dialects is offered here. The situation is very different in Middle English, when dialectal distinctiveness was the norm.

It is usual to state that there is evidence for four dialects: Old Northumbrian and Old Mercian (usually grouped together as Old Anglian), Old Kentish and West Saxon. However, for all varieties except West Saxon the evidence is fragmentary and difficult to interpret, and the geographical expressions 'Kentish', 'Northumbrian', etc. are probably best seen as typological notions rather than as specifically localised. And of course there are large parts of the country with hardly any material remains at all, e.g. East Anglia.

Dialectal distinctions in OE are found in transmission (i.e. spelling and phonology – insofar as the latter can be reconstructed), grammar and (it appears) lexicon. Details of dialectal usage can be found in the standard OE grammars, e.g. A. Campbell, *Old English Grammar* (Oxford: Clarendon Press, 1959), R. Hogg, *A Grammar of Old English I: Phonology* (Oxford: Blackwell, 1992).

Chapter 4

Middle English

4.1 Introduction

Middle English (ME) is the term used to describe the varieties of English spoken and written from about 1100 to about 1500. ME differed from OE in terms of its status and function. After the Norman Conquest of 1066, the OE written standard, Late West Saxon, gradually fell into disuse. Latin took over from English the documentary functions of the medieval state, and French, the language of the conquerors, at first competed with English as the language of literary culture. Of course, English continued to be employed both in speech and in writing. Indeed, there is much more surviving written ME than OE material, and English not only remained the primary spoken language of the vast majority of the population of England but also was rapidly adopted by the descendants of the Norman-French invaders. However, in writing at least, the function of English was for much of the period a local one, catering for local literary tastes and used for the contemporary equivalent of primary education.

As a result, there was no normative form of written English (let alone spoken English) for most of the ME period. Since English had a local rather than a national function, it made pedagogic sense to develop writing systems which reflected closely local patterns of vernacular speech and which were therefore capable of being taught on a 'phonic' basis. Thus, when ME was employed in the written mode after 1066, it reflected historical changes and dialectal variation which had been disguised by OE written standardisation, with local patterns of spelling (reflecting, albeit conventionally, local pronunciations), grammar and even lexicon. Since the constraints of the OE standardised usage had been lifted, the full impact of the very substantial contact between English and Scandinavian was expressed in the written mode only after the Norman Conquest. Moreover, ME was profoundly affected by contact with French, above all in lexis.

During the course of the ME period, English re-established itself as an elaborated language of prestige, available for a whole range of literary and documentary functions. As English began once again to take on these national functions, it became communicatively necessary to develop new national norms; and a new standard form of written English, this time based on the usage of London, began to emerge from the fifteenth century onwards. This was generally adopted by the early printers, who in turn provided a norm for private usage from the sixteenth century onwards. At the same time, major changes in the pronunciation of English took place, and new vocabulary, reflecting humanist learning and the discoveries of European explorers, entered the language. These features mark the beginnings of Early Modern English (EModE), and will be pursued further in Chapter 5.

Because of the variety of ME, it is not possible to write a grammar of it in the same way as can be done for West Saxon. In a sense, every ME text has its own grammar. But since most students begin their ME studies with the writings of Chaucer, the usage of the best Chaucerian manuscripts may be taken as a good reference point.

Although I have not hesitated to draw upon other texts where illustration of some common point is required, the principal texts chosen as a source of examples in this chapter are those Chaucerian texts given in Part II: the *Pardoner's Tale*, parts of the *General Prologue*, and the *Parson's Tale*. All these texts are taken from the Ellesmere Manuscript of the *Canterbury Tales* (San Marino, California, Huntington Library EL 26.C.9), a copy of the *Tales* which dates from the first decade after Chaucer's death (*ca.* 1399). The Ellesmere text has been chosen because it is by far the best-known manuscript, the basis of most modern editions, and its forms will be or will become familiar to most readers of this book. In some crucial features, though, notably in the inflexion of the adjective, the Ellesmere MS seems to deviate from Chaucer's usage more than other important early MSS. The best-known of these is probably the Hengwrt MS, now Aberystwyth, National Library of Wales, MS 392, which, although almost certainly copied by the same scribe as the Ellesmere text, differs from it linguistically in certain respects.

NOTE: There is a continuing controversy about the precise details of Chaucer's language. In brief, some scholars hold that a manuscript of a late medieval scientific text, *The Equatorie of the Planetis* in MS Cambridge, Peterhouse 75.I, is a Chaucerian holograph, and is evidence for the poet's own usage; others hold that this argument is not yet proven. Given this controversy, it seems inappropriate in an introductory textbook such as this to refer to this text. Moreover, the interest of the *Equatorie*, though considerable for specialists in Chaucerian studies and in late medieval science, is rather restricted, and the range of linguistic usages is necessarily somewhat limited.

Chaucerian/quasi-Chaucerian English was not a ME national norm in its own day; indeed, for much of the ME period, no national norm existed. The comparative familiarity of 'Chaucerian' English to the modern reader is really to do with the vagaries of historical development; Chaucer's English, the English of late-fourteenth-century London, happens to be a principal ancestor of Present-Day standard English and therefore shares features with it. There is considerable linguistic variation, not only between ME texts but also (frequently) internally, within a single text. To give an idea of the range of variation in ME, short annotated passages from other texts have also been given in Part II; for details, see the Introduction to the selection of Texts B, p. 176.

The bulk of this chapter is divided into four main parts: Spelling and Pronunciation, Syntax, Paradigms and Lexicon. Cross-references are given throughout. In each case, the usage is for the most part that of the Ellesmere text, and examples are generally drawn from there. Thus the usage presented here is largely that of a particular manuscript of Chaucer's works; although for convenience the term 'Chaucerian usage' is employed, this is simply a shorthand way of saying, 'the usage of the most authoritative Chaucerian MSS'. Other ME texts will have distinct systems.

Paragraphs of major significance for beginners are marked at the beginning and end with an arrow-icon ➔ . . ◀. The significance of unmarked material will become apparent later in students' encounters with ME texts. It is suggested that, as in Chapter 3, beginners alternate examination of Texts II in Part II below with reading portions of this chapter.

4.2 Spelling and pronunciation

4.2.1 The alphabet

➔ The alphabet used in the Ellesmere text is much like that of PDE, although a number of the letters have different sound-values from those they have today. The OE letters æ, ð and runic ƿ 'wynn' disappeared early in the ME period, being replaced by *a/e*, *th/þ* and *w* respectively. ◀

OE runic *þ* 'thorn' is retained in ME times until the advent of printing at the end of the fifteenth century, especially in the north and west of England, but it tends to be replaced by *th* as the ME period progresses. It is found rarely in the Ellesmere text, and there largely only in some determiners (e.g. THE, THAT). In the North, it tends to be written in a way which makes it identical to *y*, and indeed some early printers in the sixteenth century adopt the expedient of using *y* to represent *þ* in some determiners, e.g. *ye* THE. Such usages have developed as an 'archaistic' practice in PDE, cf. YE OLDE TEA SHOPPE.

OE *ʒ* was retained by some scribes, commonly to represent [x] and [j], but also sporadically [w] and occasionally [z]; it is as this last that it is still used in some varieties of present-day cursive handwriting. It does not occur in the Ellesmere text, which uses *gh* medially and *y* initially instead of *ʒ*. *g* replaced *ʒ* for [g]; [g] was known to the Anglo-Saxons, but was restricted to texts in Latin. *c* and *k* develop their present-day distribution in the lexicon during this period.

The letter *h* seems to have been used as a diacritic mark to indicate some kind of modification of the letter it followed: thus the development of *th*, *sh* (or *sch*) for OE *sc*, *gh* (which tended to replace *ʒ* medially), *ch* for some realisations of OE *c*, and *wh* for OE *hw*.

The letters *u* and *v* were used interchangeably to represent both vowel [u, ʊ] and consonant [v], with *v* generally being used initially, *u* elsewhere.

In OE, *y* had represented a close rounded front vowel [y], but that vowel appears to have been unrounded in many dialects of late OE, merging with OE *i* [i]. *y* then came to be used interchangeably with *i*, especially in environments where contemporary handwriting could be confusing, e.g. before or after *m*, *n*, *u*; all these letters could be written using the 'minim' stroke ɩ: *m*, *n*, *u*. *o* was used for *u* in similar environments. This accounts for the PDE spellings COME (OE *cuman*), LOVE (OE *lufu*), which could potentially appear as *cmue* and *lnue* in ME.

In words like *how* and *broun*, *ou*, *ow* replaced OE *ū*. In many varieties of ME, *e*, *o* and sometimes *a* could be doubled to indicate 'length' and this practice remains in PDE with regard to E, O (e.g. GOOD, FEED); cf. ME *good* GOOD, *fleen* FLEE, *taak* TAKE. *o(o)* also appeared in London ME for words which had *ā* in Old English, e.g. *sto(o)n* STONE (OE *stān*), *ho(o)m* HOME (OE *hām*).

4.2.2 Pronunciation

➔ Our knowledge of ME **pronunciation** derives from the analysis of rhyming verse, reconstruction from later and earlier states of the language, and the interpretation of spelling. As with OE pronunciation, there remain a number of controversial points, and the account given here is very general; also as with OE, it is very important for students not to worry too much about the precise pronunciation of ME. An extremely useful fact is that PDE spelling, if interpreted carefully, provides a good indication of Chaucerian usage. As with OE, the key point about Chaucerian English is that, except in a few special cases governed by convention, all letters were pronounced. For the terminology employed, see Chapter 2, p. 20ff. ←

As in OE, **stressed monophthongal vowels** fell into two major classes: long and short. It is not usual to signal these differences in ME texts, so long vowels have not been marked with macrons as in Chapter 3. There is indirect evidence that the long and short vowels of OE developed qualitative as well as quantitative distinctions during the transition to ME, so that the short vowels were more open in quality than their long equivalents. By about 1400, London English seems to have had something like the following inventory of monophthongal vowel-sounds: [iː, ɪ, eː, ɛː, ɛ, aː, a, ɔː, ɔ, oː, uː, ʊ].

The short vowels [ɪ, ɛ, a, ɔ, ʊ] were generally spelt *i, e, a, o, u*, and for the most part appear as such in PDE spelling. Those forms where an *o* was used for *u* in minim environments (see p. 95 above), e.g. PDE COME, LOVE, generally occur in present-day southern English dialects with the pronunciation [ʌ]; PDE /ʌ/ is not phonemic in ME.

The long vowels [iː, eː, ɛː, aː, ɔː, oː, uː] were generally spelt *i/y/ij, e/ee, e/ee, a/aa, o/oo, o/oo* and *ou/ow* respectively. For various reasons (see Chapter 5 below), PDE spelling gives a good indication of the distribution of these sounds in ME. PDE practice is to signal these vowels either by adding a 'silent E' as a diacritic mark, or by adding an additional vowel-symbol. Here are some examples, with PDE pronunciations for the most part as in RP and GenAm. In some cases, marked with a double asterisk **, the present-day pronunciation given is similar to that found in Modern Scots, which has not developed the (slightly) confusing diphthongal sounds found in southern English prestigious accents.

ME	PDE	PDE example	ME example
[iː]	[aɪ]	LIFE	[liːf] *lyf, lif*
[eː]	[iː]	MEET	[meːtən] *meten*
[ɛː]	[iː]	MEAT	[mɛːtə] *mete*
[aː]	[eː]**	NAME, TAKE	[naːmə, taːk] *name, taak*
[uː]	[aʊ]	HOW, TOWN	[huː, tuːn] *how, toun*
[oː]	[uː]	MOOD	[moːd] *mo(o)d*
[ɔː]	[oː]**	BOAT, HOME	[bɔːt, hɔːm] *bo(o)t, ho(o)m*

During the sixteenth century there were sporadic shortenings of earlier long vowels, which produced in some present-day varieties a distinction in pronunciation between such pairs as FOOD: GOOD, READ: BREAD. Here the present-day spelling is the key to understanding late medieval practice; in ME times, the pairs of words were pronounced with the same vowel.

In **the vowels of unstressed syllables**, the old qualitative distinctions were already becoming obscured in late OE times. This pattern continued in ME: Chaucer's unstressed vowel-sounds seem to have been [ə, ɪ]. Both are usually spelt *e, i/y* in the Ellesmere MS, e.g. *olde̲, swery̲ng*.

The major difference between OE and ME vowel-systems was in **diphthongs**; the OE diphthongs had monophthongised and merged with other sounds, and new diphthongs had emerged in the system through vocalisations of consonants and borrowings from French. Chaucer's system seems to have been as follows:

[aɪ] *ai, ay, ei, ey*, e.g. DAY, GREY
[ɔɪ] *oi, oy*, e.g. *joye* JOY*
[ʊɪ] *oi, oy*, e.g. *poynt* POINT*
[aʊ] *au*, e.g. *saugh* SAW (verb)
[ɔʊ] *ow*, e.g. *knowe(n)* KNEW
[ɛʊ] *ew*, e.g. *lewd* IGNORANT (cf. PDE LEWD)+
[ɪʊ] *ew*, e.g. *newe* NEW

* quite possibly no longer distinguished in Chaucerian pronunciation
+ very few words in Chaucerian English seem to have been pronounced with [ɛʊ]: besides *lewed, fewe* FEW, *shewe(n)* SHOW and *beautee* BEAUTY are the most important.

The **consonant**-system of Chaucerian English was much the same as that found in Present-Day RP and GenAm. The inventory of consonant-sounds in Chaucerian English seems to have been only a little different from that of PDE: [p, b, t, d, k, g, tʃ, dʒ, f, v, θ, ð, s, z, ʃ, h, m, n, l, r, w, ʍ, j] were all phonemic in ME. The major differences between ME and PDE usages are:

(a) Chaucerian English does not seem to have had any 'silent' letters. Thus *white*, *myghte* were pronounced [ʍiːtə, mɪxtə] respectively.

(b) *gh*, *ʒ* were pronounced [x] medially; *ʒ* was pronounced [j] initially. (*ʒ* is not found in the Ellesmere MS of *The Canterbury Tales*, but is common in other important early Chaucerian MSS.) The usual PDE pronunciation of *gh*, i.e. 'silent GH', appears from the fifteenth century onwards; the pronunciation with [f] in ENOUGH, ROUGH, etc. began to appear from the fifteenth century, but spellings such as *boft* BOUGHT, *dafter* DAUGHTER, showing that the present-day distribution of pronunciations had not become settled, still appear in the eighteenth century; see p. 133.

(c) *Nacioun* NATION, *sure*, etc. were pronounced with [sj] rather than with PDE [ʃ].

(d) Initial *w*, *k*, *g* were all pronounced in Chaucer's language in words like *write(n)*, *gnawe(n)*, *kne(e)* KNEE. It seems likely that their employment reflects contemporary secondary articulations of the consonant, e.g. *wr* possibly indicates the pronunciation of /r/ with lip-rounding.

(e) [ʍ, w] remained distinct phonemes in Chaucer's language, /ʍ, w/: thus *wyn* WINE [wiːn], *while* WHILE [ʍiːl]. However, the beginnings of the present-day southern English pronunciation, which has merged the two sounds on /w/, is indicated in some ME dialects, e.g. *wan* WHEN.

➔ This description of Chaucer's pronunciation is necessarily a limited sketch; as with OE, you will see different accounts in different handbooks and editions. It is however, broadly in line with most modern views. As in Chapter 3, it is very important not to worry too much about getting ME pronunciation absolutely correct. Quite apart from anything else, there was certainly a very broad spectrum of accents available to choose from in late medieval London at the time Chaucer lived there. ⬅

4.3 Syntax

This section is to do with the various functions the various forms carry out; for details of forms, constant reference should be made to section 4.4, using the Thematic Index in Part III. For the grammatical terminology employed, see section 2.5.

➔ In ME, **inflexions** are less important for indicating the relationships between words than they were in OE, so ME is in general much easier for present-day readers to understand – although its greater apparent familiarity can sometimes lead readers to skate over quite significant differences of meaning between ME and PDE. ←

The ME pattern emerged in the following way. The inflexional systems of OE become obscured during the Late OE and ME periods, probably for a variety of interacting reasons. Nouns, adjectives and determiners are no longer marked for grammatical gender. Verb-endings have been markedly reduced in variety. Case-endings are no longer so distinctive, and are no longer as useful in distinguishing grammatical function. In place of the OE case-system, ME adopts alternative primary strategies to express the relationships between phrases. Optional patterns of OE element-order, which were a matter of stylistic choice in OE, become fixed patterns indicating phrasal relationships, and prepositions, which could often be omitted in OE, are adopted in a much more widespread fashion in ME.

➔ Although the grammatical configuration of Chaucerian English is much more like that of PDE than is OE, there remain differences in detail. Chaucerian English represents a mid-point in the typological sequence OE : ME : PDE; it contains some forms and constructions which point back to OE usage, and others which point forward to later developments. ←

4.3.1 The noun phrase

Chaucerian English distinguishes **case**, **agreement** and **number**. Grammatical **gender** is only rarely distinguished in ME, and it is not a characteristic of Chaucerian usage.

The noun phrase: Case, number and agreement

➜ In Chaucerian English, **nouns** are inflected for **number** (singular/plural), and for the **case** of genitive singular (no case distinction is made in the plural). There are fragmentary traces of the old dative case, but these need not concern us here. There are some paradigmatic differences between ME and PDE, though these are, unsurprisingly, mostly to do with the greater number of variant paradigms which survive from OE into ME. Function within the clause is now marked primarily by word-order. Only pronouns are still regularly marked for case (as indeed, broadly speaking, they are in PDE). ◄

➜ **Agreement**, however, remains important in the ME noun phrase, notably with regard to some adjectives and some determiners, although the paradigmatic variation in modifiers is considerably less than in OE. ◄

4.3.2 Pronouns

➜ As in OE and PDE, ME **pronouns** are categorised by **person**, i.e. first/second/third. Singular third person pronouns (the equivalent of HE/SHE/IT, i.e. *he, s(c)he, it*) are selected on the basis of the sex (i.e. 'natural gender') of the noun to which they refer; the grammatical gender of OE grammar is by Chaucer's time no longer a feature. As in PDE, pronouns can be inflected according to case; cf. *he/his/him* HE/HIS/HIM, etc. ◄

➜ *Thou, ye,* etc. have special uses in ME. The distinction is roughly comparable with the *tu/vous* distinction in French, where *thou* is not only singular but also intimate and *ye* is regarded as more formal as well as plural. The situation became more complex in EModE (see pp. 134–5). ◄

The **indefinite pronoun** *man* ONE is treated as a third person pronoun; in some varieties of ME, it appears as a reduced form *me*.

The so-called **ethic dative pronoun** used to reinforce a subject-pronoun is fairly common in ME, e.g.:

1 *he wole <u>him</u> no thyng hyde*
   HE WILL HIDE NOTHING.

This usage is archaic in PDE, though it was still common in EModE.

The regular **relative pronouns** *that/þat*, *(þe/the)* *which(e)* *(that)*, etc. are used in relative clauses, although the relative pronoun is sometimes omitted altogether; the present-day distinction between 'human' WHO(M) and 'non-human' WHICH is not regularly made in ME, e.g.:

2   *This yongeste, which that wente to the toun*
    THIS YOUNGEST (MAN), WHO WENT TO THE TOWN

3   *if a preest be foul, on <u>whom</u> we truste . . .*
    IF A PRIEST IN <u>whom</u> we trust is foul . . .

which(e) can be inflected along the lines of adjectives (see pp. 114–15) to signal the plurality of its referent, e.g.:

4   *<u>whiche</u> they weren*
    WHO THEY WERE

Sporadically *whiche* is used with singular reference when preceded by *the*, e.g. *the <u>whiche</u> pointz* WHICH POINTS. *Who(m)/whos* are basically **interrogative pronouns** in ME. However, *whom* and *whos* can be used as relative pronouns in ME, although *who* seems not to be so used.

The noun phrase: Adjectives

➔ The form of some monosyllabic **adjectives** is governed by the number of the nouns they modify, e.g. *old man* OLD MAN, *olde men* OLD MEN. Moreover, as in OE, there are **strong** and **weak** paradigms for these adjectives in Chaucerian English, whereby, if the adjective is preceded by the determiners THE, THAT, THIS, THOSE, THESE, the weak form is used. Elsewhere, the strong paradigm was generally used. ←

➔ By Chaucer's time the formal distinctiveness of these paradigms was very slight, e.g. *this olde man* THIS OLD MAN, *this man is old* THIS MAN IS OLD. This distinction seems to have been found only in formal London speech, and had ceased to be observed in Northern Middle English; in the generation after Chaucer it had died out altogether throughout the English-speaking area. ←

NOTE: Chaucer commonly uses a strong form of the adjective after *a(n)*. This is because *a(n)* was not used as an indefinite article in OE, and thus *an* in *an oold man* simply sustains the inherited strong usage which would have been regular in an OE indefinite phrase, e.g. *eald mann.*

Chaucer also uses a weak adjective in vocative constructions, i.e. when persons are addressed directly; this is an OE usage (see p. 54, NOTE). Eg.:

5   *Nay, olde cherl, by God, thou shalt nat so*
   NO, OLD PEASANT, BY GOD, THOU MUST NOT (DO) SO.

The scribe of the Ellesmere MS has some difficulties with *-e* in adjectives, apparently because it is not a living part of his own language (as it was with Chaucer). When the Ellesmere scribe copied the Hengwrt MS he seems for various reasons to have reproduced Chaucer's usage more closely, and thus the distribution of *-e* is much more regular. In the Hengwrt MS, *-e* is omitted in 'weak' positions only in the speech of the young northern students in *The Reeve's Tale*, but this deviation is probably Chaucerian, and part of the poet's practice of reproducing northern speech-habits; adjectival *-e* disappeared in northern dialects long before it disappeared in the south.

A few adjectives were inflectionally marked in imitation of French usage, e.g. *weyes espirituels* SPIRITUAL PATHS. In this case, also in imitation of French usage, the adjective follows the noun (this can also occur without marking the adjective for agreement, e.g. *heestes honurable* HONOURABLE COMMANDMENTS, rhyming with *the firste table*). It seems likely that phrases such as *theues stronge* are employed for rhyming purposes.

Many adjectives did not follow this pattern and did not inflect to indicate singular/plural, strong/weak; even in Chaucerian English the usage was dying out. For details of adjectival paradigms and for indications of which adjectives were inflected and which were not, see 'Paradigms' pp. 114–15 below.

Adjectives are frequently used in ME as the head words of phrases which in PDE would more usually be expressed with supplementary nouns, e.g. *the yongeste* THE YOUNG (MEN).

The noun phrase: Determiners

➔ As in PDE, a few **determiners** agree in number with the nouns they modify, though the formal markers can differ somewhat. Some determiners inflect, e.g. *thise men* THESE MEN, cf. *this man* THIS MAN. However, most determiners, such as *the*, do not inflect. An indefinite article *a(n)*, derived from the OE numeral *ān* ONE, was becoming more widespread along PDE lines; *an* was used when the following word began with a vowel, *a* elsewhere. Since *a(n)* was a 'new' form, its syntactic role differed slightly from that of the other determiners with regard to the adjective; see pp. 101–2 above. ←

The noun phrase: Numerals

None of the cardinal **numerals** inflects in Chaucerian usage, as a few did in OE, and their usage is much as in PDE. One common practice, which still occurs in certain PDE dialects, is the use of an endingless noun after a numeral, e.g. *foure and twenty yere* TWENTY-FOUR YEARS. Such usages are generally accounted for as survivals of the OE numeral + genitive plural construction, or of OE nouns with an endingless plural. The sequence of numbers in *foure and twenty* may also be noted. It is comparatively rare in present-day varieties of English, but not unknown; cf. also Present-Day German *vier und zwanzig*.

4.3.3 The verb phrase

➔ The special set of grammatical categories involved in the **verb phrase** and discussed in Chapter 3 above are relevant to ME studies as well, i.e. agreement, finiteness, simple and complex verb phrases, person, tense, mood, aspect and voice. Since all these grammatical categories are relevant for ME (and indeed EModE) as well as OE studies, they are not defined again here; see pp. 40–4. Of course, the formal expression of these categories was not the same in ME as in OE; see pp. 115–19. ←

ME uses both **simple** and **complex** verb phrases for various purposes. A feature of OE often retained into ME is the 'split' between auxiliary and lexical verbs in complex verb phrases, e.g.:

6 *he kan no difference fynde*
HE CAN FIND NO DIFFERENCE.

The verb phrase: Agreement, person and number

➔ As in OE, there is **agreement** between subject and predicator, e.g. *he bindeth* HE BINDS; *they binden* THEY BIND. Finite verbs are thus inflected according to **person** and **number**, e.g. *I binde, thou bindest, he bindeth, they binde.* ←

The verb phrase: Tense and aspect

→ Finite verbs are also inflected for **present and preterite tense**, e.g. *sche loueth, sche loued.* The '**historic present**', whereby a formal present tense is used with a past-tense meaning, is not found in OE. However, it is common in Chaucerian English, e.g.:

7 *This yongeste, which that wente to the toun, ful ofte in herte he rolleth up and doun*...
THIS YOUNGEST (MAN), WHO WENT TO THE TOWN, VERY OFTEN HE REVOLVES IN HIS HEART ... ←

Complex verb phrases are also used to express tense and aspectual distinctions. With regard to the **future tense**, in ME, *wol/schal*, etc., the reflexes of OE *willan, sculan*, etc., frequently retain the lexical significance they carried in OE (**volition** and **obligation** respectively), e.g.:

8 *Oure sweete Lord God of hevene*... *wole that we comen alle to the knowleche of hym*
OUR SWEET LORD GOD OF HEAVEN ... WISHES THAT WE ALL COME TO KNOWLEDGE OF HIM

9 ...*he shal first biwaylen the synnes that he hath doon*
HE MUST FIRST BEWAIL THE SINS THAT HE HAS DONE.

However, it could be argued that they are used simply as future auxiliaries as well in examples such as

10 *Now wol I yow deffenden hasardye*
NOW I ?SHALL/WANT TO FORBID YOU (FROM PURSUING) GAMBLING.

Since volition generally implies futurity, the extension of the construction to take over expression of the simple future tense was always a potential development. Future time could also, as in OE, be expressed by the simple present tense.

Other tense and aspectual distinctions can be expressed in ME as they are in PDE, with the use of auxiliaries followed by lexical verbs, although the range of forms is not as large; thus the common PDE AM + -ING construction (e.g. I AM GOING, I WAS GOING), used to express **progressive aspect**, is not common in ME, and simple verb phrases are used instead. **Perfect aspect combined with past tense** can be expressed, as in PDE, by means of complex verb phrases. When the lexical verb is **transitive**, i.e. capable of governing a direct object, then reflexes of OE *habban* are used, e.g.:

11 *whan a man <u>hath dronken</u> draughtes thre*
   WHEN A MAN <u>HAS DRUNK</u> THREE DRAUGHTS

When the verb is **intransitive** (i.e. not capable of governing a direct object) the reflexes of PDE BE are used, e.g.:

12 *At nyght <u>was come</u> into that hostelrye wel nyne and twenty in a compaignye*
   AT NIGHT ABOUT TWENTY-NINE (FOLK) IN A COMPANY <u>HAD COME</u> INTO THAT HOSTELRY.

Gan (from OE *ginnan* BEGIN) is sometimes used as a past-tense auxiliary, e.g.:

13 *This olde man <u>gan looke</u> in his visage*
   THIS OLD MAN LOOKED INTO HIS FACE

The verb phrase: Voice

Reflexes of OE *weorþan* BECOME are still found occasionally in Chaucerian English (ME *worthe(n)*, etc.) to express **passive voice**. However, the usual methods for expressing passive voice in ME are either by using the verb *ben*, as in PDE, e.g.:

14 *He is . . . yholde the lasse in reputacioun*
   HE IS CONSIDERED . . . THE LESS IN REPUTATION.

or, as in OE, by using the indefinite pronoun *man*. The PDE construction linking passive and **progressive** elements, e.g. WAS BEING BOUND, is unknown in ME; instead the form *be* + past participle is employed, e.g.:

15 *Biforn a cors, was caried to his graue*
   IN FRONT OF A CORPSE [WHICH] WAS BEING CARRIED TO ITS GRAVE.

The verb phrase: Mood

During the course of the ME period, the formal **indicative/subjunctive mood** distinctions characteristic of OE generally collapsed, although vestiges of the older usage remain, as in PDE, in formal usage, e.g.:

16 *if that yow be so leef to fynde Deeth*
   IF YOU ARE (cf. PDE formal BE) SO DESIROUS OF FINDING DEATH.

The reflexes of PDE MAY, MIGHT – in Chaucerian English *may* and *might (e)* – became extended in meaning during the course of the ME period. Their original sense was CAN, COULD, and they usually retain these meanings in Chaucerian English, e.g.:

17 *the feend...putte in his thoughte that he sholde poyson beye, with which he myghte sleen his felawes tweye*
   THE DEVIL...PUT INTO HIS THOUGHT THAT HE SHOULD BUY THE POISON, WITH WHICH HE COULD KILL HIS TWO COMPANIONS.

However, there is an obvious semantic overlap between MAY/MIGHT 'hypothesis' and CAN/COULD 'possibility' even in PDE, and so, as the old formal subjunctive disappeared, ME *may/might*, etc. could easily be extended to take over the functions of that construction. An example such as

18 *Thanne may we bothe oure lustes al fulfille*
   THEN WE ?MAY/CAN BOTH FULFIL ENTIRELY OUR DESIRES

demonstrates the overlap.

The verb phrase: Impersonal and phrasal verbs

The main syntactic innovation in the verb phrase during the ME period was the rise of two kinds of construction: the **impersonal verb**, and the **phrasal verb**. The former, found in OE, became greatly extended in use during the ME period. It may be exemplified by *us thynketh* IT SEEMS TO US, *hem thoughte* IT SEEMED TO THEM; it was already highly restricted in context in EModE times, and has now largely disappeared. The latter construction, still common in PDE, consists of a verb followed by another element which seems closely tied to it semantically, e.g. GET UP, WAKE UP, LOOK UP. Typically, phrasal verbs in PDE are rather colloquial in register; typically also, they tend to have formal-register near-synonyms, cf. ARISE, AWAKE, CONSULT.

The verb phrase: Negation

As in OE, **negation** is expressed in ME by the negative particle *ne*, frequently assimilated to the words it precedes (e.g. *nis = ne + is*); cf. *nas* WAS NOT. In ME it is often reinforced by a postverbal particle *nat*, *nought*, etc; toward the end of the ME period, and thus usually in Chaucerian English, it became common to drop *ne* and use *nat*, etc. alone, e.g. *if he wol nat tarie* IF HE DOES NOT WISH TO WAIT. As in OE, multiple negation was not stigmatised: *he nevere yet no vileynye ne sayde* HE NEVER YET SPOKE ANY COARSE SPEECH.

4.3.4 Sentence structure

Word-order

➔ Since in ME the OE inflectional system has broken down, **word-order** patterns are much like those of PDE with the same range of prototypical and deviant usages. The usual order of elements, in both main and subordinate clauses, is SP (i.e. subject–predicator), where the predicator immediately follows the subject, e.g.:

19 *If that <u>a prynce useth</u> hasardye...*
   IF A PRINCE PRACTISES GAMBLING ...

However, this usage can, as in PDE, be deviated from for stylistic reasons in order to place some other element in thematic position in a clause or sentence, e.g.:

20 *This tresor hath Fortune unto us yiven, in myrthe and jolitee oure lyf to lyven*
   FORTUNE HAS GIVEN TO US THIS TREASURE IN ORDER TO LIVE OUR LIFE IN MIRTH AND JOLLITY.

When a complex verb phrase is employed, the lexical element tends to appear at the end of the clause, e.g.:

21 *the feend...putte in his thought that he sholde poyson beye*
THE DEVIL PUT INTO HIS MIND THAT HE SHOULD BUY
POISON. ←

Despite what has just been said, S...P (subject–predicator) is still sometimes found, especially when the object of the clause is a pronoun, e.g.:

22 *This olde man ful mekely hem grette*
THIS OLD MAN GREETED THEM VERY HUMBLY.

And a delayed verb phrase can still appear occasionally in subordinate clauses, e.g.:

23 *Whan that Aprill with his shoures soote the droghte of March*
   hath perced to the roote...
WHEN APRIL WITH ITS SWEET SHOWERS HAS PIERCED TO THE
ROOT THE DROUGHT OF MARCH...

PS (predicator–subject) is still often found when the clause begins with an adverbial, e.g.:

24 *unnethe ariseth he out of his synne*
HE SCARCELY RISES OUT OF HIS SIN (with simple verb phrase)

25 *at many a noble armee hadde he be*
HE HAD BEEN ON MANY A NOBLE MILITARY EXPEDITION
(with splitting of the complex verb phrase).

It is also found in questions, e.g.:

26 *Why lyvestow so longe in so greet age?*
WHY DO YOU LIVE SO LONG IN(TO) SUCH GREAT AGE?

NOTE: The so-called 'dummy' *do*, characteristic of PDE in such constructions, appears in EModE, and will be discussed on pp. 140–41; it is not a feature of ME question-constructions.

Sentence Structure: Clauses

➔ ME has a range of different **clause**-types, both coordinated and subordinated. These clauses are no longer generally distinguished in Chaucerian English, as they were in OE, by word-order. ←
   Coordinating conjunctions include *and, but*, etc., as in PDE, e.g.:

27 *And forth he gooth...into the toun, unto a pothecarie, <u>and</u>*
   preyde hym that he hym wolde selle som poyson...
   AND HE GOES FORTH ... INTO THE TOWN, TO AN APOTHE-
   CARY, AND BEGGED HIM THAT HE WOULD SELL SOME
   POISON . . .

Subordinate clauses can be introduced, as in OE, by a range of
subordinating conjunctions. The forms of these conjunctions are
much as in PDE, except that the particle *that* often (although not
always) appears along with *if, whan*, etc., e.g. <u>*Whan that*</u> *Aprill* ...
WHEN APRIL . . . <u>*If that*</u> *a prynce* IF A PRINCE, <u>*how that*</u> *the seconde*
heeste HOW THE SECOND COMMANDMENT, <u>*whil that*</u> *thou*
strogelest WHILE YOU STRUGGLE, <u>*er that*</u> *he dide* BEFORE HE DID;
beside <u>*whan*</u> *he came* WHEN HE CAME, <u>*if*</u> *he be baptized* IF HE IS
BAPTISED. The option of using *that* has obvious metrical advantages,
and there is evidence that metre seems to have been a determining
factor in Chaucer's selection or omission of *that* in such constructions.

Relative clauses are commonly introduced by *that* in ME. A
slightly confusing feature is that they can sometimes be separated
from the noun phrases they modify, something not possible in PDE,
e.g.:

28 *God save yow, that boghte agayn mankynde*
   MAY GOD, WHO REDEEMED MANKIND, SAVE YOU.

For other relative pronouns, see pp. 101, 114. Sometimes a relative
clause is used without a relative pronoun when that pronoun is in subject position; this usage occurs in OE and EModE, but is not known in
PDE, e.g.:

29 *Biforn a cors, was caried to his graue*
   IN FRONT OF A CORPSE, WHICH WAS BEING CARRIED TO ITS
   GRAVE.

Adverbial clauses without subordinating conjunctions are also
found in ME, e.g.:

30 *Bledynge ay at his nose in dronkenesse*
CONTINUALLY BLEEDING AT HIS NOSE IN DRUNKENNESS.

Comparative clauses are common, e.g.:

31 *And two of vs shul strenger be than oon*
AND TWO OF US MUST BE STRONGER THAN ONE.

Sometimes the conjunctions characteristic of comparative clauses are used correlatively, e.g.:

32 *right as they hadde cast his deeth bifoore, right so they han hym slayn*
JUST AS THEY HAD PLANNED HIS DEATH EARLIER, JUST SO THEY HAVE SLAIN HIM.

Sentence Structure: Some special features

Chaucerian English still retains some special features of OE sentence-structure which are not a prototypical feature of PDE usage: recapitulation and anticipation and the splitting of heavy groups. The third feature discussed on pp. 65–66, parataxis, is not so salient a feature of Chaucer's practice, but it is found in some varieties of ME.

In **recapitulation and anticipation** an anticipatory noun phrase is recapitulated later in the clause by a pronoun, e.g.:

33 *This yongeste, which that wente to the toun, ful ofte in herte he rolleth up and doun*
THIS YOUNGEST (MAN), WHO WENT TO THE TOWN, VERY OFTEN HE REVOLVES IN SPIRIT . . .

34 *The worste of hem, he spak the first word*
THE WORST OF THEM, HE SPOKE THE FIRST WORD.

35 *alle the gretteste that were of that lond, pleyynge atte hasard he hem fond*
ALL THE GREATEST WHO WERE FROM THAT LAND, HE FOUND THEM PLAYING AT GAMBLING.

The splitting of heavy groups also survives into ME, e.g.:

36 *Thy tonge is lost, and al thyn honeste cure*
YOUR TONGUE AND YOUR CARE FOR HONOURABLE THINGS ARE LOST

37 *An oold man and a povre with hem mette*
AN OLD AND POOR MAN MET WITH THEM.

Stylistic developments between OE and late ME times meant that writers could choose between the older **paratactic** style characteristic of OE and a newer **hypotactic** style which seems to have been brought into Engish through contact with French; for the difference, see definitions on pp. 65–6. Chaucerian usage was basically hypotactic, with quite complex subordination (cf., in Texts B below, lines 1–11 of the *General Prologue* extract, or the passage from the *Parson's Tale*); but some writers, such as Malory, seem consciously to have sustained the older paratactic usage as a sign of traditional values.

4.4 Paradigms

➜ Paradigms are the model patterns for the various word-classes, and this section gives an outline of ME usage, demonstrating the reflexes of the OE configuration.

The usage here represents for the most part that of the Ellesmere MS of the *Canterbury Tales*, but examples are also drawn from other texts so that a broad characterisation of ME patterns can be given. Where possible, the paradigms have been designed to correspond to those found in Chapter 3 above, so that comparisons can be made easily. ←

Since paradigmatic choice depends on syntactic function, reference should be made to section 4.3 throughout, using the Thematic Index in Part III.

4.4.1 Nouns

➜ The five OE **noun**-declensions survive into ME, but there are numerous reorganisations and merging of categories. By the time of Chaucer, there was a Basic Declension, whose essential characteristics derive from the OE General Masculine Declension, and a set of Irregular Declensions deriving from the other four OE declensions. The **Basic Noun Declension** was as follows:

Case	Singular	Plural
Nom.	*stoon* STONE	*stoones*
Acc.	*stoon*	*stoones*
Gen.	*stoones*	*stoones*
Dat.	*stoon(e)*	*stoones*

Most ME nouns are declined on this pattern, e.g. *fish* FISH, *bo(o)k* BOOK, *lond* LAND. A sub-group where the nominative singular ends in *-e* follows a generally similar pattern, e.g. *herte(s)* HEART(S), *soule(s)* SOUL(S). Sometimes the inflexional *-e-* is replaced by *-y-*, e.g. *swevenys* DREAMS; sometimes it is dropped altogether, especially in nouns of more than one syllable, e.g. *naciouns* NATIONS. It will be observed that *-e* occasionally appears in the dative case; this use is largely restricted in the Ellesmere MS to what seem to have been a few formulaic expressions, e.g. *in londe* IN (THE) LAND. ←

In Chaucerian English, there are only a few exceptions to this paradigm, and these may be termed the **Irregular Declensions**. These are relics of the OE Declensions (2)–(5), and in general they demonstrate deviant plural forms (genitive singular forms follow the Basic paradigm). Examples are: *oxen* OXEN, *eyen* EYES and the variant form *foon* FOES (beside *foos*); *feet* FEET beside *foot* FOOT, *gees* GEESE beside *goos* GOOSE; and nouns with endingless plurals such as *sheep* SHEEP, *deer* DEER and variant forms such as *thyng* THINGS, *hors* HORSES (beside *thynges*, HORSES). It will be observed that many of these exceptions are also found in PDE.

A few nouns have forms of the genitive which differ from that of the Basic declension. Some are endingless, e.g. classical names whose nominative forms end in *-s*, e.g. *Epicurus owene son* EPICURUS' OWN SON, and some native forms *my fader soule* MY FATHER'S SOUL.

In other ME texts, more of these exceptions survive; e.g., in *Sir Orfeo*, a text whose manuscript dates from the generation before Chaucer, forms such as *berien* BERRIES, *honden* HANDS are also found.

4.4.2 Pronouns

→ ME **pronouns**, as those of PDE, retain number, person and case distinctions, and are also used to signal the gender of their referents when in the third person. However, the gender reference is not based on grammatical gender, as it was in OE, but on so-called natural gender, i.e. sex-distinctions. The case-distinctions, between nominative, accusative, genitive and dative, are those defined in Chapter 3 above. ←

NOTE: The OE **dual pronoun** (see pp. 72–3 above) died out early in the ME period, so is not discussed further here.

→ The Chaucerian **pronoun-paradigms** are as follows:

First person

Case	Singular	Plural
Nom.	*I* (rarely *ich*)	*we*
Acc.	*me*	*us*
Gen.	*my(n)(e)*	*our(e)(s)*
Dat.	*me*	*us*

Second person

Case	Singular	Plural
Nom.	*thou/thow*	*ye*
Acc.	*the(e)*	*you/yow*
Gen.	*thy(n)(e)*	*your(e)(s)*
Dat.	*the(e)*	*you/yow*

Third person

	Singular			Plural
Gender	Masc.	Fem.	Neut.	All genders
Nom.	*he*	*she*	*it/hit*	*they*
Acc.	*hym/him*	*hir(e)/hyr(e)*	*it/hit*	*hem*
Gen.	*his*	*hir(e)(s)*	*his*	*hir(e)(s)*
Dat.	*hym/him*	*hir(e)/hyr(e)*	*it/hit*	*hem*

The accusative and dative in all pronouns are the same; this is because these two categories of pronoun may be considered to have merged in Chaucerian English. ←

When the subject-form of the second person singular pronoun is preceded by its verb, it frequently merges with that verb, thus: *lyvestow?* DO YOU LIVE?

The inflexion of the **relative pronoun** *which(e)* was discussed on p. 101 above; it seems that it sporadically behaved in formal terms like an adjective (see pp. 114–15). The pronoun *who* had the following paradigm: *who, whom* (acc.), *whos* (gen.). All three forms could be used as **interrogative pronouns**; *whom* and *whos* were used as relative pronouns, but *who* seems not to have been so used. By far the most common relative pronoun was *that*, which was indeclinable.

4.4.3 Determiners

➔ Chaucerian English, unlike OE, has an **indefinite article**, *a(n)* whose distribution was the same as in PDE, i.e. *an* pre-vocalically and *a* elsewhere.

The **definite article** in Chaucerian English was *the*, and was indeclinable. The OE inflected determiner equivalent to *the* (i.e. *se*, *sēo*, *pæt*, etc.) was replaced by the indeclinable forms early in the ME period.

The **demonstrative determiners** were however inflected, as in PDE agreeing with their headword in number, i.e. *that* THAT, *tho* THOSE; *this* THIS, *thise/these* THESE, but the large number of inflexions found in OE texts had disappeared. There is uncertainty as to the pronunciation of *e* in *thise*. Metrical evidence suggests that the *-e* on *thise/these* was not pronounced, and was simply a written-mode marker of plurality. ←

4.4.4 Adjectives

➔ Chaucerian English sometimes distinguishes between **strong** and **weak** paradigms of **adjectives** (cf. pp. 101–02), although the range of inflexional distinctions is considerably smaller than it was in OE times.

Chaucerian adjectives may be classified into the following groups:

(1) Adjectives derived from OE which distinguish strong and weak paradigms. These are reflexes of OE adjectives such as *eald* OLD, *gōd* GOOD, *lang* LONG, *geong* YOUNG. In Chaucerian English the paradigm is as follows:

> *old* OLD (strong singular), *olde* (strong plural), *olde* (weak singular), *olde* (weak plural)

(2) Adjectives derived from OE which do not distinguish strong and weak paradigms. These fall into two sub-groups:

Adjectives whose OE nom masc sg strong ended in *-e*, e.g. *wilde* WILD, *swēte* SWEET, *clǣne* CLEAN, *grēne* GREEN; cf. Chaucerian *wilde, sweete, clene, grene*.

Adjectives which were polysyllabic in OE, e.g. *hālig* HOLY, *lȳtel* LITTLE; cf. Chaucerian *hooly, litel*.

These adjectives are indeclinable in Chaucerian English.

(3) Adjectives derived from other languages, e.g. *large* AMPLE, GENEROUS. Such adjectives are indeclinable in Chaucerian English. The only forms in this group which occasionally inflect are those where French practices of inflexion have been transferred to English, e.g. *weyes espirituels* SPIRITUAL PATHS. ←

NOTE: A relic of the old genitive plural is occasionally found, e.g. *Oure Hoost ... was oure aller cok* OUR HOST ... WAS (AWAKENING) COCKEREL FOR ALL OF US, where *aller* is the reflex of OE *ealra*. The expression seems to be a formulaic one, and no longer productive in ME.

Comparison of adjectives follows a simple pattern very like PDE usage, with regular *-er/-re, -est* and broadly the same irregular forms as appear in PDE (e.g. *good: bettre: best(e)*).

4.4.5 Adverbs

In general, Chaucerian **adverbs** end in *-e, -ly* and (rarely) *-liche*, e.g. *brighte* BRIGHTLY, *unkyndely* UNNATURALLY, *roialliche* ROYALLY.

4.4.6 Verbs

→ As in OE and PDE, ME **verbs** fall into three categories: **weak**, **strong** and **irregular**, and the assignment of verbs to these categories is broadly in line with the assignment of such verbs in earlier and later states of the language. As is the case in OE and PDE, ME verb paradigms take account of **person**, **number**, **tense** and **mood**. ←
→ Here are three **model conjugations**: *binde(n)* TO BIND, a typical strong verb; *love(n)* TO LOVE, a typical weak verb; and

the most important irregular verb, *be(e)(n)* TO BE. These paradigms correspond to those offered for OE in Chapter 3. ←

→ (1) *binde(n)* TO BIND

	Indicative	Subjunctive
Present		
1st person sg	*binde*	*binde*
2nd person sg	*bindest*	*binde*
3rd person sg	*bindeth*	*binde*
All persons pl	*binde(n)*	*binde(n)*
Preterite		
All persons sg	*bounde*	*bounde*
All persons pl	*bounde(n)*	*bounde(n)*
Imperative:	*bind* (sg)	*bindeth* (pl)
Participles		
Present	*bindyng(e)*	Past *(y)bounde(n)* ←

→ (2) *love(n)* TO LOVE

	Indicative	Subjunctive
Present		
1st person sg	*love*	*love*
2nd person sg	*lovest*	*love*
3rd person sg	*loveth*	*love*
All persons pl	*love(n)*	*love(n)*
Preterite		
1st/3rd persons sg	*lovede*	*lovede*
2nd person sg	*lovedest*	*lovede*
All persons pl	*lovede(n)*	*lovede(n)*
Imperative:	*love* (sg)	*loveth* (pl)
Participles		
Present	*lovyng(e)*	Past *(y)loved(e)* ←

→ (3) *be(e)(n)* TO BE

	Indicative	Subjunctive
Present		
1st person sg	*am*	*be*
2nd person sg	*art*	*be*
3rd person sg	*is*	*be*
All persons pl	*be(e)(n)/* *ar(e)(n)*	*be(e)(n)/ar(e)(n)*
Preterite		
1st/3rd persons sg	*was*	*were*
2nd person sg	*were*	*were*
All persons pl	*were(n)*	*were(n)*
Imperative:	*be* (sg)	*be(th)* (pl)
Participles		
Past	*be(e)(n)*	←

NOTE: Optional elements in a number of places in these paradigms may be noted, e.g. the *y-* prefix on past participles (descended from OE *ge-*). In Chaucerian English, these optional elements were frequently employed for metrical reasons. Some optional elements were only found in certain dialects; thus, for instance, *y-* does not appear in northern varieties of ME. See the Appendix pp. 121–24 below for details of dialectal variations.

More about strong verbs

Binden can act as the general model for all strong verbs; however, as in OE and PDE, there are several classes of strong verb in ME marked by varying patterns of alternation in stem vowels. For ease of comparison with OE practice, the ME reflexes of the same classes are given here, although sometimes different model verbs have been chosen.

The principal parts given here are (1) the infinitive, (2) the third person preterite, (3) the plural preterite and (4) the past participle; the third person present singular is no longer as distinct from the rest of the paradigm as it could be in OE. It will be observed that some of the old distinctions between classes of strong verbs have disappeared. The roman numerals refer to classes of strong verb as classified in OE.

I	WRITE	*write(n)*	*wroot*	*write(n)*	*(y)write(n)*
II	CREEP	*crepe(n)*	*crepte, cre(e)pe*	*crepe(n)*	*(y)crope(n)*
III	BIND	*binde(n)*	*bounde*	*bounde(n)*	*(y)bounde(n)*
IV	BEAR	*berc(n)*	*ba(a)r, beer*	*bare(n), bere(n)*	*(y)bore(n)*
V	TREAD	*trede(n)*	*trad*	*trode(n)*	*(y)trode(n)*
VI	SHAKE	*shake(n)*	*shook*	*shoke(n)*	*(y)shake(n)*
VII	HOLD	*holde(n), helde(n)*	*held*	*helde(n)*	*(y)holde(n)*
	KNOW	*knowe(n)*	*knew*	*knewe(n)*	*(y)knowe(n)*

Some verbs which were contracted in OE (see p. 82) appear as follows in Chaucerian English. Not all variants are given.

V	SEE	*se(n)*	*saugh*	*sawe(n)*	*(y)seyn*
VI	SLAY	*slee(n)*	*slough*	*slowe(n)*	*(y)slayn*

More about weak verbs

The OE class-distinctions in weak verbs have largely died out by Chaucer's time. The only common form to display a distinctive paradigm is *have(n)* HAVE, which belonged to the OE weak Class III:

III	HAVE	*have(n)*	*hadde*	*hadde(n)*	*(y)had*

The distinction between weak Classes I and II had disappeared by Chaucer's time, although there are occasional relicts of a distinctive Class II paradigm in earlier texts such as *Sir Orfeo*, e.g. *aski* ASK (infinitive).

More about irregular verbs

As in OE, ME irregular verbs fall into two groups: (1) **preterite-present verbs**, and (2) **anomalous verbs**. Here are the principal parts of some common irregular verbs, plus the third person present singular. (nb. 'no pp.' = no recorded past participle).

Group I

KNOW	*wite(n); wo(o)t; wiste; wiste(n); (y)wist*
OWE (cf. OE OWN)	no infin.; *oweth; oughte; oughte(n); owed*
KNOW	*conne(n); can; coude; coude(n); coud*
BE ABLE TO	*mowe(n); may; myghte; myghte(n);* no pp.
BE OBLIGED TO	no infin.; *shal; sholde; sholde(n)*; no pp.
BE ALLOWED	no infin.; *moot; moste*; moste(n)**, no pp.

* Sometimes used with an evident present-tense meaning.

Group II

WANT TO	no infin.; *wil(e)/wol(e); wolde; wolde(n)*; no pp.
NOT WANT TO	no infin.; *nil(e); nolde; nolde(n)*; no pp.
DO	*doon; doth; dide; dide(n); (y)don*
GO	*goon; goth; yede/wente; yede(n)/wente(n);* *(y)gon*

4.4.7 Numerals

ME **numerals** are divided into **cardinal** and **ordinal** categories. Here are the ME cardinal numbers 1–10, 100 and 1000, and equivalent ordinals for 1st–10th in the variety of language represented by the Ellesmere and contemporary London MSS:

	Cardinal	Ordinal
1	*oon*	*first(e)*
2	*two(o)*	*seconde, secunde*
3	*thre(e)*	*thridde, thirde*
4	*four*	*ferthe, fourthe*
5	*five*	*fifthe*
6	*sixe*	*sixte*
7	*sevene*	*seventhe*
8	*eighte*	*eighthe*
9	*nine*	*ninthe*
10	*ten*	*tenthe*
100	*houndred*	
1000	*thousand*	

4.5 Lexicon

➜ As with the OE lexicon, it is probably best to study ME vocabulary in the context of a general history, e.g. Barber (1993), Baugh and Cable (1993), Strang (1970). These notes simply indicate some general points. ←

4.5.1 Borrowing

A characteristic feature of ME is its habit of borrowing from other languages to increase its wordstock. There seem to have been two reasons for this hospitality towards loanwords: (1) there was large-scale contact between English-speakers and users of other languages, notably varieties of Scandinavian and French, and (2) since ME was a much less inflected language than OE, it was easier to adapt words from foreign languages for the syntactic structures of the borrowing language.

There are three main sources of loanwords into English during the ME period: Scandinavian, Latin and French.

Many **Scandinavian** words were actually borrowed into the spoken mode during the OE period but had been 'hidden' by the standardised written record and only appeared in ME times. Most express very common concepts, cf. PDE BAG, BULL, EGG, ROOT, UGLY, WING, and it is noticeable that Scandinavian has supplied English with such basic features as the third person plural pronoun, THEY/THEM/THEIR. Some, though not all, of these forms are found in Chaucerian English; Chaucer still uses *ei* (from OE) rather than *egg*, and only the nominative form of the third person plural pronoun derived from Scandinavian (thus he uses Scandinavian-derived *they* beside OE-derived *hem, hire*).

A number of **Latin** words came directly into English during the ME period, largely as learned words carried over in the translation of Latin texts, e.g. *testament, omnipotent*, although some may have come into English through French, e.g. *purgatorie*. However, the great wave of Latin borrowings into English takes place from the fifteenth century onwards, with the rise of humanism, and is really a feature of EModE studies (see Chapter 5 below).

By far the largest number of words borrowed into English during the ME period are taken from varieties of French. Up to the thirteenth century these borrowings were rather few and reflected the role of French as the language of the ruling class (cf. PDE JUSTICE, OBEDIENCE, MASTERY, PRISON, SERVICE, all of which are first found in English during the early ME period). Most of these words were adopted from Norman French, sometimes demonstrated by the distinctive form of the adopted word in PDE compared with its Present-Day French cognate, e.g. WAR (ME and Norman French *werre*): Present-Day French *guerre*, CARPENTER (ME and Norman French *carpenter*): Present-Day French *charpentier*. However, after that date, French words from the Central French dialects enter the language at a great rate, reflecting the cultural status of Central France; it seems to have become customary for the higher social classes in England to signal their class-membership by studding their English with French-derived vocabulary. Chaucer's lexicon is rich with words derived from French, e.g. *honour, chivalrie, curteisie, compaignye, tendre* – all of which have survived barely changed into PDE.

4.5.2 Word-formation

More subtly, French usages were also adopted to augment patterns of English word-formation, e.g. the extension of the French adjectival suffix to words with native English roots such as KNOWABLE, UNSPEAKABLE.

4.5.3 Changes of meaning

There were some changes of meaning between OE and ME, largely to do with the reorganisation of the lexicon consequent upon words being borrowed from French; thus *mood* in Chaucerian English is closer in meaning to that of PDE MOOD, since an older meaning had been taken over by a French loanword, viz. SPIRIT.

4.6 Appendix: On Middle English dialects

For reasons given on pp. 92–93 above, ME is the period when dialect-variation is most fully expressed in the written mode. Some awareness of dialectal usages is essential to a proper understanding of ME structure, even though advanced dialectological analysis is a comparatively complex matter.

ME dialects have been traditionally categorised as follows: Northern (including Lowland Scotland), East Midland (including London), West Midland and Southern, with distinctively Scots, East Anglian and Kentish sub-dialects. However, closer study soon reveals that these groupings are extremely general typological notions, and that in reality the ME materials present us with a dialect continuum, rather like that of PDE spoken dialects.

Bearing this fact in mind, it is nevertheless possible to present an extremely rough characterisation of the five groupings. Only a few criteria, diagnostic in collocation, have been chosen to illustrate each dialect-region, and it should be emphasised that this is a highly simplified sketch. Anyone interested in pursuing matters further is strongly urged to consult the standard work on Middle English dialectology, A. McIntosh, M.L. Samuels and M. Benskin eds., *A Linguistic Atlas of Late Mediaeval English* (Aberdeen: Aberdeen University Press, 1986), especially the General Introduction to Volume I; see also M. Laing ed., *Middle English Dialectology* (Aberdeen: Aberdeen University Press, 1988) for a collection of classic essays.

Northern

(1) *a*-spellings for OE $\bar{a}$, e.g. *stane* STONE, beside *stoon*, etc. in other dialects

(2) *ui*, *uCe*-spellings for OE $\bar{o}$, e.g. *guid/gude* GOOD, beside *go(d)(e)* in other dialects

(3) *-es/-is* type inflexions for both 3rd person present singular and present plural of verbs, e.g. *standis* STANDS

(4) *-and* as the present participle inflexion

(5) *scho* for PDE SHE

(6) Early occurrence of *th*-type 3rd person plural pronouns in all cases, e.g., *thay, thaim, thair*

(7) Early loss of weak/strong adjective distinction, e.g. *the strang strif* THE VIOLENT STRUGGLE, *the strif is strang*

(8) Distinctively northern vocabulary, with a high level of borrowing from Scandinavian, e.g. *til* TO, *fra* FROM

(9)   *y* and *þ* are written identically, as *y*

(10)   Scots texts form a distinctive sub-group, becoming more distinctive as the fifteenth century progresses. Characteristic features include *quh-* for PDE WH- in words such as WHAT, WHO, WHICH (*quhat, quha, quhilk*), etc.

West Midland

(1)   *o*-spellings for OE *a* when followed by a nasal, e.g. *mon* MAN, beside *man* etc. in other dialects

(2)   *u, uy*-spellings for OE *y*, e.g. *fuyr* FIRE

(3)   *e*-spellings for WS *æ* in *dei* DAY (cf. WS *dæg*), etc.

(4)   In verbal inflexion, *-eth* for 3rd present singular, *-e(n)* for present plural.

(5)   Retention of *eo*-spelling in words like *(s)heo* SHE

(6)   Retention of weak/strong adjective distinction, e.g. *the longe wey, the wey is long*

East Midland

(1)   *a* for OE *a* + nasal and WS *æ*, and *i, y* for OE *y*: *man, day, fir(e)*

(2)   *o(o)* for OE *ā*, e.g. *stoon*

(3)   In verbal inflexion, *-eth*, etc. for third person present singular, *-e(n)* for present plural.

(4)   Mixture of native and borrowed forms in 3rd person plural paradigm is characteristic, i.e. *they, hem, her(e)*, etc.

(5)   Present participle in *-ing(e)* etc., past participle in *-en* in words such as *bounden*. Some East Anglian texts have *-and(e)* as the present participle inflexion, as in northern dialects, and this form also occurs in certain mid-fourteenth-century London texts.

(6)   Retention of weak/strong adjective distinction

(7)   East Anglian texts form a distinctive sub-group, with (e.g.) *x*- for PDE SH- in words like *xal* SHALL, *xulde* SHOULD etc., and *qu-* for WH- in *quan* WHEN, etc.

Southern

(1)   *v* for initial *f* in OE, e.g. *vox* FOX. (*z* is found initially for *s* in a few south-eastern ME texts in *zunne* SUN, etc. It is likely that in southern varieties of ME initial *s* was generally pronounced voiced.)

(2)   In South-Western, *u, uy* for OE *y*; in Kentish, *e* is much more common as the reflex of OE *y* – thus Kentish *zenne* SIN, OE *synne*

(3)   Conservative verbal inflexion: *-th* for third present singular (e.g. *comth* COMES), *-eth*, etc. for present plural.

(4)   Past participle commonly with *y-* prefix, e.g. *ybounde*

(5)   Retention of weak/strong adjective distinction

(6)   Overall, Southern English dialects are conservative in inflectional patterns, with, e.g. retention of grammatical gender until the mid-fourteenth century (see also (3)–(5) above).

The above features are only representative sets of dialectally distinctive forms, and the lists of forms could of course have been greatly extended.

Chapter 5

Early Modern English

5.1 Introduction

The era 1500–1700 is traditionally described by English historical linguists as the period of Early Modern English (EModE). The external events which determine these dates are the arrival of printing in England in 1475, and the founding of the modern British state in 1707, with the Act of Union between England, Wales and Scotland. These two events may seem of very different kinds, yet they have a cultural significance with major implications for linguistic development. Printing was adopted – and succeeded – because of the emergence of mass literacy and the consequent demands of a reading public which could not be satisfied by the old scribal system of text-production. The Act of Union was also the prerequisite for the development of the British Empire, the primary political means by which the English language was projected beyond the British Isles to become the dominant language of late-twentieth-century culture.

The implications of this cultural setting are numerous, but one is perhaps most obvious to present-day readers of EModE: it is, in the written mode, a standardised language which, although allowing of a greater degree of variation than would be considered desirable in the twentieth century, is nevertheless an homogeneous phenomenon in comparison with, say, ME. English now had a national function, and the formal expression of the written language was modified to conform with that function. As the Tudor scholar Nicholas Grimald put it, it became *a great aduantage to waxe vniforme* in the written mode.

In comparison with ME it is fairly easy to give a sketch of prototypical usage based upon written texts. It will be observed that there remains a good deal of minor linguistic variation between and within the illustrative texts presented here; this written variation reflects only partially the spoken variation of the time. This situation only became stabilised during the course of the seventeenth century as teachers and printers settled on single usages for each word, generally those adopted in the Authorised Version of the Bible, printed in 1611. Such practices of uniformity were plainly function-ally significant. Protestant culture before, during and after the Civil War demanded mass literacy as a religious duty, and the rise of the 'spelling-book' during the period must have both fed this demand and established normative patterns which filtered into other registers (e.g. private letters).

EModE is much closer to PDE than either OE or ME, and it can seem at first glance rather familiar. And, indeed, the practice of presenting (e.g.) the works of Shakespeare in normalised spelling can lull twentieth-century readers into believing that there is no difference between EModE and PDE usage – a belief which can be deceptive.

This chapter is divided into four parts: Spelling and Pronun-ciation, Syntax, Paradigms and Lexicon. This division is for ease of subsequent reference, and it is not intended that you should read straight through the parts in the order given here. Cross-references are given throughout. An attempt has been made to draw examples from the Texts in Part II, but I have not hesitated to draw upon other texts where illustration of some common point is required.

Paragraphs of major significance for beginners are marked at the beginning and end with an arrow-icon ➔ . . ←. The significance of unmarked material will become apparent later in students' encounters with EModE texts. It is suggested that, as in Chapter 3 above, beginners alternate examination of Texts C in Part II with reading portions of this chapter. It must be emphasised that the outline of EModE given here is a very limited sketch, giving only a bare outline of the principal characteristics of this state of the language. Students wishing to take the subject further should refer to books in the Annotated Bibliography, notably Barber (1976) and Görlach (1991).

5.2 Spelling and pronunciation

5.2.1 The alphabet

➔ Shakespeare's alphabet is much like that of PDE: *th* has replaced *þ*, and it will be observed that the passages taken from the First Folio do not use *y* in words like *ye* THE. ←

v/u are often distributed in EModE texts as in ME, i.e. interchangeably to represent both vowel and consonant, with *v* generally being used initially, *u* elsewhere, e.g. *vnfashionable* UNFASHIONABLE, *proue* PROVE. This situation changed during the seventeenth century, and later-seventeenth-century printers developed the modern distribution. *vv* is occasionally used for *w*, e.g. *vvhich* WHICH.

y is still sometimes used where PDE would have *i*, e.g. *poynt* POINT. *j* is rarely used, except in roman numerals e.g. *vij* 7. EModE printers use *i* instead in words like *maiesticall* MAJESTICAL, *iot* JOT, *Iacob* JACOB.

c generally has its PDE distribution, but it does sometimes vary with *s*, e.g. *choise* CHOICE beside *peace* PEACE. In final position it was usual for PDE -IC to appear as *-ick(e)*, e.g. *physick* MEDICINE, *franticke* FRANTIC.

The forms *æ* and *œ* occasionally appear in EModE texts, but as a result of the adoption of Latin conventions, e.g. *Cæsar*, *Æglogue* ECLOGUE, *œconomie* ECONOMY. *ph* is sometimes used, as a quasi-learned practice, where PDE has F, e.g. *phanaticall* FANATICAL.

For PDE final -Y, *-ie* frequently appears, e.g. *verbositie* VERBOSITY, *ortagriphie* ORTHOGRAPHY beside *deformity* DEFORMITY. Final *-e*, which had ceased to have a grammatical function in late ME, is often added to words by printers as an aid to the justification of type or simply as a decorative feature, e.g. *poore* POOR, *franticke* FRANTIC. It also developed a diacritic function (see pp. 128–29 below).

z seems to have had an uncertain status in Shakespeare's time. In *King Lear*, one character insults another by calling him *thou whoreson zed, thou unnecessarie letter*, which seems indicative of at least some contemporary views. The status of the letter remains uncertain in PDE; cf. frequent confusion over -ISE/-IZE.

5.2.2 Diacritics

Final *-e* ceased to have a grammatical function in late ME (see above), and it begins during the EModE period to take on a special role as a diacritic. It retains these roles in PDE. One present-day function is indicated by the different present-day pronunciations of FAT, FATE, etc. In PDE, the vowel A has distinct pronunciations in these two words, usually signalled by the presence or absence of -E;

historically, this is a difference between vowels which were short and long respectively in late ME. In EModE, it became generally conventional to distinguish the historically long vowel by adding -e, e.g. *while* WHILE, *sore* SORE, *onely* ONLY.

This practice did cause difficulties with pairs such as WRITE, WRITTEN (from OE *wrītan, (ge)writen)* where the distinction of meaning was carried by the vowel-length alone. Thus it became conventional (although not consistently so) to signal an historically short vowel with a following double consonant, e.g. *merry* MERRY, *fellow* FELLOW, *Forrest* FOREST. In PDE, this doubling often fails when the consonant is at the end of a word, but in EModE doubling is frequent in that position, e.g. *expell* EXPEL, *stopp* STOP. -ick is used instead of expected -icc, presumably for aesthetic reasons, e.g. *politick* POLITIC. A final -e is often added after the doubled letter by analogy with forms of the WRITTEN, GLADDER type, e.g. *glasse* GLASS, *Sunne* SUN (beside *Sun*), *stuffe* STUFF.

Some letters in PDE have ambiguous 'phonic' significance, and it was during EModE that it became conventional (though not consistently so) to distinguish them using -e, e.g. *strange* STRANGE, *peace* PEACE (beside *scarse* SCARCE).

Capitalisation of letters in EModE does not follow the PDE practice. Various systems existed until the end of the nineteenth century, when the PDE usage, where only words at the beginning of sentences and proper names are capitalised, became stabilised. This practice contrasts with that found in present-day German, where nouns are capitalised wherever they appear in the sentence; such a usage does appear for a time in eighteenth-century English, but has not been sustained. In the First Folio of Shakespeare's works, any noun, verb or adjective could be capitalised.

In the texts taken from the First Folio – and unlike in the texts illustrating Chapters 3 and 4 – the **punctuation** of the original has been retained since it seems to follow a fairly clear system; however, this system was not that of PDE. In PDE, punctuation is grammatical, i.e. designed to reflect the grammatical structure of the written word, and is part of the pragmatic apparatus of the written system, designed to help the reader. In the First Folio, punctuation is rhetorical, reflecting much more closely the pauses and emphases of speech: it is thus designed to help those whose primary encounter with the text would be through listening. Grammatical punctuation did not become dominant in English writing until the end of the seventeenth century, and there is still an observable tension between the rhetorical and grammatical traditions even in present-day written discourse.

For the use of the apostrophe, see p. 137 below.

5.2.3 Pronunciation

Our knowledge of EModE pronunciation is derived from several sources. As with ME, the analysis of verse, spelling and loanwords, and reconstruction from later and earlier states of the language are important sources of information. But this material is supplemented by the very considerable evidence supplied by the first writers on the English language, the spelling reformers (sometimes referred to as **orthoepists**), the early phoneticians and the authors of such works as rhyming dictionaries, handbooks for foreigners learning English, and shorthand manuals. Very often their work is made problematic by certain prescriptivist attitudes – they sometimes describe how they think things *ought* to be pronounced, rather than what is actually said – and the lack of a commonly accepted set of conventions for signalling pronunciation makes comparisons between writers difficult. But many of them are excellent observers of their own language. (For a discussion, see Smith 1996: Chapter 2.)

An extra complexity, strongly indicated in the evidence, is that there were evidently social and generational as well as geographical factors involved in the adoption of a particular accent.

The pronunciation suggested here is that of middle-aged, middle-class Londoners living at around 1600. Such people are most likely to have made up the bulk of Shakespeare's audience, and seem to have been the main readership for the orthoepistical and phonetic works of the period. However, it should be remembered that there is considerable contemporary evidence for other accents (see the Appendix to this chapter, p. 154–5).

➔ The details of EModE pronunciation can seem confusing. But, as a rule of thumb, PDE **spelling** can be used as good (if indirect) evidence for EModE pronunciation, since the correlation of written letter and spoken sound-segment was fairly close in the London accent. As in studying OE and ME, it is important not to worry too much about the details of EModE pronunciation; as in ME times, there was a wide range of accentual variation and the language was in a considerable state of flux consequent on urbanisation. ←

Between ME and EModE, the histories of the short and long vowels diverged. The **short vowels** of late ME, [ɪ, ɛ, a, ɔ, ʊ], seem to have been broadly stable in EModE times; the vowel [ʌ], characteristic of Southern English accents today, only emerged in some varieties as a distinct phoneme, /ʌ/, after Shakespearean times, and therefore should not be distinguished from /ʊ/. /ʌ/, of course, is still not generally found in northern English varieties of PDE.

The ME **long vowels** however had undergone a marked change of distribution within the lexicon by EModE times. This change is referred to as the **Great Vowel Shift**; as its name suggests, it is *the* major development in the history of English phonology. The details and the causes of the phenomenon need not detain us here. The following table gives the correspondences between ME, EModE and PDE pronunciation (RP and GenAm) for the reflexes of the late ME long vowels, plus the PDE spelling of an illustrative form (which was of course established in EModE times). As in the sections on pronunciation in Chapters 3 and 4, which may be compared with the table here, a double asterisk ** indicates that the pronunciation given is similar to that found in present-day Scots, used for the reasons given on pp. 25 and 96.

ME	EModE	PDE	Present-day example
[iː]	[əɪ]	[aɪ]	LIFE
[eː]	[iː]	[iː]	MEET
[ɛː]	[eː]	[iː]	MEAT
[aː]	[ɛː]	[eː]**	NAME
[uː]	[əʊ]	[aʊ]	HOW, TOWN
[oː]	[uː]	[uː]	MOOD
[ɔː]	[oː]	[oː]**	BOAT, HOME

There were in EModE sporadic shortenings of some late ME long vowels in particular contexts, especially ME [ɛː, oː] when followed by [d, t, θ, v, f] in monosyllabic words. However, this is not a consistent process, and the modern outputs vary; cf. PDE DEAD beside MEAD, FLOOD beside MOOD. The variation in the present-day pronunciation of -OO- in FLOOD, GOOD is due to the shortening happening at different times. It is probably simplest for the beginner when reconstructing EModE pronunciation to assign [eː] to all 'PDE -EA- words' and [uː] to all 'PDE -OO- words'; the shortening process was probably continuing in Shakespeare's time, so some speakers at least would have been using such pronunciations.

The **vowels of unstressed syllables** are, as in Chaucer's English, [ə, ɪ]. However, the distribution of these vowels changed considerably between ME and EModE times, since EModE does not have certain inflexions still maintained in Chaucerian English, e.g. the distinction between strong and weak adjectives (see pp. 101–02). In the advancing pronunciation of the period, [ə, ɪ] may be generally considered to have the present-day distribution, where they are used in unstressed words (i.e. 'grammatical' words like A, THE) or in the unstressed syllables of lexical words (e.g. WRITT<u>E</u>N). It is likely, however, that in formal usages an attempt was made to distinguish less-stressed vowels more clearly, especially in loanwords. Thus for example *affection* AFFECTATION was probably pronounced variously as [ə'feksjən] and [a'fɛksjəʊn].

Diphthongs in EModE are a mixture of inherited forms and those which were the result of the Great Vowel Shift. Shakespeare's system was probably as follows:

[aɪ] in words such as DAY, GREY, etc. In PDE, words containing this diphthong have fallen in with those containing ME [aː] NAME, etc., but they were still distinguished in careful speech in the seventeenth century.

[ɔɪ, ʊɪ] had probably merged into [ɔɪ] by Shakespeare's time in the speech of many, but others still kept the reflexes of the two distinct. There was also some cross-influencing between the two sets even amongst those speakers who maintained a distinction. Given the complex problems, it is probably best for beginners simply to use the present-day pronunciation in words such as JOY, POINT, etc., while being aware of other possible pronunciations.

[əɪ] The reflex of ME [iː], the result of the Great Vowel Shift.

[aʊ] In PDE, words which contained this diphthong generally have [ɔː], e.g. LAW, VAULT, and it seems likely that this new pronunciation was already current in Shakespeare's time; however, some conservative speakers probably still used the older pronunciation.

[ɔʊ] In PDE, words which contained this diphthong generally have (in Scottish accents) [o(ː)] etc., e.g. KNOW, OWE, and have thus merged with the reflexes of ME [ɔː]. However, in Shakespeare's time some conservative speakers probably still retained a diphthongal pronunciation.

[ɛʊ, ɪʊ] had probably merged into [ɪu] by Shakespeare's time in words such as LEWD, NEW etc. The present-day pronunciation with [ju] was also probably current in the speech of many folk.

[əʊ] The reflex of ME [uː], the result of the Great Vowel Shift.

Consonants are generally as in ME and, indeed, as in PDE, the main differences from the ME/PDE systems being:

(a) The emergence in London English of a new phoneme, /ŋ/ in SING, etc. This phoneme is of course still not phonemic in varieties of present-day Northern English, although it is contextually used, e.g. [sɪŋg] SING.

(b) The loss in London English of ME [x]. There is some evidence for the retention of this sound in the middle of the sixteenth century, but by Shakespeare's time it was no longer used. It has left its mark on the spelling-system, with *gh*; but as in PDE this cluster seems either to have been silent (cf. PDE THOUGHT, SLAUGHTER, THOUGH), or pronounced with [f] (cf. PDE DRAUGHT, LAUGHTER, ENOUGH). Some uncertainty about the distribution is indicated by EModE spellings such as *dafter* DAUGHTER, *boft* BOUGHT.

(c) In EModE, *r* is still pronounced wherever it was written; there are no 'silent Rs' as in present-day Southern British English, e.g. JAR [dʒaː]. London English *ca.* 1600 was, like present-day General American, what is known as a 'rhotic' accent. Indeed, there is some evidence that high-status speakers continued to be rhotic in English until quite late in the nineteenth century, as witnessed by analyses carried out by scholars at the time.

(d) In formal EModE speech, [w, ʍ] are still kept as distinct phonemes, with minimal pairs *while* WHILE, *wile* TRICK. However, it seems certain that they were no longer distinct phonemes for many speakers, as indicated by Shakespeare's puns on *white* WHITE, *wight* BEING, CREATURE. This pronunciation was not complete in standardised spoken Southern English before the eighteenth century; the distinction is still retained in present-day Scots and Scottish English.

(e) *Nation, sure, measure*, etc. are in EModE, as in ME, still pronounced by most speakers with [sj, zj] rather than with PDE [ʃ, ʒ]. However, the present-day usage must have already been current among some speakers, since Shakespeare puns on *shooter* and *suitor* in the play *Love's Labour's Lost*.

(f) Initial *w, g, k* were all pronounced in ME in words like PDE WRITE, GNAW, KNEE. During Shakespeare's time, these older pronunciations disappeared; this is indicated by Shakespeare's puns on *ring* and *wring*, *knight* and *night*, *knot* and *not*.

5.3 Syntax

➜ Within this section are included three fundamental areas of syntax: the **noun phrase**, the **verb phrase** and **sentence structure**. As in Chapters 3 and 4, this section deals with the functions the various forms carry out; for details of forms, constant reference should be made to the 'Paradigms' section p. 145–53, using the Thematic Index in Part III. For the grammatical terminology employed, see Chapter 2. ←

➜ In general, EModE grammar is very like PDE, although there remain a few features which are more characteristic of earlier stages of the language. There are also a few EModE innovations which have failed to survive into PDE, most notably in the verb phrase. ←

5.3.1 The noun phrase

➜ As in Chaucerian English and in PDE, EModE **nouns** are inflected for **number** (singular/plural), and for the **case** of genitive singular (no case distinction is made in the plural). Function within the clause is signalled by word-order; and, as in PDE, only pronouns are regularly marked for cases other than genitive singular. ←

Agreement and the noun phrase

➜ **Agreement** within the noun phrase is restricted, as in PDE, to signalling number-relations between certain determiners and the headwords they modify, e.g. *these Pockets*; *this Son of Yorke*. Agreement remains important in relating subjects to predicators. ←

Pronouns and the noun phrase

➜ **Pronouns** are, as in OE, ME and PDE, categorised by **person**, i.e. first/second/third; singular third-person pronouns are selected on the basis of the sex of the noun to which they refer, and may thus be categorised in accordance with 'natural' **gender**. ←

➜ As in ME, *thou*, *ye*, etc. had special uses in EModE, originally comparable with the *tu*, *vous* distinction in French. By

EModE times, *ye, you*, etc. had developed as the common, unmarked form of address; *thou* by 1600 had developed as a marked, familiar form which could be used both positively and negatively (see, for instance, the interplay of *thou*, etc. and *you* in the passage from *King Lear* in Text C). By the end of the seventeenth century *thou* was restricted to non-standard varieties, and to special kinds of religious discourse (including use by certain Nonconformist sects, such as the Quakers, which emphasised communal equality and familiarity). ←

NOTE: The use of *thou*, etc. as the **pronoun of address to God** seems something of an anomaly, and various explanations have been put forward to account for this practice. Possibly the most plausible is that *thou* is a precise translation from languages where the second person pronouns were distinguished by number but not by social status. Since the singularity of God is an important point of theology, it would seem important to EModE translators to emphasise this in their choice of pronoun.

The dominant **relative pronouns** at the beginning of the EModE period are *that* and (to a lesser extent) *which/the which. Who, whom, whos(e)* remain as **interrogative pronouns**, though, as in ME, *whom/whos* can also be used as relative pronouns. During the course of the sixteenth century, the interrogative pronoun *who* became extended in function and started to be used as a relative pronoun as well. By Shakespeare's time, *that* and *which* were still common, but *who* had begun to be used regularly when the pronoun referred to a human antecedent, e.g.:

1   *I met a foole,/Who laid him downe . . .*

Shakespeare also occasionally uses *as* as a relative pronoun, a usage attested in PDE but regarded as non-standard, e.g.:

2   *that kind of Fruite,/As Maides call Medlers.*

Pronouns were also used (though not invariably) in **imperative constructions** where they would be omitted in PDE, e.g.:

3   *Sit you downe Father: rest you.*

It seems likely from the contexts in which they occur that the use of pronouns in such constructions was felt to be more polite and less peremptory than when they were omitted.

Unlike in PDE, pronouns can occasionally be used as head-words in noun phrases containing modifying elements, e.g. *the cruellest shee; hee of Wales.*

The **ethic dative** is still found in EModE, e.g.:

4 *I met a foole, who laid him downe, and bask'd him in the Sun.*

In PDE, such expressions are replaced with forms such as HIMSELF; such forms indeed begin to appear during the ME period but they were only slowly adopted.

Adjectives and the noun phrase

Adjectives follow the PDE pattern, and are no longer marked, as they were still in Chaucerian English (cf. p. 101), for definiteness or plurality. However, there are still a few features remaining of the older patterns. Postmodifying adjectives are found rather more frequently than in PDE, especially in verse, e.g. *Inductions dangerous*; and sometimes their position within the noun phrase varies from present-day usage, especially in vocative expressions, e.g. *Goode my Lorde*. For adjectives subjected to the splitting of heavy groups, see p. 144 below. Adjectives continue as in ME to be used as the heads of noun phrases rather more frequently than in PDE, e.g.:

5 *the poore haue cry'de.*

Determiners and the noun phrase

→ Determiners generally follow the PDE pattern in terms of function. However, determiners could co-occur with pronouns in phrases such as *this my Vertue*, where in PDE the construction would be THIS VIRTUE OF MINE. In demonstratives a distinction was made between *this/these, that/those* and *yon/yond(er)*. The last of these forms was used when the referent was distant from both speaker and hearer, e.g.:

6 *When yond same star that's westward from the pole.* ←

Numerals and the noun phrase

Numerals are used much as in PDE. Constructions common in ME such as *three & twenty* are still common. Numerals do not necessarily modify an uninflected headword, e.g. *three & twenty years.*

The noun phrase: A note about possessives

In PDE, possession can be expressed either through a **genitive (possessive) phrase**, e.g. JOHN'S BOOK, or through a **prepositional phrase**, e.g. THE BOOK OF JOHN. In EModE, three ways of expressing possession were available. Two of these are those found in PDE, e.g. _Cæsars_ Funerall (with a genitive phrase), _the vices of thy Mistris_ (with a prepositional phrase). The third construction uses the **possessive pronoun** _his_ (and occasionally _her, their_), e.g. _the Count his gallies_ THE COUNT'S GALLEYS. The usage is common in, although not restricted to, situations where the possessive noun ends in _-s_ when uninflected, e.g. _Mars his heart_ THE HEART OF MARS.

It will have been observed that there is no **apostrophe** in _Cæsars_, where one would be required in PDE. The use of the apostrophe, when it was used at all, was highly variable in EModE. Its primary use was to signal the elision of some element in a word or phrase, e.g. _hee's_ HE'S, _find'st_, but it was frequently omitted altogether, e.g. _Heres a Scull now_. By analogy it spread to other contexts, e.g. _ha's_ HAS, _cry'de_ CRIED. Its use with _-s_ on nouns, again probably an analogous procedure, was sporadic only and found with both possessive and plural inflexions. The PD usage, whereby -'s is used for the possessive singular and -s' for the possessive plural, was not formalised until at least a century after Shakespeare. (For _its, it's_ see pp. 147–48ff. below.)

When a genitive phrase contained a modifying element, that element was sometimes separated from the headword it modifies in a way which would be unusual in PDE, e.g. _this same Scull sir, was Yoricks Scull, the Kings Jester_ THIS VERY SKULL, SIR, WAS THE SKULL OF YORICK, THE KING'S JESTER.

5.3.2 The verb phrase

→ The special set of grammatical categories involved in the verb phrase and discussed in Chapters 2, 3 and 4 above are relevant to EModE studies as well, i.e. agreement, finiteness, simple and complex verb phrases (including the role of _will/shall_, etc), person, tense, aspect, voice and mood, transitivity, negation. For definitions of these notions, see Chapter 2; for the equivalent forms in Chapters 3 and 4, see the Thematic Index in Part III. ←

The verb phrase: Agreement, person and number

➔ As in OE and ME, and as in PDE, predicators **agree** with their subjects in **person** and **number**, e.g. *I speake not; my gorge rises; we make Lome*. Thus the basic structure of relationships within the verb phrase, and between the verb phrase and other parts of grammar, are very similar to those found in PDE. ⬅

The verb phrase: Tense and aspect

➔ Finite verbs are inflected for **present and preterite tense**, e.g. *she loueth, she loued*. The '**historic present**' continues to appear in EModE, in colloquial usage, e.g.:

7   *he got a many fishhooks... then he gets many Counters and puts them in his pocket also* (see Görlach 1991: 325–326) ⬅

Complex verb phrases are also used in EModE to express **tense** and **aspectual** distinctions. The EModE reflexes of PDE WILL, SHALL still retain something of the lexical significance carried by OE *willan* and *sculan*, viz. **volition** and **obligation** respectively, e.g.:

8   *which he would call abhominable*
WHICH HE WOULD WISH TO CALL ABOMINABLE

9   *Thou shalt haue one*
YOU MUST HAVE ONE

and cf. the force of *Thou shalt not* in the Ten Commandments in the Bible. However, there is evidence of the *will*-type being used for simple futurity, e.g.:

10   *'twil serue*
IT WILL SUFFICE.

In the eighteenth century, the distribution of SHALL/WILL as **future auxiliaries** was determined by prescriptivist grammarians who were aware of the older meanings. It thus became customary, when expressing future tense, to use SHALL, etc. with first person subjects and WILL, etc. with second and third person subjects. To assign SHALL, etc. to second and third person subjects (as in YOU SHALL DO WHAT I SAY), when simply intending to express futurity, was felt to assert dominance over that subject on the part of the speaker in a way which could be construed as face-threatening (insulting, intimidating, etc.). This subtlety is probably lost on PDE speakers, and explains why the distinction between WILL and SHALL in expressing future time is dying out. In some parts of the English-speaking area, this usage was rarely adopted (e.g. in Scotland).

Perfect aspect combined with past tense can be expressed as in PDE, by means of complex verb phrases. When the lexical verb is **transitive**, i.e. when the verb is capable of taking a direct object, then reflexes of PDE HAVE are used, e.g.:

11 *He <u>hath brought</u> many Captiues home to Rome.*

With **intransitive** verbs, i.e. verbs not capable of taking a direct object, it remains common practice in EModE (though not invariably) to employ the reflexes of PDE BE, e.g.:

12 *The King himselfe <u>is rode</u> to view their Battaile.*

A very common feature of the PDE tense/aspect system is the use of the **progressive** category of verb phrases, e.g. HE IS LOVING, HE WAS LOVING, HE HAS BEEN LOVING. Although such constructions are known in EModE, they are rare, and generally the simple present is used, e.g. *Soft, he wakes* QUIETLY, HE IS WAKING UP.

The verb phrase: Voice

One PDE usage, the passive progressive/passive perfect construction HE IS BEING LOVED, HE HAS BEEN LOVED, is not recorded in EModE. Otherwise, **passive voice** is expressed in EModE as in PDE, by means of the auxiliary BE, e.g.:

13 *That eyelesse head of thine, <u>was</u> first <u>fram'd</u> flesh/To raise my fortunes.*

The verb phrase: Mood

As in ME, formal **indicative/subjunctive mood** distinctions are few, but still to be found, e.g.:

14 *If it <u>were</u> so, it was a greeuous Fault*

15 *And if King <u>Edward be</u> as true and iust*
16 *If thou <u>consider</u> rightly of the matter*
17 *Where <u>be</u> your Iibes now?*

However, sometimes the formal distinction is no longer observed, e.g.:

18 *If euer thou <u>wilt</u> thriue*

(where *wilt* is historically an indicative form)

The reflexes of PDE MAY/MIGHT still seem to sustain something of their older meaning in, e.g.,

19 *the Letters that he speakes of/May be my Friends*
20 *To what base vses we may returne Horatio*
21 *why of that Lome..might they not stopp a Beere-barrell?*

The verb phrase: The auxiliary DO

→ Perhaps the most interesting auxiliary in EModE is the reflex of PDE DO, since this emerged as a new usage in EModE times, but subsequently became restricted again. DO was used as a lexical verb in OE with causative sense, e.g. *Dōþ þæt þæt folc sitte* MAKE THE PEOPLE SIT. However, in the sixteenth and seventeeth centuries it underwent a marked widening of usage, and by the middle of the sixteenth century it could appear in five contexts:

(a) negative direct questions, e.g.:
     Didst thou not heare a noyse?
(b) affirmative direct questions, e.g.:
     Did this in Cæsar seeme Ambitious?
     Dost thou thinke Alexander lookt o'this fashion i'th'earth?
(c) negative declarative sentences, e.g.:
     You do not giue the Cheere.
(d) negative imperatives, e.g.:
     Do not muse at me my most worthy Friends.
(e) affirmative declarative sentences, e.g.:
     You all did loue him once
     You all did see ... I thrice presented him a Kingly Crowne.

(e) has now died out. For the use of *do* in negation, see p. 141 below. ←

The expansion and subsequent contraction of the DO-construction is a controversial matter among historical linguists, and will not be pursued further here. See the Annotated Bibliography for further reading.

The verb phrase: The impersonal construction

The **impersonal construction** is still in use in EModE, but has become much restricted in use in comparison with ME. Only *methinks* and *methought* appear commonly in the works of Shakespeare, e.g.:

22 *Me thinkes there is much reason in his sayings*

and Shakespeare never uses **himthought*, **usthinks*, **youthinks*, etc. It seems that, by Shakespeare's time, *methinks* was simply a fossil expression rather than a reflection of a still-productive usage.

The verb phrase: Negation

Negation was usually expressed either by placing *not* after the finite verb (*I know not*) or between *do* and the finite verb (*You do not giue*); the negating particle could also be suffixed to auxiliaries such as *can*, e.g.:

23 *since I cannot proue a Louer.*

Multiple negation is still occasionally found in Shakespeare's writings, e.g.:

24 *I cannot goe no further*
 I CANNOT GO ANY FURTHER,

but it is becoming rarer. There is evidence that the PDE abbreviated negative auxiliaries DON'T, WON'T, CAN'T etc. were in existence in speech in Shakespeare's time.

5.3.3 Sentence structure

Word-order

➜ Word-order patterns in EModE are much like those in ME and in PDE, contrasting with OE usage. The usual order of elements, in both main and subordinate clauses, is SP (i.e. subject–predicator), where the predicator immediately follows the subject, e.g.:

25 *this Scul has laine* in the earth three & twenty years
26 which *he would call* abhominable.

When a complex verb phrase is employed, the lexical element can still occasionally be separated from the auxiliary, e.g.:

27 *Whose Ransomes, did the generall Coffers fill*
28 *Which he did thrice refuse.* ←

'Predicator–subject' word order is still found fairly frequently in EModE, especially when the clause begins with an adverbial, e.g.:

29 *Heere hung those lipps*
30 *then am I the Prisoner.*

Auxilary and lexical verbs are separated in

31 *greeuously hath Cæsar answer'd it.*

As in PDE, PS-order appears in questions, e.g. *is he dead?*, and, also as in PDE, with the DO-auxiliary (see p. 140 above).

Of course, these prototypical patterns of word-order may be departed from for stylistic reasons, e.g.:

32 *Plots haue I laide* (with initial direct object).

Sentence Structure: Clauses

➜ Like OE and ME, EModE has a range of different clause-types, both coordinated and subordinated. As in ME, clause-types in EModE are no longer generally distinguished by element-order. ←

Coordinating conjunctions in EModE include *and*, *but*, etc., e.g.:

33 *But Brutus sayes, he was Ambitious:/ And Brutus is an Honourable man.*

As in OE and ME, in EModE there is a range of **subordinating conjunctions**. As in ME, the forms of these conjunctions are much as in PDE, except that the particle *that* often appears after *if, when*, etc., e.g.:

34 *When that the poore haue cry'de,*

beside

35 *when he shold pronounce debt.*

The most interesting deviations from PDE usage occur with the **relative clause**. For details of the relative pronouns available in EModE, see p. 135. above. In the following examples, the relative pronoun is underlined:

36 *One that hath bin a Courtier...*
37 *the Letters that he speakes of/ May be my Friends;*
38 *this is abominable, which he would call abhominable*
39 *I thrice presented him a Kingly Crowne,/ Which he did thrice refuse*
40 *I met a Foole,/ Who laide him downe, and bask'd him in the Sun*
41 *He hath strange places cram'd/ With obseruation, the which he vents/ In mangled formes*
42 *Were such things here, as we doe speake about?*

The choice of relative pronoun is determined in EModE, as in PDE, by a range of quite complex factors.

Another usage, not illustrated in the Shakespeare texts in Part II, is to omit the relative pronoun altogether, e.g.:

43 *The labour we delight in, Physicks paine*
   THE LABOUR (WHICH) WE ARE PLEASED TO DO IS A CURE FOR PAIN

44 *heere's a night pitties neither Wisemen, nor Fooles*
   HERE IS A NIGHT (WHICH) PITIES NEITHER WISE MEN NOR FOOLS

Constructions such as *The labour we delight...* still occur in PDE; constructions such as *heere's a night...*, where the omitted relative pronoun occupies the subject position within the relative clause, are no longer found. Both constructions are of course found in ME; see p. 109.

Relative clauses can frequently be separated from the phrases they modify, e.g.:

45 *the Sword is out/ That must destroy thee*
THE SWORD WHICH MUST DESTROY YOU IS DRAWN

46 *So should he looke, that seemes to speake things strange*
SO OUGHT HE WHO IS ABOUT TO BRING FRESH NEWS LOOK.

Other clause types, e.g. **adverbial**, **comparative**, follow broadly the same pattern as in PDE, with some minor variations in usage. For details of these minor variations, see books on EModE cited in the Annotated Bibliography (e.g. Barber 1976, Görlach 1991).

Sentence Structure: Some special features

As in ME, recapitulation and anticipation and the splitting of heavy groups are to be found in EModE. See pp. 66, 110.

Recapitulation and anticipation is a construction whereby an anticipatory noun phrase is recapitulated later by a pronoun, e.g.:

47 *my two <u>Schoolefellowes</u>,/ Whom I will trust as I will Adders fang'd,/ <u>They</u> beare the mandat*
48 *Alas poor <u>Yorick . . . he</u> hath borne me on his backe a thousand times . . .*

Sometimes a pronoun-subject is unexpressed where it would be in PDE, e.g.:

49 *Nor do we finde him forward to be sounded,/ But with a crafty Madnesse [HE] keepes aloofe.*

Sometimes this practice is extended to a complete subject-phrase, e.g.:

50 *we rip their hearts,/ [TO RIP] Their Papers is more lawful.*

The **splitting of heavy groups** is still a feature of EModE grammar, notably with regard to the modifying adjective, e.g.:

51 *An honest mind and plaine.*

However, this construction is not invariably used, cf.:

52 *such insociable and poynt deuise companions.*

By Shakespeare's time, the **paratactic** style would have been regarded as very old-fashioned; complex **hypotaxis** was regarded as the best model for English prose style. For further details, see the Annotated Bibliography.

5.4 Paradigms

→ This section gives an outline of EModE forms representing the reflexes of the OE configurations. As elsewhere in this chapter, the patterns presented are those of the First Folio; most examples are drawn from the Texts in Part II, but examples have been taken from elsewhere in the First Folio where necessary. ←

→ Since paradigmatic choice depends on syntactic function, constant reference to the 'Syntax' section should be made, using the Thematic Index in Part III. ←

5.4.1 Nouns

→ The configuration of the EModE noun-declensions is essentially the same as that found in late ME. In Shakespeare's time, therefore, there was a Basic Noun Declension whose essential characteristics derive from the OE General Masculine Declension, and a set of Irregular Declensions. The **Basic Noun Declension** in Shakespearean English was as follows:

Case	Singular	Plural
Nom.	*stone* STONE	*stones*
Acc./Dat.*	*stone*	*stones*
Gen.	*stones*	*stones*

*The distinction between Acc. and Dat. was not really a meaningful one in EModE, but is sustained here to enable easy comparison with the paradigms given in Chapters 3 and 4.

Almost all EModE nouns are declined as *stone*. In PDE, genitives are distinguished in writing by the use of the apostrophe, e.g. STONE'S, STONES'; for the use of the apostrophe in EModE, see p. 137. ←

A minor variant pattern is supplied by the occasional habit of using *his*, *her*, etc. instead of the genitive inflexion, e.g. *Sejanus his Fall*.

A few nouns follow **irregular declensions**. Most of these are relics of the other OE paradigmatic patterns, e.g. *eyen* EYES, *shoon* SHOES, *horse* HORSES (beside *horses*). There are of course also those relic forms which have survived into PDE, e.g. *oxen*, *feet*, *sheep*. A minor set of innovations was derived from the reinterpretation of older forms. *Dice*, originally a plural of *die* (still occasionally used in PDE), was an old plural which has come to be reinterpreted as singular. The PDE form PEA is a new singular which first appeared in the seventeenth century, derived from the older singular *pease* which was reinterpreted as a plural.

5.4.2 Pronouns

➔ EModE pronouns, as those of PDE, retain number, person and case distinctions, and are also used to signal the gender of their referents when in the third person. As in ME, this gender-reference is based on so-called natural gender, i.e. sex-distinctions. ⬅

➔ The EModE **pronoun-paradigms** are as follows:

First person

Case	Singular	Plural
Nom.	*I*	*we*
Acc.	*me*	*us*
Gen.	*my, mine*	*our(s)*
Dat.	*me*	*us*

Second person

Case	Singular	Plural
Nom.	*thou*	*ye/you*
Acc.	*thee*	*you*
Gen.	*thy, thine*	*your(s)*
Dat.	*thee*	*you*

Third person

Gender		Singular		Plural
	Masc	Fem	Neut	All genders
Nom.	*he, a*	*she*	*it/'t*	*they*
Acc.	*him*	*her*	*it/hit*	*them/'em*
Gen.	*his*	*her, hers*	*his/its/it's*	*their(s)*
Dat.	*him*	*her*	*it/hit*	*them/'em*

It will be observed that, as in ME, the accusative and dative in all pronouns are the same; this is because these two categories of pronoun may be considered to have merged in Chaucerian English. ←

In PDE, it is usual to distinguish the use of, e.g., MY/MINE by position; thus PDE distinguishes between MY HAT and THE HAT IS MINE. In EModE, *my* and *mine* can both be used as pre-modifiers. Their distribution in this position is comparable with that used for PDE A/AN; *my*, etc. is used when the modified element begins with a consonant, *mine*, etc. when the modified element begins with a vowel or *h*, as well as in postmodifying expressions such as *of mine*. Thus we have examples such as *That eyelesse head of thine*; *thy Mistris*; *a poore thing but mine own*. However, advanced speakers were beginning to transfer forms of the *my*-type to all positions, e.g. *my own*, *my head*; both forms appear in the First Folio.

For the distinct functions of *thou, ye/you*, etc., see pp. 134–5 above. *Ye* is conservative in Shakespeare's time, and alternates with *you* in subject-position.

Reduced forms of the third person pronoun are commonly represented in writing. *A* HE occurs in some ME dialects, but seems to have been extended into more widespread use in EModE as a general reduced form of *he*, e.g. *a pou'rd a Flaggon of Renish on my head once*. *'em* is still used in many varieties of PDE speech, but is often represented in EModE writing, e.g. *Call 'em*. *'t* is also common, e.g. *'Twere* IT WERE, *'twil* IT WILL; cf. the PDE abbreviated form IT'LL.

The possessive of *it* can be either *his* or *its/it's* in EModE. The former is the inherited form, but that it was already regarded as problematic is indicated by the habit, widespread in (e.g.) the Authorised Version of the Bible, of replacing it with the periphrasis *thereof*, e.g. *The falle thereof was great. Its/it's* seems to have been formed by analogy with the usual possessive/genitive inflexion. In

PDE, it has become conventional for the possessive pronoun to be written without an apostrophe, ITS, leaving IT'S as an abbreviation for IT IS. However, in EModE both forms were used for the possessive pronoun.

In EModE, the principal **relative pronouns** are *that, which, who* (also *whom, whose*) and *the which*; the pronoun is also sometimes omitted where it would be present in PDE. For details of use and examples, see p. 135. *Who, whom* and *whose* could also be used as **interrogative pronouns**, as in PDE, e.g. *Whose doe you thinke it was?*

5.4.3 Determiners

➜ In general, the **determiners** of EModE are much the same as in PDE. The articles are *a(n)* (indefinite) and *the* (definite); a reduced form of *the, th(')*, is occasionally found indicated in writing, e.g. *i'th Forrest* IN THE FOREST. The demonstratives are as in PDE: *that/those, this/these*; however, another demonstrative, *yon/yond(er)* is also used. For the functions of these forms, see p. 136. ⬅

5.4.4 Adjectives

➜ The weak/strong distinction in **adjectives**, characteristic of OE and still vestigial in ME, is no longer observed in EModE (see p. 136 above and references there cited). **Comparison of adjectives** is much as in PDE, except that there is more frequent variation between the FREER/MORE FREE types, giving examples such as *perfecter* (where PDE would have MORE PERFECT), *more sweet* (where PDE would tend to have SWEETER). Sometimes the two methods of comparison can be combined, e.g. *the most vnkindest cut of all.* ⬅

5.4.5 Adverbs

➜ In general, EModE **adverbs** follow the same patterns as in PDE. One slight difference from PDE practice is the occurrence of forms which are identical in form with the adjective, e.g. *'Tis Noble spoken* IT IS NOBLY SPOKEN. Such forms derive from analogy with those adverbs which ended in *-e* in OE, e.g. *fæste* FIRMLY (cf. PDE FAST in STAND FAST, etc.). Another difference between EModE and PDE is the wide range of intensifying adverbs in use, e.g. *sore*, *right*, *passing*, where PDE would use VERY. ←

5.4.6 Prepositions

→ The **prepositions** of EModE are much as PDE. A notable feature, signalled in the written mode, is their appearance in reduced form, e.g. *i'th Forrest* IN THE FOREST. ←

5.4.7 Verbs

→ As in OE, ME and PDE, EModE verbs fall into three categories: **weak**, **strong** and **irregular**. As is the case at other stages of the language, EModE verb paradigms take account of **person**, **number**, **tense** and **mood**. ←

→ Here are three **model conjugations**: (1) *bind(e)* TO BIND, a typical strong verb; (2) *loue* TO LOVE, a typical weak verb; and (3) the most important irregular verb, *be* TO BE. These paradigms correspond to those offered in Chapters 3 and 4 above. ←

→ (1) *bind(e)* TO BIND

	Indicative	Subjunctive
Present		
1st person sg	*bind(e)*	*bind(e)*
2nd person sg	*bind(e)st*	*bind(e)*
3rd person sg	*bindeth*	*bind(e)*
All persons pl	*bind(e)*	*bind(e)*
Preterite		
1/3 persons sg	*bound(e)*	*bound(e)*
2nd person sg	*bound(e)st*	*bound(e)*
All persons pl	*bound(e)*	*bound(e)*

Imperative: *bind(e)*

Participles
Present   *binding(e)*   Past   *bound(e)* ←

→ (2) *loue* TO LOVE

	Indicative	Subjunctive
Present		
1st Person Sg	*loue*	*loue*
2nd Person Sg	*lou(e)st*	*loue*
3rd Person Sg	*loueth*	*loue*
All Persons Pl	*loue*	*loue*
Preterite		
1st, 3rd Persons Sg	*loued*	*loued*
2nd Person Sg	*louedst*	*loued*
All Persons Pl	*loued*	*loued*

Imperative: *loue*

Participles:
Present   *louing(e)*   Past   *loued* ←

→ (3) *be* TO BE

	Indicative	Subjunctive
Present		
1st Person Sg	*am*	*be*
2nd Person Sg	*art, beest*	*be*
3rd Person Sg	*is*	*be*
All Persons Pl	*are*	*be*
Preterite		
1st Person Sg	*was*	*were*
2nd Person Sg	*wast, wert*	*were*
3rd Person Sg	*was*	*were*
All Persons Pl	*were*	*were*

Participles:
Present: *being*   Past: *been, bin* ←

The paradigms given in (1)–(3) are the most commonly used forms in EModE. There were several variant forms. Perhaps the most important of these is to do with the third person singular present, where -(e)s can sometimes appear for -eth, as in PDE; the form with -(e)s occurs first in northern dialects of ME but subsequently spread south. There is some evidence that -(e)s was in common use in London speech some time before it was signalled in writing; Shakespeare, in his late play *Pericles*, seems to be referring to this practice in the line *Who wanteth it and sayes he wants it?*

More about strong verbs

Bind can act as the general model for all strong verbs, except that -en is frequently retained as a past participle ending, even in PDE. However, as in OE and ME, there are several classes of strong verb in EModE marked by varying patterns of alternation in stem vowels. For ease of comparison with OE and ME practice, the EModE reflexes of the same classes are given here.

The principal parts (i.e. those forms from which a complete paradigm of the verb can be generated) given here are the infinitive, the preterite (all persons save second singular) and the past participle. It will be observed that many of the distinctions between the principal parts of the strong verbs have collapsed; this seems to have been one of the reasons for the (temporary) adoption of DO-constructions in phrases such as *he did eat*, since the inherited present and preterite forms would in many dialects have become identical in pronunciation. Moreover, some formal distinctions between classes characteristic of OE or ME have also disappeared. It should also be noted that there is a good deal of variation within the various paradigms, since analogous processes operated to confuse the various classes.

I	WRITE	*write*	*wrote*	*written*
II	CREEP	*creep(e)*	*crope*	*cropen*
III	BIND	*bind(e)*	*bound(e)*	*bound(e)*
IV	BEAR	*bear(e)*	*bare, bore*	*borne*
V	TREAD	*tread(e)*	*trad, trod*	*trodden*
VI	SHAKE	*shake*	*shook*	*shaken*
VII	HOLD	*hold*	*held*	*holden, held*
	KNOW	*know(e)*	*knew(e)*	*known*

The above forms may be taken as representative of each class. There was a fair degree of variation, caused by the forces of analogy; thus, for example, the preterite of *write* is also recorded as *wrate*, *writ* at various times and in various texts during the course of the EModE period.

Another source of variation was the co-existence of weak and strong forms of the same verb, since analogy caused the transfer of many strong verbs into the weak paradigm and (more rarely) of weak verbs into the strong paradigm. For instance, the principal parts of HELP are recorded both as *help, holp*, and *holpen* and as *help, helped* and *helped* (the latter, of course, being the PDE configuration); PDE DIG is a strong verb, but in EModE the preterite of *dig* is commonly *digged*.

More about weak verbs

Loue may act as a model for all weak verbs. The only major source of variation is indicated by the spelling-variation between *-ed* and *-'d*, e.g. *abhorred, offer'd*. It seems likely that the pronunciation of *-e-* in such environments was an option which could be exercised or ignored for metrical reasons.

More about irregular verbs

Here are the principal parts of some common irregular verbs. The forms listed are (1) the first person singular present, (2) the second person singular present, (3) the present plural, (4) the preterite (all persons, save second singular), (5) the second person singular preterite. There are many variant forms; to save space, minor spelling variants (e.g. *shold/should*) have not been included here.

	(1)	(2)	(3)	(4)	(5)
CAN:	*can*	*canst*	*can*	*could*	*couldst*
DARE:	*dare*	*darest*	*dare*	*durst*	*durst*
MAY:	*may*	*mayst*	*mowe*	*might, mought*	*mightst*
SHALL:	*shall*	*shalt*	*shall*	*should*	*shouldst*
WILL:	*will, woll(e)*	*wilt*	*will, woll(e)*	*would*	*wouldst*

5.4.8 Numerals

➔ The EModE **numerals** were the same as those of PDE. One minor point: the present-day pronunciation of ONE with initial [w-], which originated in western dialects of ME, seems to have become widely adopted in EModE. ✦

5.5 Lexicon

➔ The details of EModE lexical development are complex, and are probably best studied as part of a general historical survey; see further Barber (1993), Baugh and Cable (1993), Strang (1970) and Görlach (1991: chapter 7). The notes offered here simply indicate some general characteristics of EModE vocabulary. ✦

5.5.1 Borrowing

The EModE period was one of large-scale borrowing into English from a range of other languages, above all from the classical languages. Humanism acted as a spur to 'enriching' the language through borrowing from Latin and Greek, and many words derived from Latin make their first appearance in the English lexicon during the EModE period. This process of borrowing seems to have been quite conscious, and was recommended by many contemporary authorities on style, generally termed **neologisers**. In fact, borrowing became such a marked feature of EModE written discourse that a reaction set in, and several **purist** and 'archaising' writers during the period attempted to replace these Latinate borrowings, which they famously condemned as **inkhorn terms** (i.e. the pretentious language of the over-learned), with native-derived words. Perhaps the best-known of the latter is Edmund Spenser. Purist writers tried to find equivalents for the new classical loanwords, e.g. *cleavesomeness* DIVISIBILITY, *unthroughfaresom* IMPENETRABLE; as the fate of these examples in PDE indicates, the purists were generally unsuccessful.

Words from the Romance languages, especially French and Italian, continued to enter the language in great numbers. However, perhaps the principal new source of loanwords into English resulted from the encounter between Europeans and the peoples they met during the trading and imperial expansions of the period. A few examples will illustrate the range of loans, some of them direct and others transmitted to English through other European languages: *pariah* (from Tamil), *potato* (from Quechua, the lingua franca of the Inca empire), *chocolate* (from Nahuatl/Aztec). For further details, see p. 14 above.

5.5.2 Word-formation

As in ME, words were adapted through affixation to carry out new roles. Often words produced in this way were derived from loanwords; and sometimes there was a period of competition between different forms before one was settled upon (cf. the forms *propension, propenseness, propensitude, propensity,* all of which are recorded in the *Oxford English Dictionary*. Only the last of these forms has survived into PDE).

5.5.3 Changes of meaning

Finally, some mention should be made of changes of meaning between EModE and PDE. These are too numerous to list in this handbook, although a few are illustrated in the apparatus accompanying the Texts in Part III. Perhaps the most important point to make is that present-day readers are most often confused by changes in meaning of quite common words. A good example is *presently*, which in EModE means IMMEDIATELY, etc., while in most varieties of present-day British English it means AFTER A SPACE OF TIME. Interestingly, 'presently' still seems to have its older meaning in some varieties of Scots and North American English.

5.6 Appendix: Evidence for EModE dialects

Although EModE is much more standardised in the written mode than ME, there is nevertheless a surprising amount of evidence for dialectal usage during the EModE period, much of it still unexamined by scholars. For further information, see the Annotated Bibliography on pp. 223–7. As an example of dialectal usage, the passage from *King Lear* in Part II pp. 223–7 below might be briefly analysed.

As indicated in the Texts, the passage is set on the road to Dover in Kent. Edgar, disguised as a local rustic, defends his blinded father from the wicked steward Oswald, and adds to his disguise by adopting a rustic form of speech. His language is a mixture of non-standard features, e.g.:

(1) *z* for S, *v* for F in *zwaggerd* BLUSTERED, *volk* FOLK are evidently attempts to indicate initial voiced fricatives. They were a common feature in southern dialects in Shakespeare's day; they are no longer a feature of Present-Day Kentish dialect, having receded westward.

(2) Also southern is the form *ch-* or *che* for I, e.g. *chud* I SHOULD, *chill* I WILL, *che vor'ye* I WARRANT YOU; the *ch-* type form derives from the full form of the pronoun in OE and ME, *ic/ich*.

(3) However, *ice* I SHALL is a northern construction, while *Ballow* CUDGEL seems to be an item of Nottinghamshire dialect vocabulary.

It would appear that Shakespeare is here simply adopting a kind of 'stage-dialect' rather than more accurate representation of Kentish. Parallels have been drawn between the variety represented here and similar features found in the Devonshire dialect portrayed in *The London Prodigal* of 1605, which was also performed by Shakespeare's company.

Part two

Illustrative Texts

About the texts

This part of the book consists of a set of illustrative texts to accompany Chapters 3–5. The texts are divided into three sections: Section A (Old English Texts), Section B (Middle English Texts) and Section C (Early Modern English Texts). Texts spanning the transition between OE and ME, and between ME and EModE, are also included. For pedagogic reasons, the editorial principles adopted vary from text to text, and between sections.

Texts relate for the most part to those in standard editions and readers, with some modifications and emendations to enable them better to serve the purposes of beginners. Some in Section C are drawn from books printed while the authors of the texts in question were still alive or had died only shortly before.

Students will find it useful to supplement these texts with others in order to find their own examples. Particularly recommended as a source-book is Burnley 1992.

For references to grammatical structures, see the Thematic Index in Part III.

Old English Texts

In this section Texts (1)–(6) have been normalised into Early West Saxon, for reasons given in the Preface and in the note on p. 46. The punctuation of all texts in this section is editorial, since the originals were only irregularly punctuated; the punctuation is designed to help the modern reader. Texts (1), (2) and (4), taken from the OE translation of the Bible, and Text (3), from the *Anglo-Saxon Chronicle*, have been rewritten to remove obscurities or irregularities which may confuse beginners, in the same way that texts designed for foreign learners of PDE are frequently rewritten; they are also accompanied by very literal translations. For normalised but otherwise unmodified versions of these texts, see Sweet (1953). Texts (5) and (6), Cædmon's *Hymn*, and a selection of two passages from *The Dream of the Rood*, however, have not been rewritten, although they have been normalised; for easily accessible, non-normalised versions of these texts, see H. Sweet (rev. D. Whitelock), *Sweet's Anglo-Saxon Reader* (Oxford: Clarendon Press, 1967). Texts (7) and (8), a portion of a homily by Ælfric and a passage from the great OE epic poem *Beowulf*, have been neither rewritten nor normalised, and may act as 'bridge' texts to more advanced work. Notes on some difficulties of translation and interpretation for passages (6)–(8) appear at the end of each passage.

All the vocabulary for the texts in Section A appears in the OE Glossary in Part III.

(1) The Man Who Built His House on Sand

This text is a version of the well-known New Testament parable (see Matthew 7.24–27).

Se wīsa wer timbrode his hūs ofer stān. Þā cōm þær micel flōd, and þær blēowon windas, and āhruron on þæt hūs, and hit ne fēoll: sōþlīce, hit wæs ofer stān getimbrod.

Þā timbrode se dysiga wer his hūs ofer sandceosol. Þā rīnde

hit, and þǣr cōm flōd, and blēowon windas, and āhruron on þæt hūs, and þæt hūs fēoll; and his hryre wæs micel.

Translation

The wise man built his house on stone. Then a great flood came there, and winds blew there, and fell down upon the house, and it did not fall: truly, it was built on stone.

    Then the foolish man built his house on sand [lit. sand-gravel]. Then it rained, and a flood came there, and winds blew, and fell down upon the house, and the house fell; and its fall was great.

(2) Abraham and Isaac

This text is a version of the well-known Old Testament story (Genesis 22).

God cwæþ tō Abrahāme: 'Nim þīnne sunu Isaāc, and far tō þǣm dūnum, and geoffra hine þǣr uppan dūne.'

    Þā ārās Abrahām on þǣre nihte, and fērde mid twǣm cnapum tō þǣm dūnum, and Isaāc samod. Hīe ridon on assum. Þā on þone þriddan dæg, þā hīe þā dūne gesāwon, þā cwæþ Abrahām tō þǣm twǣm cnapum þus: 'Andbidiaþ ēow hēr mid þǣm assum!'

    Isaāc bær þone wudu tō þǣre stōwe, and Abrahām bær his sweord and fȳr. Isaāc þā āscode Abrahām his fæder: 'Fæder mīn, hwǣr is sēo offrung? Hēr is wudu.' Se fæder cwæþ: 'God forescēawaþ, mīn sunu, him self þā offrunge.'

    Þā cōmon hīe tō þǣre stōwe; and hē þǣr wēofod ārǣrde on þā ealdan wīsan. Þā band hē his sunu, and his sweord ātēah. Þā hē wolde þæt weorc beginnan, þā clipode Godes engel arodlīce of heofonum: 'Abrahām!' Hē andswarode sōna. Se engel him cwæþ tō: 'Ne ācwele þū þæt cild!'

    Þā geseah Abrahām ramm betwix þǣm brēmlum; and hē āhōf þone ramm tō þǣre offrunge.

Translation

God said to Abraham: 'Take your son Isaac, and go to the hills, and offer [i.e. sacrifice] him there upon a hill.'

    Then Abraham arose in the night, and went with two servants to the hills, and Isaac as well. They rode on asses. Then on the third day, when they saw the hills, then Abraham said to the two servants thus: 'Wait here with the asses!'

Isaac carried the wood to the place, and Abraham carried his sword and fire. Isaac then asked Abraham his father: 'My father, where is the offering? Here is wood.' The father said: 'God himself, my son, will provide the offering.'

Then they came to the place, and he there raised an altar in the old manner. Then he bound his son, and drew his sword. When he was about to carry out [lit. wished to begin] the deed, then God's angel called quickly from heaven [lit. heavens]: 'Abraham!' He answered at once. The angel said to him: 'Do not kill the child!'

Then Abraham saw a ram amongst the brambles; and he raised up the ram as the offering.

(3) **From the _Anglo-Saxon Chronicle_**

This text is a modified version of a passage from the _Anglo-Saxon Chronicle_. The Chronicle, which was begun during the later part of the reign of Alfred the Great, is an annalistic record of events since ancient times, compiled from the Bible, the writings of scholars like Bede, notes made in the margins of the mathematical tables used to calculate the date of Easter, and old traditions. Convenient translations of the Chronicle are by G.N. Garmonsway (London: Dent, 1954), and by M. Swanton (London: Dent, 1996).

Anno 449. Hēr Martiānus and Valentīnus onfēngon rice, and rīcsodon seofon winter. And on hiera dagum Hengest and Horsa, fram Wyrtgeorne gelaþode, Bretta cyninge, gesōhton Bretene on þǣm stede þe is genemned Ypwines-flēot, ǣrest Brettum tō fultume, ac hīe eft on hīe fuhton. Se cyning hēt hīe feohtan ongēan Peohtas; and hīe swā dydon, and sīge hæfdon swā hwǣr swā hīe cōmon. Hīe þā sendon tō Angle, and hēton him sendan māran fultum. þā sendon hīe him māran fultum. þā cōmon þā menn of þrim mǣgþum Germānie: of Ealdseaxum, of Englum, of Īotum.

455. Hēr Hengest and Horsa fuhton wiþ Wyrtgeorne þǣm cyninge in þǣre stōwe þe is genemned Æglesþrep; and his brōþor Horsan man ofslōg. And æfter þǣm Hengest fēng to rice, and Æsc his sunu.

457. Hēr Hengest and Æsc fuhton wiþ Brettas in þǣre stōwe þe is genemned Crecganford, and þǣr ofslōgon fēower þūsend wera. þā forlēton þā Brettas Centland, and mid micle ege flugon tō Lundenbyrig.

Translation

Anno 449. In this year [lit. here] Martianus and Valentinus succeeded to [lit. received] kingship, and ruled seven years. And in their days Hengest and Horsa, invited by Vortigern, king of [the] Britons, came to Britain at the place which is called Ebbsfleet, first as a help to [the] Britons, but they afterwards fought against them. The king commanded them to fight against [the] Picts; and they did so, and had victory wherever they came. Then they sent to Angeln, and told them to send more help. They then sent to them more help. Then the men came from three tribes in Germany: from [the] Old Saxons, from [the] Angles, from [the] Jutes.

455. In this year Hengest and Horsa fought against Vortigern the king in the place which is called Aylesford; and his brother Horsa was slain [lit. one slew his brother Horsa]. And after that Hengest and Æsc his son succeeded to kingship [lit. Hengest succeeded to kingship, and Æsc his son].

457. In this year Hengest and Æsc fought against [the] Britons in the place which is called Crayford, and there slew four thousand men [lit. of men]. The Britons then abandoned Kent, and with great fear fled to London.

(4) Daniel

This text is a version of the well-known biblical story (Daniel 6).

On Cyres cyninges dagum wrēgdon þā Babilōniscan þone wītegan Daniēl, for þǣm þe hē hiera dēofolgield tōwearp. Hīe cwǣdon ānmōdlīce tō þǣm cyninge: 'Gief ūs Daniēl, þe ūrne god Bēl tōwearp. Gif þū hine forstande, wē fordīlgiaþ þē and þīnne hīred.'

þā geseah se cyning þæt hīe ānmōde wǣron, and þone wītegan him geaf. Hīe þā hine āwurpon intō ānum sēaþe, on þǣm wǣron seofon lēon.

On þǣm seofoþan dæge fērde se cyning tō þāra lēona sēaþe, and inn beseah. Hwæt! Daniēl wæs sittende gesundfull onmiddan þǣm lēom. þā clipode se cyning mid micelre stefne: 'Mǣre is se God þe Daniēl on belīefþ.' And hē þā mid þǣm worde hine ātēah of þǣm scræfe, and hēt inn weorpan þā þe hine ǣr fordōn woldon. þā wurdon þæs wītegan ēhteras āscofene betwix þǣm lēom, and hīe þǣrrihte mid grǣdgum ceaflum hīe ealle tōtǣron.

Translation

In the days of King Cyrus, the Babylonians accused the prophet Daniel, because he overthrew their idol. They said unanimously to the king: 'Give us

Daniel, who overthrew our god Baal. If you protect him, we [will] destroy you and your family.'

Then the king saw that they were unanimous, and gave them the prophet. They then threw him into a pit, in which [there] were seven lions.

On the seventh day, the king went to the lions' pit, and looked in. Lo! Daniel was sitting safe and sound in the midst of the lions. Then the king called with a great voice: 'Glorious is the God in whom Daniel believes.' And he then with that word took him out of the pit, and commanded to be thrown in [lit. to throw in] those who had wanted [lit. wanted formerly] to destroy him. Then the prophet's persecutors were thrust among the lions, and they straightway with greedy jaws tore them all to pieces.

(5) Cædmon's Hymn

The story of Cædmon is well known from Book IV, chapter 24 of the Venerable Bede's *Ecclesiastical History*, which should be consulted for the context of this poem. A convenient account of the poem's genesis in context, with references, appears in S.A.J. Bradley, *Anglo-Saxon Poetry* (London: Dent, 1982). Visitors to Westminster Abbey in London will see the stone placed to the memory of Cædmon in 'Poets' Corner'.

Salient to a modern reader will be the sustained use of alliteration, which is structural in OE verse, just as rhyme is basic to much later verse. The basic metrical unit in OE poetry was the half-line; these were linked together in pairs by alliterating syllables. Although distinct licence was allowed for the purposes of stylistic foregrounding, nevertheless pairs of lines such as *heofon tō hrōfe* and *hālig Scieppend* were commonplace. This poem indicates the basic pattern; in the four stressed syllables of a prototypical pair of alliterative half-lines, the first three should alliterate. The poem also illustrates, amongst other things, the formulaic nature of OE verse, exemplified here by the number of synonyms for God. On verse-form in OE, see Mitchell and Robinson (1995).

Nū sculon herian	heofonrīces Weard,
Metodes mihte	and his mōdgeþanc,
weorc Wuldorfæder,	swā hē wundra gehwæs
ēce Dryhten,	ōr onstealde.
Hē ærest scōp	eorþan bearnum
heofon tō hrōfe	hālig Scieppend.
þā middangeard	mancynnes Weard
ēce Dryhten,	æfter tēode
fīrum foldan	Frēa ælmihtig.

Translation

Now [we] must praise [the] Guardian of [the] heavenly kingdom, [the] power of God and his conception, [the] work of [the] Father of Glory, in that He, eternal Lord, established [the] beginning of every marvellous thing. He, holy Creator, first created heaven as a roof for children of men. Then [the] Guardian of mankind, eternal Lord, almighty Master, afterwards adorned [the] earth for living beings.

(6) From *The Dream of the Rood*

This poem is recorded in its fullest form in the Vercelli Book, a late-tenth-century West Saxon manuscript which was left in Northern Italy in Anglo-Saxon times. Vercelli is on the road to Rome; the manuscript was either abandoned or forgotten there by a pious Anglo-Saxon pilgrim. An earlier Old Northumbrian version of a Cross-poem also survives, carved in runic script, on the late-seventh-/early-eighth-century Ruthwell Cross overlooking the Solway Firth in what is now south-west Scotland. The poet of the Vercelli Book seems to have drawn upon this traditional material in producing his own version; OE poetic composition was a process of re-creation and assimilation rather than a striving for absolute originality.

The Vercelli poem is a dream-vision in which the Cross on which Christ was crucified appears to a Dreamer-Narrator and speaks to him. The basic rhetorical device on which the poem hangs is **prosopopoeia**, i.e. assigning character and speech to an inanimate object. Section (a) is from the beginning of the poem; section (b) is from the speech of the Cross, and describes the Crucifixion of Christ. It will be observed that the Cross describes Christ as a Germanic warrior; the Anglo-Saxons understandably saw Christianity in terms of their own culture. There are many editions of the poem; a convenient translation appears in S.A.J. Bradley, *Anglo-Saxon Poetry* (London: Dent, 1982).

Notes on difficulties of interpretation are given at the end of each section of the poem. Words and phrases giving rise to such notes are under-lined.

(a) Lines 1–12

Hwæt, ic swefna cyst   secgan wylle,
hwæt <u>mē gemǣtte</u>   tō midre nihte
siþþan reordberend   reste wunedon.
<u>þūhte mē</u> þæt ic gesāwe   syllicre trēow
on lyft lǣdan   lēohte bewunden,   5
bēama beorhtost.   Eall þæt bēacen wæs
begoten mid golde;   gimmas stōdon
fægere æt foldan scēatum,   <u>swylce þǣr fīfe wǣron</u>
<u>uppe on þǣm eaxlegespanne</u>.   Behēoldon þǣr <u>engeldryhta fela</u>

fǣgere þurh forþgesceaft;   ne wæs þǣr hūru fracodes gealga,
ac hine þǣr behēoldon   hālige gāstas,   11
men ofer moldan,   and eall þēos mǣre gesceaft.

(2) *mē gemǣtte*, (4) *þūhte mē*. These two constructions are impersonal, a usage found in OE but more common in Middle English. Translate as I DREAMT and IT SEEMED TO ME respectively.

(8)–(9) *swylce þǣr fīfe wǣron/uppe on þǣm eaxlgespanne* LIKEWISE THERE WERE FIVE UP ON THE INTERSECTION. The reference here seems to be to the stigmata, the five wounds of Christ, which injury the Cross is envisaged as sharing.

(9) *engeldryhta fela* MANY ANGEL-MULTITUDES, i.e. MANY MULTITUDES OF ANGELS. Note that *fela*, here placed after the noun it modifies, causes that noun to inflect in the genitive.

(b)   Lines 29–50

'þæt wæs geara iū   (ic þæt gȳta geman)
þæt ic wæs āhēawen   holtes on ende,   30
āstyred of stefne mīnum.   <u>Genāmon mē þǣr strange fēondas,</u>
geworhton him þǣr tō wæfersȳne,
          hēton mē hiera wergas hebban;
bǣron mē þǣr beornas on eaxlum,
          oþ þæt hīe mē on beorg āsetton;
gefæstnodon mē þǣr fēondas genōge.
          Geseah ic þā Frēan mancynnes
efstan elne micle,   þæt hē mē wolde on gestīgan.   35
þǣr ic þā ne dorste   ofer Dryhtnes word
būgan oþþe berstan,   <u>þā ic bifian geseah</u>
<u>eorþan scēatas.</u>   Ealle ic mihte
fēondas gefyllan,   hwæþre ic fæste stōd.
<u>Ongyrede hine þā geong hæleþ,</u>   þæt wæs God ælmihtig,
strang and stīþmōd;   gestāh hē on gealgan hēanne,   41
mōdig on monigra gesyhþe,   þā hē wolde mancynn lȳsan.
Bifode ic þā mē se beorn ymbclypte;   <u>ne dorste ic hwæþre</u>
                                 <u>būgan tō eorþan;</u>
<u>feallan tō foldan scēatum,</u>   <u>ac ic scolde fæste standan.</u>
Rōd wæs ic ārǣred,   āhōf ic rīcne cyning,   45
heofona hlāford,   hyldan mē ne dorste,
þurhdrifon hīe mē mid deorcum næglum;   on mē sindon þā dolg
                               gesīene,
opene inwidhlemmas;   ne dorste ic hiera ǣnigum sceþþan.

Bysmeredon hīe <u>unc būtū</u> ætgædere;   eall ic wæs mid blōde
                                       bestēmed,   49
begoten of þæs guman sīdan,   siþþan hē hæfde his gāst
                                         onsended.

(31) *Genāmon mē þǣr strange fēondas* (lit.) TOOK/SEIZED ME THERE
STRONG ENEMIES, i.e. STRONG ENEMIES TOOK/SEIZED ME THERE. It will
be observed that many clauses in this passage begin with the lexical verb:
geworhton, hēton (32), *bǣron* (33), etc. This usage seems to be thematically
governed; by foregrounding the verbs through the use of (slightly) deviant
syntax, the poet wishes to draw our attention to the sequence of actions
undertaken at the Crucifixion.

(37–38) *þā ic bifian geseah/ eorþan scēatas* WHEN I SAW THE SURFACE(S)
OF THE EARTH TREMBLE. This clause refers to the earthquake which
accompanied the Crucifixion (Matthew 27: 51).

(40) *Ongyrede hine þā geong hæleþ* THEN (THE) YOUNG HERO
UNDRESSED HIMSELF. An ironic (?) reversal of the 'arming of the hero'
scene characteristic of the epic-genre, found in the *Iliad* and *Aeneid* as well
as in *Beowulf*.

(43–44) *ne dorste ic hwæþre būgan tō eorþan;/ feallan tō foldan scēatum,
ac ic scolde fæste standan* NEVERTHELESS I DID NOT DARE TO BOW TO
(THE) EARTH, TO FALL TO EARTH'S SURFACES, BUT I HAD TO STAND
FIRM. The Cross is torn between its bond of loyalty towards Christ – something felt by all natural objects, and the Cross is of course in origin a tree –
and the duties of execution assigned to it. Such conflicts, often termed 'heroic
dilemmas', are commonplace in Germanic heroic literature.

(49) *unc būtū* BOTH OF US (TWO). The poet uses the dual pronoun.

(7) From Ælfric's *Life of King Oswald*

This passage is taken from one of Ælfric's *Lives of the Saints*, a sermon-cycle
composed in the last decade of the tenth century. Ælfric wrote most of his
works while he was a monk at Cerne Abbas, Dorset, before, in 1005, becoming abbot of Eynsham in Oxfordshire. Ælfric was a prolific writer, compos-
ing not only three cycles of homilies (two sets of *Catholic Homilies*, and the
Lives of the Saints) but also various other works of an educational nature,
including a *Grammar* and a *Colloquy*, both designed to help in the teaching
of Latin. He is generally regarded as the most important and versatile prose-
writer of late Anglo-Saxon England, only rivalled by his contemporary
Wulfstan. A convenient text of the *Homily* appears in H. Sweet (rev.
D.Whitelock), *Sweet's Anglo-Saxon Reader* (Oxford: Clarendon Press, 1967).
Translations of other works by Ælfric, accompanied by an account of his life,
are conveniently available in M. Swanton, *Anglo-Saxon Prose* (London:
Dent, 1975).
    King Oswald was the great royal saint of the Kingdom of Northumbria;
his regnal dates are 633–641. The Northumbrian kings had a special devotion

to the cult of the Cross, demonstrated by the appearance of the cross-symbol on their coins and by their collection of relic fragments allegedly taken from the True Cross on which Christ was crucified; and Oswald's raising of a cross at 'Heavenfield' can be related to the erection of great stone crosses as hegemony symbols on the borders of the ancient Northumbrian kingdom. The most famous of these crosses is of course that at Ruthwell; see p. 165 above.

There are notes on difficulties of interpretation at the end of each section of the passage given here. Words and phrases giving rise to such notes are underlined. References are to numbered sentences.

(1) Æfter þan þe Augustīnus tō Engla lande becōm, wæs sum æþele cyning, Ōswold gehāten, on Norþhymbra lande, gelȳfed swȳþe on God. (2) Sē fērde on his iugoþe fram his frēondum and māgum tō Scotlande on sǣ, and þǣr sōna wearþ gefullod, and his gefēran samod þe mid him sīþedon.

(3) Betwux þām wearþ ofslagen Ēadwine his ēam, Norþhymbra cynincg, on Crīst gelȳfed, fram Brytta cyninge, Cedwalla gecīged, and twēgen his æftergengan binnan twām gēarum; and se Cedwalla slōh and tō sceame tūcode þā Norþhymbran lēode æfter heora hlāfordes fylle oþ þæt Ōswold se ēadiga his yfelnysse ādwæscte. (4) Ōswold him cōm tō, and him cēnlice wiþ feaht mid lȳtlum werode, ac his gelēafa hine getrymde, and Crīst him gefylste tō his fēonda slege.

(5) Ōswold þā ārǣrde āne rōde sōna Gode tō wurþmynte, ǣr þan þe hē tō þām gewinne cōme, and clypode tō his gefērum: (6) 'Uton feallan tō þǣre rōde, and þone Ælmihtigan biddan þæt hē ūs āhredde wiþ þone mōdigan fēond þe ūs āfyllan wile. (7) God sylf wāt geare þæt wē winnaþ rihtlīce wiþ þysne rēþan cyning tō āhreddenne ūre lēode.' (8) Hī fēollon þā ealle mid Ōswolde cyninge on gebedum; and syþþan on ǣrne mergen ēodon tō þā gefeohte, and gewunnon þǣr sige, swā swā se Eallwealdend him ūþe for Ōswoldes gelēafan; and ālēdon heora fȳnd, þone mōdigan Cedwallan mid his micclan werode, þe wēnde þæt him ne mihte nān werod wiþstandan.

(9) Seo ylce rod siþþan þe Ōswold þǣr ārǣrde on wurþmynte þǣr stōd, and wurdon fela gehǣlde untrumra manna and ēac swilce nȳtena þurh þā ylcan rōde, swā swā ūs rēhte Bēda. (10) Sum man fēoll on īse, þæt his earm tōbærst, and læg þā on bedde gebrocod forþearle, oþ þæt man him fette of þǣre foresǣdan rōde sumne dǣl þæs mēoses þe hēo mid beweaxen wæs, and se ādliga sōna on slǣpe wearþ gehǣled on þǣre ylcan nihte þurh Ōswoldes geearnungum.

(11) Sēo stōw is gehāten 'Heofonfeld' on Englisc, <u>wiþ þone langan weall þe þā Rōmaniscan worhtan</u>, þǣr þǣr Ōswold oferwann þone wælhrēowan cynincg. (12) And þǣr wearþ siþþan ārǣred swīþe mǣre <u>cyrce</u> Gode tō wurþmynte, þe wunaþ ā on ēcnysse.

(1) *Augustīnus* St Augustine, apostle to the Anglo-Saxons, brought Christianity to Kent in 597.

gelȳfed (WHO) BELIEVED. Relative clauses without expression of the relative pronoun are fairly common in OE.

(2) *Sē fērde* HE TRAVELLED. The determiner *sē* is here being used instead of a pronoun.

wearþ gefullod, and his gefēran samod WAS BAPTISED TOGETHER WITH HIS COMPANIONS (lit. WAS BAPTISED, AND HIS COMPANIONS AS WELL). For the use of *weorþan* + past participle, and for 'the splitting of heavy groups', of which this is an example, see Chapter 3, pp. 59, 66.

(3) *Betwux þām = Betwix þǣm* MEANWHILE (lit. BETWEEN THOSE) *cynincg = cyning; heora = hiera*

(4) *him cōm tō* CAME TO HIM (lit. HIM CAME TO). The delayed preposition, especially with pronouns, is a characteristic OE usage.

(7) *tō āhreddenne* TO RESCUE. This is an example of the inflected infinitive construction.

(8) *Hī = Hīe*
þæt him ne mihte nān werod wiþstandan THAT NO TROOP COULD STAND UP TO HIM. *ne . . . nān* is a 'double negative' construction.

(9) *wurdon fela gehǣlde untrumra manna and ēac swilce nȳtena* MANY SICK MEN AND ALSO LIKEWISE ANIMALS WERE HEALED. *Fela* MANY has here been separated from the elements it modifies, both of which are in the genitive plural.

(11) *wiþ þone langan weall þe þā Rōmaniscan worhtan* BY THE LONG WALL WHICH THE ROMANS MADE (i.e. Hadrian's Wall). *worhtan = worhton*.

(12) *cyrce = cirice*

(8) From *Beowulf*

Beowulf is the greatest epic poem surviving from Anglo-Saxon times. The materials on which the poet drew are ancient: some elements derive from the history of the Germanic 'homeland' in Scandinavia, others from folklore. Yet these ancient materials have been transformed by a later Christian writer. The narrative of the poem is centred on the hero Beowulf's three great battles, against the ogre Grendel (in the hall of Hrothgar, king of the Danes), against Grendel's mother (underwater) and, after a space of time, against a dragon (involving exposure to fire). Such a bald description makes the poem sound something like a comic-strip adventure. However, twentieth-century criticism has revealed the religious elements, elegiac and homiletic, which underlie the poem and which are employed in a sophisticated and highly wrought manner. The comparison with the epics of Homer and Virgil is a valid one.

There are numerous translations of *Beowulf*. That contained in S.A.J. Bradley, *Anglo-Saxon Poetry* (London: Dent, 1982) is a convenient prose version, but it is worth looking at verse translations as well. Recommended are those by K. Crossley-Holland (London: Macmillan, 1968), E. Morgan (Aldington: Hand and Flower Press, 1952) and M. Alexander (Harmondsworth: Penguin, 1973), all the work of practising poets. The best editions are those by F. Klaeber (the major scholarly edition; Lexington: Heath, 1950) and G. Jack (the best students' edition, but with much of interest for advanced scholars; Oxford: Clarendon Press, 1994). This passage, with a few minor modifications, follows these editions.

The passage given below comes from early in the poem (lines 64–125). Hrothgar, king of Denmark, has erected a great hall appropriate to his royal dignity and expressive of the personal bonds between him and his retainers: Heorot, whose name has usually been taken to correspond to the hart, a creature with royal significance in ancient Germanic society. In the hall, men drink mead; they receive gifts; they listen to *hearpan swēg* HARP'S MUSIC. Thus far we are reminded of the tribal societies recorded by the Roman writer Tacitus in his *Germania* (for which see H. Mattingly and S.A. Hanford trans. *Tacitus: The Agricola and the Germania*, Harmondsworth: Penguin, 1970). But the poem to which the king and his courtiers listen nevertheless appears to correspond in subject-matter to that in Cædmon's *Hymn* (see Text (5) above), a deeply Christian poem.

Heorot is therefore in origin a place of joy. However, there are one or two ominous hints of evils to come, e.g. *heaðowylma bād* (IT) AWAITED HOSTILE FLAMES; and the *swutol sang scopes* SWEET SONG OF (THE) POET awakens the demon who lurks on the frontiers of tribal society. This semi-human monster is called Grendel – a phonaesthetically significant name (cf. PDE GRIM, GRIND, GRUFF, etc.). Grendel is infuriated by the presumption of the humans, and he attacks Heorot, carrying off thirty of Hrothgar's retainers. The situation is only resolved when Beowulf, a prince of the Geatish tribe living in what is now southern Sweden, hears of Hrothgar's troubles and decides to prove his valour by destroying Grendel.

Interpretative notes appear at the end of the passage. Words and phrases giving rise to such notes are underlined in the text.

þā wæs Hrōðgāre	herespēd gyfen,	
wīges weorðmynd,	þæt him his winemāgas	65
georne hȳrdon,	oðð þæt sēo geogoð gewēox,	
magodriht micel.	Him on mōd be-arn,	
þæt healreced	hātan wolde,	
medoærn micel	men gewyrcean	
þonne yldo bearn	æfre gefrūnon,	70
ond þǣr on innan	eall gedǣlan	
geongum ond ealdum,	swylc him God sealde	

būton folcscare   ond feorum gumena.
Dā ic wīde gefrægn   weorc gebannan
manigre mǣgþe   geond þisne middangeard,   75
folcstede frætwan.   Him on fyrste gelomp,
ǣdre mid yldum,   þæt hit wearð ealgearo,
healærna mǣst;   scōp him Heort naman
<u>sē þe his wordes geweald</u>   <u>wīde hæfde</u>.
Hē <u>bēot</u> ne ālēh,   bēagas dǣlde,   80
sinc æt symle.   Sele hlīfade
hēah ond horngēap;   heaðowylma bād,
lāðan līges;   ne wæs hit lenge þā gēn,
þæt se ecghete   <u>āþumswēoran</u>
æfter wælnīðe   wæcnan scolde.   85

Dā se ellengǣst   earfoðlīce
þrāge geþolode,   sē þe in þȳstrum bād,
þæt hē dōgora gehwām   drēam gehȳrde
hlūdne in healle;   þǣr wæs hearpan swēg,
swutol sang scopes.   Sægde sē þe cūþe   90
frumsceaft fīra   feorran reccan,
cwæð þæt se Ælmihtiga   eorðan worhte,
wlitebeorhtne wang,   swā wæter bebūgeð,
gesette sigehrēþig   sunnan ond mōnan
lēoman tō lēohte   landbūendum,   95
ond gefrætwade   foldan scēatas
leomum ond lēafum,   līf ēac gesceōp
cynna gehwylcum   <u>þāra ðe</u> cwice hwyrfaþ.

Swā ðā drihtguman   drēamum lifdon,
ēadiglīce,   oð ðæt <u>ān</u> ongan   100
fyrene fremman   fēond on helle.
Wæs se grimma gǣst   Grendel hāten,
mǣre mearcstapa,   sē þe mōras hēold,
fen ond fæsten;   fīfelcynnes eard
wonsǣli wer   weardode hwīle,   105
siþðan <u>him Scyppend</u>   <u>forscrifen hæfde</u>
<u>in Cāines cynne</u>.   þone cwealm gewræc
ēce Drihten,   þæs þe hē Ābel slōg.
<u>Ne gefeah hē þǣre fǣhðe,</u>   <u>ac hē hine feor forwræc,</u>
<u>Metod for þȳ māne</u>   mancynne fram.   110
þanon untȳdras   ealle onwōcon,

eotenas ond ylfe   ond orcnēas,
swylce gīgantas,   <u>þā</u> wið Gode wunnon
lange þrāge;   hē him ðæs lēan forgeald.

Gewāt ðā nēosian,   syþðan niht becōm,   115
hēan hūses,   hū hit Hring-Dene
<u>æfter bēorþege</u>   gebūn hæfdon.
Fand þā ðǣr inne   æþelinga gedriht
swefan æfter symble;   sorge ne cūðon,
wonsceaft wera.   Wiht unhǣlo,   120
grim ond grǣdig,   gearo sōna wæs,
rēoc ond rēþe,   ond on ræste genam
þrītig þegna;   þanon eft gewāt
hūðe hrēmig   tō hām faran,
mid þǣre wælfylle   wīca nēosan.   125

(66) *oðð þæt = oþ þæt*

(68) *hātan wolde* (HE) WANTED. The subject-pronoun is often left unexpressed in verse, as here.

(79) *sē þe his wordes geweald wīde hæfde* HE WHO HAD AUTHORITY WIDELY IN HIS SPEECH, i.e. the power to announce law. Kings in Anglo-Saxon times exercised power directly, through the *verbum regis* THE WORD OF THE KING. *Sē þe* is a relative construction, marked by a combination of determiner and relative particle.

(80) *bēot* VOW, BOAST. The 'heroic boast' is a frequent phenomenon in ancient Germanic literature. For a classic example, see an Old Icelandic text, the *Heimskringla* of Snorri Sturluson (1178–1241). In the portion of this text known as *King Olaf Tryggvasson's Saga*, chapter 35, Snorri gives an account of the baroquely ingenious vows of the Jómsborg Vikings. For a convenient translation of this text, see S. Laing (rev. J. Simpson), *Snorri Sturluson: Heimskringla, Part I (The Olaf Sagas)* (London: Dent, 1964).

(84) *āþumswēoran* An 'irregular' dative-plural = BETWEEN SON-IN-LAW AND FATHER-IN-LAW. The lines *þæt se ecghete āþumswēoran/ æfter wælnīðe wæcnan scolde* may be translated as THAT THE VIOLENT HATRED BETWEEN SON-IN-LAW AND FATHER-IN-LAW HAD TO ARISE AFTER (i.e. THROUGH) DEADLY ENMITY. These lines refer to something treated at greater length later in the poem, future conflict between Danes and another tribe, the Heathobards – which Hrothgar had tried to halt by marrying his daughter Freawaru to Ingeld, a prince of the Heathobards.

(98) *þāra ðe* Another example of a relative construction using determiner and relative particle.

(100) *ān* ONE modifies *fēond* ENEMY in the following line.

(106–107) *him Scyppend forscrifen hæfde/ in Cāines cynne* The reference here is to the banishment of Cain and his descendants after the killing of Abel; see Genesis 4.

(109–110) *Ne gefeah hē þǣre fǣhðe, ac hē hine feor forwræc/ Metod for þȳ māne mancynne fram* NOR DID HE (i.e. Cain) GAIN JOY FOR THAT HOSTILE ACT, BUT HE, GOD, BANISHED HIM FAR AWAY FROM MANKIND BECAUSE OF THAT CRIME.

(113) *þā* The determiner is here used in place of a relative particle.

(117) *æfter bēorþege* AFTER BEER-DRINKING. The ritual and social role of drinking-bouts and feasting in ancient Germanic society is well attested; see, for instance, Tacitus, *Germania*, chapter 22.

Middle English Texts

In this Section Texts (1)–(3) are taken from the Ellesmere MS of the *Canterbury Tales* (now MS San Marino, California, Huntington Library 26. C. 9, formerly Earl of Ellesmere's MS), and represent the 'prototypical' ME generally described in Chapter 4. These versions correspond to those in the *Riverside Chaucer* (ed. L. Benson *et al.*, Oxford: Oxford University Press, 1988), but with some modifications of punctuation; the texts have also been checked against transcriptions of the manuscript.

Texts (4)–(8) are given as short representative selections from larger works written earlier and later in the ME period, or in places other than London. Text (9) is an example of less formal writing, i.e. a late-fifteenth-century letter. A gloss is supplied for Texts (1)–(3), (8) and (9) at the end of each passage; translations for Texts (4)–(6) are given, again at the end of each passage. Since ME punctuation is idiosyncratic and often fairly sparse in many manuscripts, editorial punctuation is used here.

(1) From *The General Prologue to the Canterbury Tales*

The Canterbury Tales, from which Texts (1)–(3) are taken, was Chaucer's last major work, undertaken largely in the last decade of the fourteenth century. Chaucer's aim was to present a series of stories within a linking framework. Such a structure was fashionable among contemporaries; it is exemplified in English by John Gower's *Confessio Amantis*, which was completed in its first form in 1390, and in Italian by Boccaccio in his *Decameron*. The chosen framework for Chaucer's poem was that of a pilgrimage to the shrine of Thomas Becket (martyred 1170) at Canterbury, perhaps the most important cult-centre in England during the later Middle Ages.

Text (1) is the opening of the cycle of tales: *The General Prologue*. The complex syntax, beginning with two lengthy adverbial clauses which themselves contain subordinate elements, reflects the complexity of the underlying thought, with its reference to medieval thinking on the processes of nature in relation to the grander workings of the universe. The opening is reminiscent of the opening of the dream-visions with which Chaucer began his poetic career (*The Book of the Duchess*, *The House of Fame*, *The*

Parliament of Fowls); but in contrast to these texts the vision encountered is a real medieval event, a pilgrimage.

A marginal glossary has been supplied. Glossed words are underlined in the text. Interpretative notes for words and phrases marked with small Roman numerals (^{i, ii} etc.) appear at the end of the passage.

Whan that Aprill with his shoures soote	SWEET SHOWERS
The droghte of March hath perced to the roote,	DROUGHT; PIERCED
And bathed euery veyne in swich licour	VEIN; SUCH LIQUID
Of which vertu engendred is the flour;ⁱ	
Whan Zephirusⁱⁱ eek with his sweete breeth	5
Inspired hath in euery holt and heeth	BREATHED LIFE INTO; GROVE
The tendre croppes, and the yonge sonne	SHOOTS
Hath in the Ram his half cours yronne,ⁱⁱⁱ	
And smale foweles maken melodye,	
That slepen al the nyght with open ye^{iv}	10
(So priketh hem nature in hir corages),	INCITES; SPIRITS
Thanne longen folk to goon on pilgrimages,	LONG, DESIRE
And palmeres^v for to seken straunge strondes,	FOREIGN SHORES
To ferne halwes, kowthe in sondry londes^{vi};	DISTANT SHRINES
And specially from euery shires ende	15
Of Engelond to Caunterbury they wende,	
The hooly blisful martir for to seke,	
That hem hath holpen whan that they were seeke.	SICK

ⁱ *of which vertu engendred is the flour* BY WHICH POWER THE FLOWER IS ENGENDERED.

ⁱⁱ *Zephirus* ZEPHYRUS, THE WEST WIND OF SPRING.

ⁱⁱⁱ *the yonge sonne/ Hath in the Ram his half cours yronne* THE YOUNG SUN HAS RUN HIS HALF-COURSE IN THE RAM (i.e. the sign of Aries). Chaucer's interest in astrology is well attested, not least by his composition of a text-book on the subject for his son, *A Treatise on the Astrolabe*. The sun is 'young' because the solar year has just begun with the spring equinox.

^{iv} *with open ye* WITH OPEN EYE(S). This seems to have been an original observation by Chaucer. In the *Riverside Chaucer* it is noted that 'one can rarely see a bird with its eyes closed, since most birds have two sets of eye-lids, and that which they use for blinking is transparent.'

^v *palmeres* PILGRIMS TO THE HOLY LAND. Such pilgrims were known as 'palmers' because they carried a palm-branch as a sign that they had been to Palestine.

^{vi} *kowthe in sondry londes* KNOWN IN VARIOUS LANDS.

(2) From *The Pardoner's Tale*

The *Pardoner's Tale* has a considerable mythic pedigree. Readers of 'The King's Ankus' in Rudyard Kipling's *The Jungle Books* will have encountered an analogous narrative, the theme of which Kipling borrowed from an ancient Buddhist fable. However, the story has been transmuted by Chaucer into a sharply realised medieval situation, offered in the form of a sermon on the theme of *Radix malorum est cupiditas* ('the root of evils is cupidity'). That the Pardoner is notoriously corrupt and deceitful adds an extra degree of interest and creative tension to that interplay of tale and teller which is a characteristic of the cycle.

The passage offered here is from the beginning of the Pardoner's narrative. It describes the way in which the three young *riotoures* set off to seek death, guided by a mysterious old man – and find it, disguised as a pile of gold.

A marginal glossary has been supplied. Glossed words are underlined in the text. Interpretative notes for words and phrases marked with small Roman numerals ([i], [ii] etc.) appear at the end of the passage.

But, sires, now wol I telle forth my tale.	
Thise riotoures thre of whiche I telle,	DEBAUCHERS
Longe erst er prime rong of any belle,	BEFORE THE FIRST HOUR
Were set hem in a tauerne to drynke,	
And as they sat, they herde a belle clynke	5
Biforn a cors, was caried to his graue.	CORPSE [WHO] WAS
That oon of hem gan callen to his knaue:	CALLED
'Go bet,' quod he, 'and axe redily	QUICKLY; ASK
What cors is this that passeth heer forby;	PAST
And looke that thou reporte his name weel.'	10
'Sire', quod this boy, 'it nedeth neuer-a-deel;	SERVANT; IT'S NOT
	AT ALL NEEDED
It was me toold er ye cam heer two houres.	
He was, pardee, an old felawe of youres,	COMPANION
And sodaynly he was yslayn tonyght,	14 SLAIN
Fordronke, as he sat on his bench vpright.	VERY DRUNK;
	STRAIGHT
Ther cam a privee theef men clepeth Deeth,	STEALTHY; CALL
That in this contree al the peple sleeth,	
And with his spere he smoot his herte atwo,	
And wente his wey withouten wordes mo.	19
He hath a thousand slayn this pestilence.	DURING THIS PLAGUE
And, maister, er ye come in his presence,	
Me thynketh that it were necessarie	
For to be war of swich an aduersarie.	

Beth redy for to meete hym eueremoore;
Thus taughte me my dame; I sey namoore.'   25
'By Seinte Marie!' seyde this taverner,
'The child seith <u>sooth</u>, for he hath slayn this yeer,   TRUTH
<u>Henne</u> ouer a mile, withinne a greet village,   HENCE
Bothe man and womman, child, and <u>hyne</u>, and page;   SERVANT
I <u>trowe</u> his habitaciouns be there.   30 BELIEVE
To been <u>auysed</u> greet wysdom it were,   FOREWARNED
Er that he dide a man a dishonour.'
'Ye, Goddes armes!' quod this riotour,
'Is it swich peril with hym for to meete?
I shal hym seke by wey and <u>eek</u> by strete,   35 ALSO
I make <u>auow</u> to Goddes <u>digne</u> bones!   PROMISE; NOBLE
Herkneth, felawes, we thre been al ones;
Lat ech of vs holde vp his hand til oother,
And ech of vs bicomen otheres brother,
And we wol sleen this false traytour Deeth.   40
He shal be slayn, he that so manye sleeth,
By Goddes dignitee, er it be nyght!'
Togidres han thise thre <u>hir trouthes plight</u>   PLEDGED
                                                                    THEMSELVES

To lyue and dyen ech of hem for oother,
As though he were his owene <u>ybore</u> brother.   45 BY BIRTH
And vp they <u>stirte</u>, al dronken in this rage,   JUMPED
And forth they goon towardes that village
Of which the taverner hadde spoke biforn.
And many a grisly ooth thanne han they sworn,
And Cristes blessed body they <u>torente</u> –   50 TORE APART
Deeth shal be deed, if that they may hym <u>hente!</u>   SEIZE
Whan they han goon nat fully half a mile,
Right as they wolde han troden ouer a stile,
<u>An oold man and a poure</u> with hem mette.   AN OLD AND POOR
                                                                    MAN

This olde man ful mekely hem grette,   55
And seyde thus, 'Now, lordes, <u>God yow see!</u>'   MAY GOD SAVE
                                                                    YOU

The proudeste of thise riotoures three
Answerde agayn, 'What, <u>carl</u>, with sory grace!   FELLOW
Why <u>artow</u> al <u>forwrapped</u> saue thy face?   ART THOU; WRAPPED
                                                                    UP

Why <u>lyuestow</u> so longe in so greet age?'   60 DO YOU LIVE
This olde man gan looke in his visage,
And seyde thus: 'For I ne kan nat fynde
A man, though that I walked into <u>Ynde</u>,   INDIA
Neither in citee ne in no village,
That wolde chaunge his youthe for myn age;   65
And therfore moot I han myn age <u>stille</u>,   QUIETLY
As longe tyme as it is Goddes wille.
<u>Ne Deeth, allas, ne wol nat han my lyf</u>.ⁱ
Thus walke I, lyk a restelees <u>kaityf</u>,   WRETCH
And on the ground, which is my moodres gate,   70
I knokke with my staf, bothe erly and late,
And seye 'Leeue mooder, leet me in!
Lo how I <u>vanysshe</u>, flessh, and blood, and skyn!   WASTE AWAY
Allas, whan shul my bones been at reste?
Mooder, with yow wolde I chaunge my <u>cheste</u>   75 STRONGBOX
That in my chambre longe tyme hath be,
Ye, for an <u>heyre clowt</u> to wrappe me!'   HAIRCLOTH
But yet to me she wol nat do that grace,
For which ful pale and <u>welked</u> is my face.   WITHERED
'But, sires, to yow it is no curteisye   80
To speken to an old man vileynye,
But he trespasse in word or elles in dede.
<u>In Hooly Writ ye may yourself wel rede</u>:ⁱⁱ
'Agayns an oold man, <u>hoor</u> vpon his heed,   GREY/WHITE (OF
    HAIR)

Ye sholde arise'; wherfore I <u>yeue</u> yow <u>reed</u>,   85 GIVE; ADVICE
Ne dooth vnto an oold man noon harm now,
Namoore than that ye wolde men did to yow
In age, if that ye so longe <u>abyde</u>.   REMAIN ALIVE
And God be with yow, where ye go or ryde!
I moot go thider as I haue to go.'   90
'Nay, olde cherl, by God, thou shalt nat so,'
Seyde this oother hasardour anon;
'Thou partest nat so lightly, by Seint John!
Thou spak right now of <u>thilke</u> traytour Deeth,   THAT SAME
That in this contree alle oure freendes sleeth.   95
Haue heer my trouthe, as thou art his espye,
Telle where he is or thou shalt it <u>abye</u>,   PAY FOR IT
By God and by the hooly sacrement!

For soothly thou art <u>oon of his assent</u>   IN LEAGUE WITH HIM
To sleen vs yonge folk, thou false theef!'   100
'Now, sires,' quod he, 'if that yow be so <u>leef</u>   DESIROUS
To fynde Deeth, turne vp this croked wey,
For in that groue I lafte hym, by my <u>fey</u>,   FAITH
Vnder a tree, and there he wole abyde;
Noght for youre boost he wole him no thyng hyde.
Se ye that <u>ook</u>? Right there ye shal hym fynde.   106 OAK
God saue yow, <u>that boghte agayn mankynde</u>,   WHO REDEEMED
                                    MANKIND

And yow amende!' Thus seyde this olde man;
And euerich of thise riotoures ran
Til he cam to that tree, and ther they founde   120
Of <u>floryns</u> fyne of gold ycoyned rounde   GOLD COINS
Wel ny an eighte busshels, as hem thoughte.
No lenger thanne after Deeth they soughte,
But ech of hem so glad was of that sighte,
For that the floryns been so faire and brighte,   125
That doun they sette hem by this precious hoord.

ⁱ *Ne Deeth, allas, ne wol nat han my lyf* NOR DOES DEATH, ALAS, WANT TO HAVE MY LIFE

ⁱⁱ See Leviticus 19: 32.

(3) From *The Parson's Tale*

The Parson's Tale may not seem to modern readers to be a prototypically Chaucerian piece of writing, but the evidence is that Chaucer had a very clear notion that his collection should end with it. That the issues raised in the earlier stories find some sort of resolution is signalled, for instance, by the persistent verbal echoes in the *Tale* of significant phrases from other texts within the larger cycle. The *Tale* is a tract on penance, appropriate for the culmination of a pilgrimage. Its teller calls it a *myrie tale in prose*, and it may be taken as a fair example of Chaucer's prose style. The passage given comes at the very beginning of the *Tale*, and is worth comparing with other ME prose texts, especially Text (8).

    A notable feature of the language of the passage is the use of the subordinate clause; in Chaucer's time, the extensive use of subordination was regarded as an elegance, approved of by the best writers. For another example of a similar phenomenon carried out in a more extreme fashion, see Text (7) below. Such a characteristic derives from French traditions; however, constructions such as *a ful noble wey and a ful covenable* A VERY NOBLE AND VERY SUITABLE WAY (lit. A VERY NOBLE WAY AND SUITABLE) derive clearly from the OE pattern known as the 'splitting of heavy groups'.

A glossary for this passage follows immediately after it, with words grouped by line number. Interpretative notes are included in the glossary. All words and phrases which are glossed or discussed are underlined in the text.

(1) Oure sweete Lord God of heuene, that no man wole perisse but wole that we comen alle to the knoweleche of hym and to the blisful lif that is perdurable, amonesteth vs by the prophete Ieremie, that seith in thys wyse: (2) 'Stondeth vpon the weyes, and seeth and axeth of olde pathes (that is to seyn, of olde sentences) which is the goode wey, and walketh in that wey, and ye shal fynde refresshynge for youre soules, etc.' (3) Manye been the weyes espirituels that leden folk to oure Lord Ihesu Crist and to the regne of glorie. (4) Of whiche weyes ther is a ful noble wey and a ful covenable, which may nat fayle to man ne to womman that thurgh synne hath mysgoon fro the righte wey of Ierusalem celestial; and this wey is cleped Penitence, of which man sholde gladly herknen and enquere with al his herte to wyten what is Penitence, and whennes it is cleped Penitence, and in how manye maneres been the acciouns or werkynges of Penitence, and how manye speces ther been of Penitence, and whiche thynges apertenen and bihouen to Penitence, and whiche thynges destourben Penitence.

(5) Seint Ambrose seith that Penitence is the pleynynge of man for the gilt that he hath doon, and namoore to do any thyng for which hym oghte to pleyne. (6) And som doctour seith, 'Penitence is the waymentynge of man that sorweth for his synne and pyneth hymself for he hath mysdoon.' (7) Penitence, with certeyne circumstances, is verray repentance of a man that halt hymself in sorwe and other peyne for his giltes. (8) And for he shal be verray penitent, he shal first biwaylen the synnes that he hath doon, and stidefastly purposen in his herte to haue shrift of mouthe, and to doon satisfaccioun, and neuere to doon thyng for which hym oghte moor to biwayle or to compleyne, and to continue in goode werkes, or elles his repentance may nat auaille. (9) For, as seith Seint Ysidre, 'He is a iapere and a gabbere and no verray repentant that eftsoone dooth thyng for which hym oghte repente.' (10) Wepynge, and nat for to stynte to do synne, may nat auayle. (11) But nathelees, men shal hope that euery tyme that man falleth, be it neuer so ofte, that he may arise thurgh Penitence, if he haue grace; but certeinly it is greet doute. (12) For, as seith Seint Gregorie, 'Unnethe ariseth he out of his synne, that is charged with the charge of yuel vsage.' (13) And therfore repentant folk, that

stynte for to synne and <u>forlete</u> synne <u>er that</u> synne forlete hem, hooly chirche holdeth hem <u>siker</u> of hire sauacioun. (14) And he that synneth and verraily repenteth hym <u>in his laste</u>, hooly chirche yet hopeth his sauacioun, by the grete mercy of oure Lord Ihesu Crist, for his repentaunce; but taak the siker wey.

(1) *that no man wole perisse* A seemingly clumsy expression, but the sense is fairly clear; it may be translated as WISHING NO ONE TO PERISH.
perdurable ETERNAL, EVERLASTING
amonesteth ADMONISHES

Ieremie JEREMIAH (the prophet; for the quotation in (2), see Jeremiah 6: 16)

(2) *sentences* TEACHINGS, OPINIONS

(4) *covenable* SUITABLE
mysgoon GONE AMISS
wyten KNOW
cleped CALLED
speces KINDS, SORTS
apertenen and bihouen BELONG TO AND ARE NECESSARY FOR

(5) *Seint Ambrose* The quotation comes from a sermon mistakenly ascribed to Saint Ambrose (*c.* 339–397), one of the principal early Christian writers known as the Doctors of the Church (the others being Augustine, Jerome and Pope Gregory the Great).
pleynynge LAMENT

(6) *waymentynge* LAMENTING
pyneth TORMENTS
mysdoon DONE AMISS

(8) *hym oghte* HE OUGHT. An impersonal construction.

(9) *Ysidre* ISIDORE OF SEVILLE. The quotation comes from the *Sentences* of Isidore of Seville. Isidore (*c.* 560–636) was Archbishop of Seville in *c.* 600. His *Etymologies* was a standard encyclopedic work for scholars throughout the Middle Ages.
iapere JESTER
gabbere FOOLISH TALKER
eftsoone IMMEDIATELY

(10) *stynte* STOP

(11) *doute* DOUBT

(12) *Seint Gregorie* SAINT GREGORY. Gregory the Great (*c.* 540–604) was Pope, saint and Doctor of the Church (see (5) *Seint Ambrose* above). His best-known works are probably the *Moralia in Job* and the *Pastoral Care*.
unnethe SCARCELY
yuel vsage EVIL CUSTOM

(13) *forlete* ABANDON

>*er that* BEFORE
>*siker* SURE

(14) *in his laste* AT HIS END (i.e. DEATH)

(4) From *The Peterborough Chronicle*

In comparison with the passages from the *Canterbury Tales*, Text (4) dates from the very earliest part of the ME period. *The Peterborough Chronicle* (MS Oxford, Bodleian Library, MS Laud Misc. 636) is a version of the *Anglo-Saxon Chronicle* which was copied and continued after the Norman Conquest. It thus spans the transition between OE and ME, and indeed there are parts of the *Peterborough Chronicle* which seem to be more OE than ME in character.

The passage given below is the annal for the year 1135, part of the so-called Final Continuation to the *Peterborough Chronicle*. Examination of the passage soon reveals many features which point back to the OE period, notably in word-order; but there are also features which point forward. Thus in spelling, *w* and *uu* appear instead of the OE 'wynn'; there are features which indicate that the OE ancestor of the dialect of the *Peterborough Chronicle* was not West Saxon but Old Anglian (e.g. *ald* OLD for WS *eald*); there are French loanwords, e.g. *Pais* PEACE; and even in word-order there are indications of new patterns (e.g. *se king Henri* THE KING HENRY beside *Henri cyng*; cf OE *Ælfred cyning* KING ALFRED).

The author of the Final Continuation was not a simple, objective annalist of events; he had a particular (monastic, local) point of view to put across and this sometimes led him into exaggeration. But the annals for this period, when combined with evidence from other sources, indicate that the mid-twelfth century was indeed a turbulent time when, as a phrase from elsewhere in the *Peterborough Chronicle* puts it, *Christ slep, and his halechen* CHRIST AND HIS SAINTS SLEPT.

The standard edition of the text is that by C. Clark (Oxford: Clarendon Press, 1970). The text here differs only in some minor details of presentation; e.g. for the MS form 7 used for AND, *and* appears throughout this passage.

A literal translation of the passage appears immediately after it. There are three biographical notes, signalled by small Roman numerals in the text, appended after the translation.

(1) Millesimo cxxxv. On þis gære for se king Henri ouer sæ æt te Lammase.[i] (2) And Ðat oþer dei þa he lai an slep in scip, þa þestrede þe dæi ouer al landes and uuard þe sunne suilc als it uuare thre niht ald mone, an sterres abuten him at middæi. (3) Wurþen men suiðe ofuundred and ofdred, and sæden ðat micel þing sculde cumen herefter: sua dide, for þat ilc gær warth þe king ded ðat oþer dæi efter Sancte Andreas massedæi on Normandi. (4) þa þestreden sona þas landes, for æuric man sone ræuede oþer þe mihte. (5) þa namen his sune and his frend and brohten his lic to Engleland and

bibirieden in Redinge. (6) God man he was and micel æie wes of him: durste nan man misdon wið oðer on his time. (7) Pais he makede men and dær. (8) Wua sua bare his byrthen gold and sylure, durste nan man sei to him naht bute god. (9) Enmang þis was his nefe cumen to Engleland, Stephne de Blais;[ii] and com to Lundene; and te Lundenisce folc him underfeng and senden æfter þe ærcebiscop Willelm Curbuil; and halechede him to kinge on Midwintre Dæi. (10) On þis kinges time wes al unfrið and yfel and ræflac, for agenes him risen sona þa rice men þe wæron swikes, alre fyrst Balduin de Reduers; and held Execestre agenes him and te king it besæt, and siððan Balduin acordede. (11) Þa tocan þa oðre and helden her castles agenes him. (12) And Dauid king of Scotland[iii] toc to uuerien him. (13) Þa, þohuuethere þat, here sandes feorden betwyx heom and hi togædere comen, and wurðe sæhte, þoþ it litel forstode.

Translation

1135. In this year, the king Henry went over sea at Lammas.[i] And the second day when he lay asleep on (his) ship, then the day darkened over all lands and the sun became such as if it were a three-nights' old moon, and stars about it at midday. Men were greatly astonished and afraid, and said that a great matter ought to follow hereafter: so it did, for that same year the king died the second day after Saint Andrew's mass-day in Normandy. Then at once these lands darkened, for every man who could at once ravaged another. Then his son and his relatives took and brought his body to England and buried (it) at Reading. He was a good man, and there was much fear of him: no man dared do evilly with another in his time. He made peace for men and beasts. Whosoever carried a gold and silver burden, no man dared say to him anything except good. At this time his nephew, Stephen of Blois,[ii] had come to England; and (he) came to London; and the people of London received him and sent for the archbishop William Curbeil; and (he) sanctified him as king on midwinter's day. In this king's time, everything was strife and evil and thievery, for against him rose at once the powerful men who were treacherous ones, first of all Baldwin de Redvers; and he held Exeter against him and the king surrounded it, and afterwards Baldwin came to an agreement. Then the others seized and held their castles against him. And David, king of Scotland[iii] started to attack him. Then, despite that, their messengers travelled between them and they met together, and became at peace, although it lasted briefly.

[i] *se king Henri* Henry I (1068–1135), youngest son of William the Conqueror. Posthumously (and rather generously) styled *Beauclerc* SCHOLAR, Henry was an able if somewhat grasping monarch whose reign saw the establishment of certain significant institutions of government, such as the Exchequer.

The blending of OE *se* with the ME word-order *se king Henri* is notable; cf characteristically OE constructions such as *Ælfred cyning*.

ii *Stephne de Blais* King Stephen (*c.*1097–1154) was a grandson of William the Conqueror. Contemporaries regarded him as too genial to make a successful king, and his kingship was contested by Henry I's allegedly somewhat ferocious daughter, Matilda.

iii *Dauid king of Scotland* David I (*c.*1080–1153) was one of the great reforming kings of Scots. During his reign, monarchical authority was asserted, the first royal coinage struck, a Scottish common law produced, the Scottish church reformed, trade encouraged and the system of fortifications known as the 'burgh' system was developed. David also owned lands in England, and was therefore partly a vassal of the English rulers; as such he played an important part in the affairs of the neighbouring kingdom.

(5) From *Sir Orfeo*

This passage is taken from the version of *Sir Orfeo* in the Auchinleck MS (MS Edinburgh, National Library of Scotland, Advocates' 19.2.1). It seems likely that the poem *Sir Orfeo* was composed in the West Midlands of England; the rhyme *owy: cri* AWAY; CRY would only work in that dialect of ME, and it is interesting that in mid-line position the scribe has replaced the rarer form *owy* with more common *oway*. However, the Auchinleck MS was a London production and was probably read at the court of Edward III *ca.* 1330; there is a plausible school of opinion which holds that the MS was known to, or even owned by, Geoffrey Chaucer.

The texts copied in the Auchinleck MS give us a useful snapshot of the kind of language to be found in the London area in the generations before Chaucer. As might have been expected, the language of *Sir Orfeo* is slightly more old-fashioned than that found in the best Chaucerian MSS. Thus it will, for instance, be observed that there are two forms for SHE in the following passage, *sche* and *hye*. More subtly, analysis of the various occurrences of this pronoun in the MS indicates that *sche* is used when the pronoun is at the beginning of the clause containing it, whereas the older (and less distinctive) form *hye* occurs when the pronoun appears after the verb it governs, e.g. *Hir riche robe hye al torett* SHE TORE ASUNDER HER NOBLE GARMENT. This systematic distinction had disappeared by the time of the Ellesmere MS. Other points of linguistic interest include the use of French-derived vocabulary (e.g. *comessing* BEGINNING).

Sir Orfeo's origins lie in the classical tale of Orpheus (see e.g. Ovid, *Metamorphoses*), but it has been carefully blended with Celtic tradition and the values and traditions of contemporary romance to produce a completely new text. The passage which follows takes place just before Lady Heurodis is snatched away from her husband by the King of the Fairies; the abduction was prefigured in a dream, but Orfeo's attempt to foil the fairy-king is doomed to failure.

The standard edition of the poem is by A.J. Bliss (Oxford: Clarendon Press, 1966), which gives amongst other things a useful account of the sources and analogues of the poem. The text here varies from that edition only in minor matters of punctuation.

A literal translation of this passage appears immediately after it.

Bifel so in þe comessing of May,
When miri & hot is þe day,
& oway beþ winter-schours,
& eueri feld is ful of flours,
& blosme breme on eueri bouȝ   5
Oueral wexeþ miri anouȝ,
þis ich quen, Dame Heurodis,
Tok to maidens of priis,
& went in an vndrentide
To play bi an orchardside,   10
To se þe floures sprede & spring,
& to here þe foules sing.
þai sett hem doun al þre
Under a fair ympe-tre,
& wel sone þis fair quene   15
Fel on slepe opon þe grene.
þe maidens durst hir nouȝt awake,
Bot lete hir ligge & reste take.
So sche slepe til after none,
þat vndertide was al ydone.   20
Ac, as sone as sche gan awake,
Sche crid, & loþli bere gan make;
Sche froted hir honden & her fet,
& crached hir visage: it bled wete;
Hir riche robe hye al torett,   25
& was reueyd out of hir witt.
þe tvo maidens hir biside
No durst wiþ hir no leng abide,
Bot ourn to þe palays ful riȝt
& told boþe squier & kniȝt   30
þat her quen awede wold,
& bad hem go & hir athold.
Kniȝtes vrn & leuedis also,
Damisels sexti & mo.
In þe orchard to þe quene hye come,   35
& her vp in her armes nome,
& brouȝt hir to bed atte last,
& held hir þere fine fast;

Ac euer sche held in o cri,
& wold vp, & owy. 40

Translation

It happened thus at the beginning of May (when the day is pleasant and hot, and winter-showers are away, and every field is full of flowers, and bright blossom on every bough grows everywhere very pleasantly) this same queen, Lady Heurodis (= Eurydice) took two precious maidens and went in the mid-morning to amuse herself at an orchard's edge, to see the flowers grow and burgeon, and to hear the birds sing. They sat themselves down all three beneath a handsome grafted tree, and right away this beautiful queen fell asleep on the greensward. The maidens dared not awake her, but allowed her to lie and take rest. So she slept until after noon-time, until the mid-morning was entirely past. But as soon as she awoke, she cried and made a loathsome clamour: she scratched her hands and her feet, and tore at her face: it bled wet; she entirely tore to pieces her noble dress, and was driven out of her reason. The two maidens beside her dared no longer stay with her, but ran directly to the palace and told both squire and knight that their queen would go mad, and asked them to go and restrain her. Knights ran, and ladies as well, sixty damsels and more. They came to the queen in the orchard, and took her up in their arms, and brought her to bed at the end, and held her there very strongly: but continually she persisted in one cry, and wanted to be up, and away.

(6) From *Sir Gawain and the Green Knight*

MS London, B.L. Cotton Nero A.x contains four texts: *Sir Gawain and the Green Knight*, *Patience*, *Purity* (or *Cleanness*) and *Pearl*. These poems, which were almost certainly by the same author, were probably composed for a provincial court somewhere in the north-west Midlands, but they yield nothing in sophistication and subtlety through comparison with contemporary London products such as *The Canterbury Tales*. *Sir Gawain and the Green Knight* is a romance, but it goes beyond the confines of its genre to challenge the courtly notions which governed the behaviour and ethical sense of its probable first audience, a serious-minded provincial noble household.

Unlike *The Canterbury Tales*, *Sir Gawain and the Green Knight* sustains the old alliterative verse tradition which (with considerable revision on the way) goes back to OE times. For various reasons, this older tradition was sustained longer in the north and west of the English-speaking area than in the south and east.

The passage which follows is at the beginning of the fourth section ('Fitt') of the poem. The protagonist, Sir Gawain, is about to ride forth to meet the Green Knight, an unearthly being who entered into a strange bargain a year before, involving mutual decapitation. At the Green Knight's request, Gawain had beheaded the Green Knight as part of a challenge-game at Arthur's court a year before, on condition that he (Gawain) offered himself for execution a year later. Whereas the Green Knight seemed, magically, not to be one whit daunted by losing his head, Gawain is not convinced that he will escape so easily . . .

Linguistically, this passage makes a good comparison with the Chaucer texts. In particular, it shows several distinctive northern features, e.g. the verbal inflexions, which are generally a good indication of dialect localisation. It will be observed that it retains the widespread use of þ and ȝ.

The standard edition of the poem is by J.R.R. Tolkien and E.V. Gordon, rev. N. Davis (Oxford: Clarendon Press, 1967). This edition includes valuable supplementary material, notably on the sources and analogues of the poem. The text presented here varies from that edition only in a few details of punctuation.

A literal translation of this passage appears immediately after it. An interpretative note to line 21 (signalled by the small Roman numeral [i]) is appended to the translation.

Now neȝez þe Nw ȝere, and þe nyȝt passez,
þe day dryuez to þe derk, as Dryȝtyn biddez;
Bot wylde wederez of þe worlde wakned þeroute,
Clowdes kesten kenly þe colde to þe erþe,
Wyth nyȝe inoghe of þe norþe, þe naked to tene;   5
þe snawe snitered ful snart, þat snayped þe wylde.
þe werbelande wynde wapped fro þe hyȝe,
And drof vche dale ful of dryftes ful grete.
þe leude lystened ful wel þat leȝ in his bedde;
þaȝ he lowkez his liddez, ful lyttel he slepes;   10
Bi vch kok þat crue he knwe wel þe steuen.
Deliuerly he dressed vp, er þe day sprenged,
For þere watz lyȝt of a laumpe þat lemed in his chambre;
He called to his chamberlayn, þat cofly hym swared,
And bede hym bryng hym his bruny and his blonk sadel;
þat oþer ferkez hym vp and fechez hym his wedez,   16
And grayþez me Sir Gawayn vpon a grett wyse.
Fyrst he clad hym in his cloþez þe colde for to were,
And syþen his oþer harnays, þat holdely watz keped,
Boþe his paunce and his platez, piked ful clene,   20
þe ryngez rokked of þe roust of his riche bruny;[i]
And al watz fresch as vpon fyrst, and he watz fayn þenne
         to þonk;
   He hade vpon vche pece,
   Wypped ful wel and wlonk;   25
   þe gayest into Grece,
   þe burne bede bryng his blonk.

Translation

Now the New Year draws near, and the night passes, the day takes over from the night, as God commands; but fierce storms wakened from the world outside, clouds bitterly threw the cold to the earth, from the north with much bitterness, to torment the naked; the snow, which nipped cruelly the wild creatures, came shivering down very bitterly; the wind blowing shrilly rushed from the high (ground), and drove each valley full of very large (snow)drifts. The man who lay in his bed listened very carefully; although he locks his eyelids, he sleeps very little; by each cock that crew he was reminded of (lit. 'knew well') the appointed day. Before the day dawned, he quickly got up, for there was light from a lamp which shone in his bedroom; he called to his chamberlain, who promptly answered him, and bade him bring him his mailcoat and his horse-saddle; the other man rouses himself and brings him his clothes, and Sir Gawain is prepared (lit. 'one prepares') in a magnificent manner. First he dressed himself in his clothes to protect (himself) from the cold, and then his other armour, which was preserved carefully, both his stomach-armour and his steel plates, polished very brightly, the rings of his splendid mail-shirt made clean from rust;[i] and everything was clean as in the beginning, and he was desirous then to thank (his servants?); he had on him each piece (of armour), very well wiped and noble; the most handsome (man) as far as Greece, the warrior made (one) bring his horse.

[i] Chain armour was *rokked* (i.e. rolled) to rub the rust off; a traditional method was in a sand-barrel.

(7) From William Caxton's Preface to his edition of the *Morte Darthure*

William Caxton, England's first printer, set up his press in the precincts of Westminster Abbey in 1476; his first clients seem to have been members of the royal court and their associates. In 1485, a month before the battle of Bosworth Field when Richard III was defeated by Henry Tudor, Caxton printed his version of Sir Thomas Malory's *Morte Darthure*, carrying out numerous modifications of his original and adding an important Preface, of which the following passage is a part.

Caxton's readership expected prose works to conform to the culturally dominant French-derived styles of the time, with highly complex syntax and a good deal of subordination (see also Text (3) above) as well as a high degree of French-derived vocabulary. The introduction to the *Morte Darthure*, which is Caxton's own composition, gives a fair idea of the characteristics of this style; the passage following is a representative extract from that introduction.

The text has been included here, and not in Section III, because it is held that the most illuminating approach to late medieval English prose style is that which sees it as deriving from earlier models than as prefiguring later developments. For a discussion of usage in Malory's cycle, see 'Language and style in Malory', in A.S.G. Edwards and E. Archibald, eds, *A Companion to Malory* (Woodbridge: Boydell and Brewer, 1996), and references there cited.

For a text of Caxton's full Prologue, see N. Blake, ed., *Selections from William Caxton* (Oxford: Clarendon Press, 1973), E. Vinaver, ed., *Malory: Works* (Oxford: Oxford University Press, 1971). The text here differs little from these except in a few points of punctuation.

A glossary for this passage follows immediately after it. Glossed words are underlined in the text. An interpretative note, signalled in the text by the small Roman numeral [i], is appended after the glossary.

(1) And I, accordyng to my copye, haue doon sette it in enprynte to the entente that noble men may see and lerne the noble actes of chyualrye, the jentyl and vertuous dedes that somme knyghtes vsed in thos dayes, by whyche they came to honour, and how they that were vycious were punysshed and ofte put to shame and rebuke, humbly bysechyng al noble lordes and ladyes wyth al other estates, of what estate or degree they been of, that shal see and rede in this sayd book and werke, thagh they take the good and honest actes in their remembraunce, and to folowe the same; wherein they shalle fynde many joyous and playsaunt hystoryes and noble and renomed actes of humanyte, gentylnesse, and chyualryes. (2) For herein may be seen noble chyualrye, curtosye, humanyte, frendlynesse, hardynesse, loue, frendshyp, cowardyse, murdre, hate, vertue, and synne. (3) Doo after the good and leve the evyl, and it shal brynge you to good fame and renommee.

(4) And for to passe the tyme thys book shal be pleasaunte to rede in, but for to gyue fayth and byleue that is al trewe that is conteyned herin, ye be at your lyberté. (5) But al is wryton for our doctryne,[i] and for to beware that we falle not to vyce ne synne, but t'exersyse and folowe vertu, by whyche we may come and atteyne to good fame and renommé in thys lyf, and after thys shorte and transytorye lyf to come vnto euerlastyng blysse in heuen, the whyche He graunte vs that reygneth in heuen, the Blessed Trynyte. AMEN.

estates CLASSES
renomed RENOWNED
remommee RENOWN

[i] *al is wryton for our doctryne* A quotation from St Paul's Letter to the Romans 15: 4. This line was also famously quoted by Chaucer (see *Nun's Priest's Tale* VII. 3441–3442, and the *Retraction* 1083; references are to the *Riverside Chaucer*).

(8) From Sir Thomas Malory, *The Morte Darthur*

Until 1934, Malory's great Arthurian cycle was only known through Caxton's edition; but in that year a manuscript was discovered in the Fellows' Library of Winchester College which was soon recognised as an authoritative representation of Malory's original. Malory died in 1471, probably a prisoner as a result of his activities during the dynastic conflict known as the Wars of the Roses. The Winchester manuscript dates from the end of the fifteenth century.

Malory's prose style, with its use of parataxis in preference to hypotaxis, points back to OE traditions; and indeed several features which have been seen as radical in Malory's style (such as the handling of direct and indirect speech, and the use of 'collective' speech) can be directly paralleled in OE prose.

The language of the passage shows the steady advance of forms which are not yet found in Chaucerian texts and which are usual in later standard English; we may note for instance *theyr* THEIR, *them* THEM (cf. Ellesmere *here*, *hem*). However, there are plenty of old-fashioned features, e.g. the reversal of word-order after an initial adverbial (*Than wente syr Bors* THEN SIR BORS WENT).

The passage is taken from the last part of Malory's cycle, when the fellowship of the Round Table is collapsing. Sir Ector's lament for Lancelot, whose love for Guinevere was a key factor in that collapse, is marked by a high degree of paratactic parallelism; the use of *thou* THOU may also be noted.

For a convenient text of the complete cycle, see E. Vinaver ed., *Malory: Works* (Oxford: Oxford University Press, 1971). The text given here differs little from the equivalent passage in Vinaver (1971: 725), except in a few details of punctuation, and a few letter-forms.

A glossary for this passage follows immediately after it. Glossed words are underlined in the text.

(1) And ryght thus as they were at theyr seruyce, there came syr Ector de Maris that had seuen yere sought al Englond, Scotlond and Walys, sekyng his brother syr Launcelot; (2) and whan syr Ector herde suche noyse and lyghte in the quyre of Joyous Garde, he alyght and put his hors from hym and came into the quyre; (3) and there he sawe men synge and wepe, and al they knewe syr Ector, but he knewe not them.

(4) Than wente syr Bors unto syr Ector and tolde hym how there laye his brother syr Launcelot, dede; (5) and than syr Ector threwe hys shelde, swerde and helme from hym, and whan he behelde syr Launcelotts vysage he fyl doun in a swoun; (6) and whan he waked it were harde ony tonge to telle the doleful complayntes that he made for his brother.

(7) 'A, Launcelot' he sayd, 'thou were hede of al Cristen

knyghtes; and now I dare say', sayd syr Ector, 'thou sir Launcelot, there thou lyest, that thou were never matched of erthely knyghtes hande; (8) and thou were the <u>curtest</u> knyght that euer bare shelde; (9) and thou were the truest frende to thy louar that euer bestrade hors, and thou were the trewest lover, <u>of a synful man</u>, that euer loued woman, and thou were the kyndest man that euer strake wyth swerde; (10) and thou were the godelyest persone that euer cam emonge <u>prees</u> of knyghtes, and thou was the mekest man and the jentyllest that euer ete in halle emonge ladyes, and thou were the sternest knyght to thy mortal foo that euer put spere <u>in the reeste</u>.'

(11) Than there was wepyng and dolour out of mesure.

(2)   *quyre* CHANCEL
(8)   *curtest* MOST COURTEOUS
(9)   *of a synful man* OF ALL SINFUL MEN
(10) *prees* PRESS OF BATTLE/ THRONG
     in the reeste IN THE REST (i.e. in the special armour-attachment used to support the lance in a charge).

(9) A letter from Margaret Paston

To contrast with the prose texts of Caxton and Malory, both of which were at least in intention designed for widespread circulation, a late fifteenth-century letter concludes this section.

This letter dates from 1448, and is one of the *Paston Letters*, the largest surviving archive of private correspondence in English from the ME period. The Pastons were a Norfolk family of considerable importance and power. Although their origins were humble – at one time they were *charls* (i.e. churls, servile tenants) at Gimmingham in Norfolk – they accrued considerable lands and wealth during the fifteenth century and, when the male line died out in 1732, the head of the family was the second Earl of Yarmouth. 'Paston' is a settlement name, near the coast in the north-east corner of Norfolk.

In some ways the most energetic of the Pastons was John Paston I (so-called to distinguish him from John Paston II and III, both of whom – confusingly – were his sons). John I was born in 1421, and was educated at the local university of Cambridge and at the Inns of Court in London. At various times an MP and a JP, he was involved in local controversies and died in 1466 while in dispute with local dignitaries – disputes so heated that he had been briefly in prison in 1465.

In 1443 John I had married Margaret Mautby, a Norfolk heiress. Whenever John I was absent from home, Margaret managed their (considerable) property with some skill. John and Margaret seem to have been a formidable pair, tough in adversity and mutually supportive in asserting the Paston family's position at every possible opportunity.

The following letter describes a dispute which took place in 1448. The letter is from Margaret to John. Margaret dictated the body of this letter to one amanuensis, James Graham, and a postscript to another not identified; she herself did not write letters in her own hand.

The references in the letter need a little explication. James Gloys is a Paston servant, being the family chaplain and clerk. 'Wymondham' is John Wyndham or Wymondham, a family rival and sometime enemy; like the Pastons, his family was one recently risen, which makes the accusation that *þe Pastons and alle her kyn were charls of Gymyngham* especially cheeky. There was no doubt more of the same, which Margaret was plainly loath to dictate – *And he had meche large langage, as ye shall knowe herafter by mowthe*. In Wymondham's defence, it is worth remembering that, when John I was imprisoned in 1465, Wymondham was generous enough not only to offer Margaret hospitality but also to write John I a letter with the encouraging postscript *And how euer ye do, hold vp your manship*.

It will be observed that there is a marked difference in spelling between the body of the letter and the postscript. Whereas the body of the letter is written in a fairly colourless variety of late-fifteenth-century English, the postscript is written in markedly Norfolk dialect (cf. such forms as *xuld* SHOULD, *qwhan* WHEN, *ryth* RIGHT).

The letter is no. 129 in N. Davis ed., *Paston Letters and Papers of the Fifteenth Century* (Oxford: Clarendon Press, 1971), which is the standard edition. The text is also printed, with useful annotation, in Burnley (1992: 177–180). The main difference between the text as presented here and that in Davis and in Burnley is the reading *charls of Gymyngham* for [. . .] *myngham* for which, plus a fascinating discussion of the context of this letter, see C. Richmond, 'What a difference a manuscript makes: John Wyndham of Felbrigg, Norfolk (d.1475)', in F. Riddy ed., *Regionalism in Late Medieval Manuscripts and Texts* (Cambridge: Brewer, 1991).

A glossary for this passage follows immediately after it. Glossed words are underlined in the text.

(1) Ryght worshipfull husbond, I recomaund me to yow, and prey yow to <u>wete</u> þat on Friday last passed before noon, þe parson of Oxened beyng at <u>messe</u> in our parossh chirche, euyn <u>atte leuacion of þe sakeryng</u>, Jamys Gloys hadde ben in þe tovne and come homward by Wymondhams gate. (2) And Wymondam stod in his gate and John Norwode his man stod by hym, and Thomas Hawys his othir man stod in þe strete by þe canell side. (3) And Jamys Gloys come with his hatte on his hede betwen bothe his men, as he was wont of custome to do. (4) And whanne Gloys was ayenst Wymondham he seid þus, 'Couere thy heed!' (5) And Gloys seid ageyn, 'So I shall for the.' (6) And whanne Gloys was forther passed by þe space of iij or iiij strede, Wymondham drew owt his dagger and seid, 'Shalt þow so, knave?' (7) And þerwith Gloys turned hym and drewe owt his dagger and defendet hym, fleyng into my moderis place; and Wymondham and his man Hawys kest

stonys and dreve Gloys into my moderis place. (8) And Hawys folwyd into my moderis place and kest a ston as meche as a forthyng lof into þe halle after Gloys; and þan ran owt of þe place ageyn. (9) And Gloys folwyd owt and stod witowt þe gate, and þanne Wymonham called Gloys thef and seid he shuld dye, and Gloys seid he lyed and called hym charl, and bad hym come hymself or ell þe best man he hadde, and Gloys wold answere hym on and on. (10) And þanne Haweys ran into Wymondhams place and feched a spere and a swerd, and toke his maister his swerd. (11) And with þe noise of þis asaut and affray my modir and I come owt of þe chirche from þe sakeryng; and I bad Gloys go in to my moderis place ageyn and so he dede. (12) And thanne Wymondham called my moder and me strong hores, and seid þe Pastons and alle her kyn were charls of Gymyngham and we seid he lyed, knave and charl as he was. (13) And he had meche large langage, as ye shall knowe herafter by mowthe.

(14) After non my modir and I yede to þe Priour of Norwich and told hym al þis cas, and þe Priour sent for Wymondham and þerwhyle we yede hom ageyn and Pagraue come with vs hom. (15) And whil Wymondham was with þe Priour, and we were at hom in our places, Gloys stod in þe strete at my moderis gate and Hawys aspyed hym þere as he stod on þe Lady Hastyngis chambre. (16) Anon he come doun with a tohand swerd and assauted ageyn þe seid Gloys and Thomas my moderis man, and lete flye a strok at Thomas with þe sword and rippled his hand with his sword. (17) And as for the latter assaut þe parson of Oxened sygh it and wole avowe it. (18) And moche more thyng was do, as Gloys can tell yow by mouth. (19) And for þe perilx of þat myght happe by þese premysses and þe circumstances þerof to be eschewed, by þaduyse of my modir and oþer I send yow Gloys to attend upon yow for a seson, for ease of myn owen hert; for in good feyth I wolde not for xl li. haue suyche anoþer trouble.

(20) As touchyng my Lady Morlé, she seith þat she atte hire will wole haue þe benyfyce of hire obligacion, for hir counseyll telleth hir, as she seith, þat it is forfayt. (21) And she wole mot haue the relif until she hath your homage, &c.

(22) The Lord Moleyns man gaderyth up þe rent at gresham a gret pace, and Jamys Gresham shall telle yow more pleynly þerof at his comyng.

(23) Nomore at þis tyme, but Almyghty God haue yow in his kepyng. (24) Wreten in hast on Trynyté, Yours MARGARETE PASTON

(25) As touchyng Roger Foke, Gloys shall telle yow all, & c.

(26) <u>Qwhan</u> Wymdam seyd þat Jamys <u>xuld</u> dy I seyd to hym þat I soposyd þat he xuld repent hym jf he <u>scholw</u> hym or dede to hym any bodyly harm; and he seyd nay, he xuld never repent hym ner have a <u>ferdyng</u> wurth of harm þow he <u>kelyd</u> ȝw and hym bothe. (27) And I seyd ȝys, and he <u>sclow</u> þe lest chylde þat longyth to ȝwr <u>kechyn</u>, and jf he dede he were lyke, I sopose, to dy for hym. (28) It js told me þat he <u>xall</u> kom to London jn hast. (29) I pray ȝw be ware hw ȝe walkyn jf he be þere, for he js ful cursyd-hertyd and <u>lwmysch</u>. (30) I wot wel he wyl not set vpon ȝw manly, but I beleve he wyl styrt vpn ȝw or on sum of ȝwr men leke a thef. (31) I pray ȝw hertyly þat ȝe late not Jamys kom hom aȝen in non wyse tyl ȝe kom home, for myn hertys ese; for be my trwth I wold not þat he were hurt, ner non man þat longyth to ȝw jn ȝwr absens for xx pwnd. (32) And in gode feyth he js sore hatyd both of Wymdam and sum of hys men, and of oþer þat Wymdam tellyth to his tale as hym lyst, for þer as Wymdam tellyth hys tale he makyth hem beleuyn þat Jamys js gylty and he no þyng gylty.

(33) I pray ȝw hertyly here masse and oþer servys þat arn <u>bwn</u> to here wyth a <u>devwt</u> hert, and I hope veryly that ȝe xal <u>spede ryth</u> wele in all ȝwr materys, be the grase of God. (34) Trust veryly in God and leve hym and serve hym, and he wyl not <u>deseve</u> ȝw. (35) Of all oþer materys I xall sent ȝw wurd jn hast.

(1) *wete* KNOW
messe MASS
atte leuacion of þe sakeryng AT THE ELEVATION OF THE SACRAMENT

(8) *forthyng lof* FARTHING LOAF

(12) *hores* WHORES

(15) *Lady Hastyngis* WYMONDHAM'S WIFE

(16) *tohand* TWO-HANDED
rippled SLIGHTLY SCRATCHED

(17) *sygh* SAW

(26) *Qwhan* WHEN
xuld SHOULD
scholw SLEW

ferdyng FARTHING
kelyd KILLED

(27) *sclow* SLEW
kechyn KITCHEN

(28) *xall* SHALL

(29) *lwmysch* MALICIOUS

(33) *bwn* BOUND
devwt DEVOUT
spede SUCCEED
ryth RIGHT

(34) *deseve* DECEIVE

Early Modern English texts

In this Section Texts (1)–(6) are taken from the First Folio of the *Works* of William Shakespeare, and represent the 'prototypical' EModE generally described in Chapter 5. Texts (7)–(10) are given as short representative selections from larger works written earlier and later in the EModE period. The punctuation of the original editions has been retained in each case.

As in Sections A and B, the principle of selection adopted has been to present the reader with a fair range of texts in various registers, illustrating most of the points made in the appropriate chapter in Part I. Also as in A and B, the texts offered here should be taken as merely a starting-point for further study. All texts are preceded by a short introduction, and followed by a glossary of words and phrases potentially unfamiliar to the present-day reader. Students may also find it useful to consult the *Oxford English Dictionary*; C.T. Onions, *A Shakespeare Glossary* (Oxford: Oxford University Press, 1919) remains a handy single-volume reference tool.

Texts (1)–(6) are printed (with a few trivial and obvious corrections) in the form in which they appeared in the First Folio of 1623, which was issued seven years after Shakespeare's death by John Heminge and Henry Condell, fellow-actors and business associates of the playwright. The Norton Facsimile copy of the original is a useful resource (London: Hamlyn, 1968). How far the First Folio represents Shakespeare's own language in detail is a very debatable point; but the First Folio does at least exemplify a particular kind of EModE at the beginning of the seventeenth century. The speeches chosen here – some of the best-known in Shakespeare's works – are of course like all works of literature a stylised reflexion of natural discourse, but they do show a range of registers and conversational situations. Since these texts include a mixture of prose and verse, they are all lineated as plays, i.e. by printed line.

Texts (7)–(11) form a more eclectic selection. The passage from the Authorised Version of the Bible (7) is given since the Bible was by far the most influential text of its time and this translation in particular impacted on the stylistic choices made by contemporaries (and indeed on subsequent generations). Texts (8) and (9), prose from the Elizabethan and Commonwealth periods, reflect the evolution of prose style during the EModE period, while Text (10), a passage from Dryden's response to a Shakespearean play, enables comparison between similar registers at different times. Text (11) is a private letter from the middle of the seventeenth century, allowing a comparison with Text (9) in Section B.

(1) From *Loues labour's lost*

Love's Labour's Lost dates from 1593–4, and is one of Shakespeare's earliest comedies. It appeared at the height of the 'inkhorn controversy', and the passage quoted can only be understood in the context of contemporary debates about the nature of the vernacular (see p. 153). The passage selected here is a satire on the extremes of behaviour which appear to have resulted from the controversy. The character Holofernes (a schoolmaster = 'Pedant') represents the skilled practitioner of 'inkhornisms', while Nathaniel (= 'Curate') is the admiring student, making notes for future reference (thus the stage direction *Draw out his Table-booke*).

The discussion of the relationship between spelling and pronunciation is interesting, since it explains such PDE oddities as DEBT, DOUBT. The ME forms of these words were *dette*, *doute* respectively; the B in the PDE spelling derives from Elizabethan hypercorrection based on Latin *debitum*, *dubitum*. Holofernes's veneration for written Latin is such that he wishes these words to be pronounced with the Latin-derived hypercorrect consonants.

Lines 24–25 are corrupt in the First Folio. P. Alexander ed., *The Complete Works of William Shakespeare* (Glasgow: Collins, 1951) reads:

Hol. 'Bone'?- 'bone' for 'bene'. Priscian a little scratch'd; 'twill serve.

The reference to Priscian, clearly not understood by the printers of the First Folio, is to the sixth-century Latin grammarian Priscianus, whose works on the Latin language, notably the *Institutiones grammaticae*, were immensely influential throughout the Middle Ages and the Renaissance.

Interpretative notes appear at the end of the passage; the words and phrases they refer to are underlined.

Actus Quartus.
Enter the Pedant, Curate and Dull.

Ped. Satis quid sufficit.
Cur. I praise God for you sir, your <u>reasons</u> at dinner haue beene sharpe & <u>sententious</u>: <u>pleasant</u> without scurrillity, witty without <u>affection</u>, audacious without impudency, learned without <u>opinion</u>, and <u>strange</u> without heresie: I did

conuerse this *quondam* day with a companion of the Kings, who is intituled, nominated, or called, *Dom Adriano de Armatha.*

Ped. Noui hominum tanquam te, His humour is lofty, his discourse <u>peremptorie</u>: his tongue <u>filed</u>, his eye <u>ambitious</u>, his gate maiesticall, and his generall behauiour vaine, ridiculous, and <u>thrasonical</u>. He is too picked, too spruce, too affected, too odde, as it were, too <u>peregrinat</u>, as I may call it.

Cur. A most singular and choise Epithat,

Draw out his Table-booke,

Ped. He draweth out the thred of his verbositie, finer than the <u>staple</u> of his argument. I abhor such phanaticall <u>phantasims</u>, such insociable and <u>poynt deuise</u> companions, such <u>rackers</u> of ortagriphie, as to speake dout <u>fine</u>, when he should say doubt; det, when he shold pronounce debt; d e b t, not det: he clepeth a Calf, Caufe: halfe, hawfe; neighbour *vocatur* nebour; neigh abreuiated ne: this is abhominable, which he would call abhominable: it <u>insinuateth</u> me of infamie: *ne inteligis domine,* to make franticke, lunaticke?

Cur. Laus deo, bene intelligo.

Ped. Bome boon for boon prescian, a little scratcht, 'twil serue.

(2) *reasons* REMARKS

(3) *sententious* PITHY
     pleasant JOCULAR

(4) *affection* AFFECTATION

(5) *opinion* ARROGANCE
     strange FRESH

(9) *peremptorie* OVERBEARING
     filed POLISHED
     ambitious DESIRING

(11) *thrasonical* BOASTFUL, from the Latin personal name Thraso (see Terence, *Eunuchus*)

(12) *peregrinat* PEDANTIC

(15) *staple* FIBRE

(16) *phantasims* FANTASTIC BEINGS
      poynt deuise extremely precise

(17) *rackers* TORTURERS
      fine MINCINGLY

(21) *insinuateth* IMPLIES

6

12

22

(2) From *As you like it*

As You Like It was composed *ca.* 1600, and is thus one of Shakespeare's 'early/middle period' compositions, along with *A Midsummer Night's Dream*, *Romeo and Juliet*, and the later 'histories' (*Richard II*, *Henry IV: Parts I and II*, and *Henry V*). The play demonstrates a carefully managed (and indeed self-conscious) modulation of verse and prose; the passage quoted, a meeting between courtiers which is expressed in verse, is nevertheless a useful example of conversational interaction including some colloquialism (cf., for instance, *wagges* with the third present singular in *-es*). The two characters, Duke Senior and Jaques, are both aristocrats, but it is part of the humour of Jaques's character that he reflects on linguistic curiosity. He is here describing his encounter with the fool, Touchstone.

Interpretative notes appear at the end of the passage; the words and phrases they refer to are underlined.

Scena Septima.

Du. Sen. Why how now Monsieur, what a life is this
That your poore friends must woe your companie,
That, you look merrily.
Iaq. A Foole, a foole: I met a foole i'th Forrest,
A motley Foole (a miserable world:)   5
As I do liue by foode, I met a foole,
Who laid him downe, and bask'd him in the Sun,
And rail'd on Lady Fortune in good termes,
In good set termes, and yet a motley foole.
Good morrow foole (quoth I:) no Sir, quoth he,   10
Call me not foole, till heauen hath sent me fortune,
And then he drew a diall from his poake,
And looking on it, with lacke-lustre eye,
Sayes, very wisely, it is ten a clocke:
Thus we may see (quoth he) how the world wagges:
'Tis but an houre agoe, since it was nine,   16
And after one houre more, 'twill be eleuen,
And so from houre to houre, we ripe, and ripe,
And then from houre to houre, we rot, and rot,
And thereby hangs a tale. When I did heare   20
The motley Foole, thus morall on the time,
My Lungs began to crow like Chanticleere,
That Fooles should be so deepe contemplatiue:
And I did laugh, sans intermission
An houre by his diall. Oh noble foole,   25
A worthy foole: Motley's the onely weare.

Du. Sen. What foole is this?

Iaq. O worthie Foole: One that hath bin a Courtier
And sayes, if Ladies be but yong, and faire,
They haue the gift to know it: and in his braine, 30
Which is as <u>drie</u> as <u>the remainder bisket</u>
After a voyage: He hath <u>strange places</u> cram'd
With obseruation, the which he vents
In mangled formes. O that I were a foole,
I am ambitious for a motley coat. 35
Du. Sen. Thou shalt haue one.

(9) *in good set termes* using the technical terminology of logic
    motley parti-coloured clothing of a professional jester

(12) *diall* WATCH, TIMEPIECE (also PHALLUS; see *houre*, below)
    poake LARGE BAG (also CODPIECE; see *houre*, below)

(18–20) *houre...ripe...tale* these words apparently also have a *double-entendre* significance: WHORE . . . SEARCH . . . TAIL

(21) *morall* MORALISE (verb)

(22) *Chanticleere* traditional name for cock; see Chaucer, *Nun's Priest's Tale* and Henryson, *The Cock and the Fox*

(23) *deepe* DEEPLY (adverb)

(24) *sans intermission* WITHOUT A BREAK; *sans* is of course from French. There is some evidence that such constructions were regarded as affected (see *Love's Labour's Lost* Act V, scene ii).

(31) *drie* a technical term in contemporary medicine; a dry brain is supposed to be especially retentive in memory
    the remainder bisket ship's biscuit, used on voyages instead of bread; it was notoriously unappetising. *Remainder bisket* is LEFT-OVER BISCUIT.

(32) *strange places* FRESH (i.e. unusual) PLACES, presumably continuing the metaphorical reference to ships' stores and their stowage.

(3) From *The Tragedie of King Lear*

King Lear was composed during the first decade of the seventeenth century, probably *ca.* 1604–1605. It thus dates from roughly the same period as *Julius Cæsar, Hamlet, Othello, Twelfth Night* and *Measure for Measure*.

In the following passage, the Steward Oswald encounters the blinded Earl of Gloucester accompanied by his loyal son Edgar. Edgar appears in various guises in the play, his underlying loyalty to his father contrasting with his surface appearance, and thus emphasising a theme in many (if not all) of Shakespeare's plays of this time, that of the disjunction between appearance and reality. One of his disguises is to adopt a stage-dialect, as here. For a discussion, see the Appendix to Chapter 5 above. The passage is also a good illustration of varying power-relations between characters, expressed linguistically.

Gloucester, being blind, does not know that Edgar is his son; believing himself therefore bereft of sympathetic kindred, he makes no resistance to Oswald (*Now let thy friendly hand/ Put strength enough too't*). However, between lines 7 and 8, Edgar interposes himself.

The message read at the end of the passage is sent by Lear's daughter Goneril to Edgar's half-brother, the wicked, fair-seeming Edmund.

Interpretative notes appear at the end of the passage; the words and phrases they refer to are underlined.

Enter Steward.

Stew. A proclam'd prize: most <u>happie</u>
That eyelesse head of thine, was first <u>fram'd</u> flesh
To raise my fortunes. Thou old, vnhappy Traitor,
Breefely <u>thy selfe remember</u>: the Sword is out
That must destroy thee.   5
Glou. Now let thy friendly hand
Put strength enough too't.
Stew. Wherefore, bold Pezant,
Dar'st thou support a <u>publish'd</u> Traitor? Hence,
<u>Least</u> that th'infection of his fortune take   10
Like hold on thee. Let go his arme.
Edg. <u>Chill not let go</u> Zir,
Without vurther <u>'casion</u>.
Stew. Let go Slaue, or thou dy'st.
Edg. Good Gentlemen <u>goe your gate</u>, and let poore   15
volke passe: <u>and 'chud</u> ha'bin <u>zwaggerd</u> out of my life,
'twould not ha'bin zo long as 'tis, by a vortnight. Nay,
come not neere th'old man: keepe out <u>che vor'ye</u>, or <u>ice</u> try
whither your <u>Costard</u>, or my <u>Ballow</u> be the harde;
chill be plaine with you.   20
Stew. Out Dunghill.
Edg. Chill picke your teeth Zir: come, no matter vor your <u>foynes</u>.
Stew. Slaue thou hast slaine me: Villain take my purse;
If euer thou wilt thriue, bury my bodie,   25
And giue the Letters which you find'st about me,
To Edmund Earle of Glouster: seeke him out
Vpon the English party. Oh vntimely death, death.
Edg. I know thee well. A seruiceable <u>Villaine</u>,
As duteous to the vices of thy Mistris,   30

As badnesse would desire.

Glou. What, is he dead?

Edg. Sit you downe Father: rest you,

Let's see these Pockets; the Letters that he speakes of

May be my Friends: hee's dead: I am onely sorry   35

He had no other <u>Deathsman</u>. Let vs see:

Leaue gentle waxe, and manners: blame vs not

To know our enemies mindes, we rip their hearts,

Their Papers is more lawfull.   39

Reads the Letter.

Let our reciprocall vows be remembred. You have manie opportunities to cut him off: if your will want not, time and place will be <u>fruitfully</u> offer'd. There is nothing done. If hee returns the Conqueror, then am I the Prisoner, and his bed, my Gaole, from the loathed warmth whereof, deliuer me, and supply the place for your Labour.   45

Your (Wife so I would say) affectionate
Seruant. Gonerill.

(1) *happie* FAVOURED BY FORTUNE

(2) *fram'd* FORMED

(4) *thy selfe remember* REFLECT ON YOURSELF

(9) *publish'd* i.e. formally proclaimed

(10) *Least* LEST

(12) *Chill not let go* I DO NOT WANT TO GO

(13) *'casion* REASON

(15) *goe your gate* GO ON YOUR WAY (cf. Old Norse *gata* ROAD, a common place-name element in northern England)

(16) *and 'chud* IF I COULD
       zwaggerd BLUSTERED

(18) *che vor'ye* I WARRANT YOU
       ice I'LL

(19) *Costard* APPLE (= head; metaphorical and jocular)
       Ballow CUDGEL

(23) *foynes* THRUST (in fencing)

(29) *Villaine* probably SERF rather than with the PDE meaning

(36) *Deathsman* EXECUTIONER

(42) *fruitfully* PLENTIFULLY

(4) From *The Tragedie of Julius Cæsar*

Julius Cæsar is usually dated to 1599 by a contemporary reference; it seems to have been one of the first plays to be performed by Shakespeare's company, the Lord Chamberlain's Men, at the famous Globe Theatre.

The passage given is Mark Antony's funeral oration over the corpse of the murdered Cæsar. Its rhetorical structure may be compared with an earlier (and much less famous) speech on the same topic by Brutus, which is revealingly given in prose. Those addressed here are the lowly Plebians (1., 2. = First and Second Plebians); an Elizabethan audience would have appreciated the ironic potential underlying Antony's use of *gentle* as his term to describe them.

Interpretative notes appear at the end of the passage; the words and phrases they refer to are underlined.

Ant. You gentle Romans.
All. Peace hoe, let vs heare him.
Ant. Friends, Romans, countrymen, lend me your ears:
I come to bury *Cæsar*, not to praise him:
The euill that men do, liues after them,   5
The good is oft interred with their bones,
So let it be with *Cæsar*. The Noble *Brutus*;
Hath told you *Caesar* was Ambitious:
If it were so, it was a greeuous Fault,
And greeuously hath *Cæsar* answer'd it.   10
Heere, vnder leaue of *Brutus*, and the rest
(For *Brutus* is an Honourable man
So are they all; all Honourable men)
Come I to speake in *Cæsars* Funerall.
He was my Friend, faithfull and iust to me;   15
But *Brutus* sayes, he was Ambitious:
And *Brutus* is an Honourable man.
He hath brought many Captiues home to Rome,
Whose Ransomes, did the generall Coffers fill:
Did this in *Cæsar* seeme Ambitious?   20
When that the poore haue cry'de, *Cæsar* hath wept:
Ambition should be made of sterner stuffe,
Yet *Brutus* sayes, he was Ambitious:
And *Brutus* is an Honourable man.
You all did see, that on the *Lupercall*;   25
I thrice presented him a Kingly Crowne,
Which he did thrice refuse. Was this Ambition?
Yet *Brutus* sayes, he was Ambitious:

And <u>sure</u> he is an Honourable man.
I speake not to disprooue what *Brutus* spoke,   30
But heere I am, to speake what I do know;
You all did loue him once, not without cause,
What cause with-holds you then, to mourne for him?
O Iudgment! thou are fled to brutish Beasts,
And Men haue lost their Reason. Beare with me,   35
My heart is in the Coffin there with *Cæsar*,
And I must pawse, till it come backe to me.
1. <u>Me thinkes</u> there is much <u>reason</u> in his sayings.
2. If thou consider rightly of the matter;
Cæsar ha's had great wrong.   40

(1)   *gentle* NOBLE

(19) *generall* PUBLIC

(29) *sure* SURELY, FOR CERTAIN

(38) *Me thinkes* IT SEEMS TO ME
      reason REASONABLENESS

(5) From *The Tragedie of Hamlet*

Hamlet was composed in the first decade of the seventeenth century, and survives in several versions; it seems clear that it was modified at various times to suit different theatrical situations. Like the other plays of the period, it deals with questions of appearance and reality, transience and fortune. The passage given here, where Hamlet, accompanied by his friend Horatio, is shown Yorick's skull by the Gravedigger (= *Clo.*, i.e. Clown), includes a meditation on these themes.

The passage allows for the interplay of conversation across social classes. Several features of the Gravedigger's language mark him off as a colloquial speaker, e.g. *has* HAS (cf. Hamlet's contrasting *hath*, although see also *my gorge ris<u>es</u> at it*), *a* HE.

Interpretative notes appear at the end of the passage; the words and phrases they refer to are underlined.

Clo. Why sir, his hide is so tan'd with his Trade, that he will keepe out water a great while. And your water, is a sore Decayer of your horson dead body. Heres a Scull now: this Scul has laine in the earth three & twenty years.
Ham. Whose was it?   5
Clo. A whoreson mad Fellowes it was;
Whose doe you thinke it was?

Ham. Nay, I know not.

Clo. A pestlence on him for a mad rogue, a pou'rd a Flaggon of <u>Renish</u> on my head once. This same Scull Sir, this same Scull sir, was *Yoricks* Scull, the Kings Iester.

Ham. This?   12

Clo. E'ene that.

Ham. Let me see. Alas poor *Yorick*, I knew him *Horatio*, a fellow of infinite Iest; of most excellent <u>fancy</u>, he hath borne me on his backe a thousand times: And how abhorred my Imagination is, my <u>gorge</u> rises at it. Heere hung those lipps, that I haue kist I know not how oft, Where be your Iibes now? Your Gambals? Your Songs? Your flashes of Merriment that were wont to set the Table <u>on a Rore</u>? No one now to mock your own Ieering? Quite <u>chopfalne</u>? Now get you to my Ladies Chamber, and tell her, let her paint an inch thicke, to this <u>fauour</u> she must come. Make her laugh at that: prythee *Horatio* tell me one thing.

Hor. What's that my Lord?   25

Ham. Dost thou thinke *Alexander* lookt o'this fashion i'th' earth?

Hor. E'ene so.

Ham. And smelt so? Puh.

Hor. E'ene so, my Lord.

Ham. To what base vses we may returne *Horatio*. Why may not Imagination trace the Noble dust of *Alexander*, till he find it stopping a bunghole.

Hor. 'Twere to consider: to <u>curiously</u> consider so.   34

Ham. No faith, not a iot. But to follow him thether with <u>modestie</u> enough, & likeliehood to lead it; as thus. *Alexander* died: *Alexander* was buried: *Alexander* returneth into dust; the dust is earth; of earth we make <u>Lome</u>, and why of that Lome (whereto he was conuerted) might they not stopp a Beere-barrell?   40
Imperial *Cæsar*, dead and turn'd to clay,
Might stop a hole to keepe the winde away.
Oh, that that earth, which kept the world in awe,
Should patch a Wall, t'expell the winters <u>flaw</u>.
But soft, but soft, aside; heere comes the King.   45

(10)   *Renish*   RHENISH WINE

(15)   *fancy*   FANTASTICALNESS

(17)   *gorge*   i.e., what has been swallowed (thus Hamlet claims that he is about to vomit)

(20) *on a Rore* PROVOKE TO A ROAR OF MIRTH

(21) *chopfalne* WITH CHEEKS FALLEN IN

(23) *fauour* APPEARANCE

(34) *curiously* PARTICULARLY

(36) *modestie* MODERATION

(38) *Lome* LOAM, CLAY

(44) *flaw* SUDDEN BLAST OF WIND

(6) From *The Tragedy of Richard the Third*

Richard III was composed in the last decade of the sixteenth century, and was an immediate favourite with Elizabethan audiences. Part of the attraction lay in the figure of Richard himself, the 'Machiavel' eager to share his innermost thoughts with the audience while deceiving his victims.

The opening soliloquy which appears below establishes Richard's character at the outset of the play. Its language is highly elaborate and rhetorical, full of puns and other wordplay (e.g. on SUN/SON in *Made glorious Summer by this Son of Yorke*). This 'artificiality' about the play has sometimes been criticised; but it makes a useful comparison with the ironic attack on the language of Holofernes and others in *Love's Labour's Lost*, a near-contemporary text.

Interpretative notes appear at the end of the passage; the words and phrases they refer to are underlined.

Actus Primus. Sceena Prima.

Enter Richard Duke of Gloster, solus.

Now is the Winter of our Discontent,
Made glorious Summer by this Son of Yorke:
And all the clouds that lowr'd vpon our house
In the deepe bosome of the Ocean buried.
Now are our browes bound with Victorious Wreathes,　　　　5
Our bruised armes hung vp for Monuments;
Our sterne Alarums chang'd to merry Meetings;
Our dreadfull Marches, to delightfull Measures,
Grim-visag'd Warre, hath smooth'd his wrinkled Front:
And now, in stead of mounting <u>Barbed Steeds</u>,　　　　10
To fright the Soules of fearfull Aduersaries,
He capers nimbly in a Ladies Chamber,
To <u>the lasciuious pleasing</u> of a Lute.
But I, that am not shap'd for sportiue trickes,

Nor made to court an amorous Looking-glasse: 15
I, that am Rudely stampt, and <u>want</u> loues Maiesty,
To strut before a wonton <u>ambling</u> Nymph:
I, that am curtail'd of this faire Proportion,
Cheated of Feature by dissembling Nature,
Deform'd, vn-finish'd, sent before my time 20
Into this breathing World, scarse halfe made vp,
And that so lamely and vnfashionable,
That dogges barke at me, as I <u>halt</u> by them.
Why I (in this weake <u>piping</u> time of Peace)
Haue no delight to passe away the time, 25
Vnlesse to see my Shadow in the Sunne,
And <u>descant</u> on mine owne Deformity.
And therefore, since I cannot proue a Louer,
To entertaine these faire well spoken dayes,
I am determined to proue a Villaine, 30
And hate the idle pleasures of these dayes.
Plots haue I laide, <u>Inductions</u> dangerous,
By drunken Prophesies, Libels, and Dreames,
To set my Brother *Clarence* and the King
In deadly hate, the one against the other: 35
And if King *Edward* be as true and iust,
As I am Subtle, False, and Treacherous,
This day should *Clarence* closely be <u>mew'd vp</u>:
About a Prophesie, which sayes that G,
Of *Edwards* heyres the murtherer shall be, 40
Diue thoughts downe to my soulle; here *Clarence* comes.

(10)   *Barbed Steeds* ARMOURED HORSES

(13)   *the lasciuious pleasing* PLEASANTLY LASCIVIOUS MUSIC

(16)   *want* LACK (verb)

(17)   *ambling* UNRESTRAINED

(23)   *halt* LIMP (verb)

(24)   *piping* i.e. time in which music of the pastoral pipe is heard instead of the martial fife

(27)   *descant* COMMENT

(32)   *Inductions* INITIAL STEPS in an undertaking

(38)   *mew'd vp* COOPED UP, SHUT UP

(7) From the *Authorized Version of the Bible* (1611)

This passage is from Genesis 25: 21–34. With certain modifications it follows the edition in the *Tudor Translations* series, ed. W.E. Henley (London: Nutt, 1903).

This text is a portion of the King James Bible, the Authorised Version of 1611, *CONTEYNING THE OLD TESTAMENT, AND THE NEW: NEWLY TRANSLATED OUT OF THE ORIGINALL TONGUES: AND WITH THE FORMER TRANSLATIONS DILIGENTLY COMPARED AND REVISED, BY HIS MAIESTIES SPECIALL COMMANDEMENT.* The Authorised Version is the product of a committee of scholars, and it is therefore to be expected that its idiom represents a series of compromises. It draws heavily on earlier translations, notably William Tyndale's of 1534, and it is therefore somewhat archaic for its time – a characteristic, of course, which it shares with most present-day translations of the Bible (cf., for instance, the *New English Bible*, Oxford and Cambridge: University Presses, 1970 = NEB).

Interpretative notes appear at the end of the passage; the words and phrases they refer to are underlined. Lineation is by biblical verse.

21. And Isaac intreated the LORD for his wife, because she was barren: and the LORD was intreated of him, and Rebekah his wife conceived.

22. And the children struggled together within her; and she said, If it be so, why am I thus? And shee went to enquire of the LORD.

23. And the LORD said unto her, Two nations are in thy wombe, and two maner of people shall be separated from thy bowels: and the one people shalbe stronger then the other people: and the elder shall serve the yonger.

24. And when her dayes to be delivered were fulfilled, behold, there were twinnes in her wombe.

25. And the first came out red, all over like an hairy garment: and they called his name, Esau.

26. And after that came his brother out, and his hand tooke holde on Esaus heele; and his name was called Iacob: and Isaac was threescore yeres old, when shee bare him.

27. And the boyes grew; and Esau was a <u>cunning</u> hunter, a man of the fielde; and Iacob was a <u>plaine</u> man, dwelling in tents.

28. And Isaac loved Esau, because he did eate of his venison: but Rebekah loved Iacob.

29. And Iacob <u>sod pottage</u>: and Esau came from the field, and hee was faint.

30. And Esau said to Iacob, Feed me, I pray thee, with that same red pottage: for I am faint; therefore was his name called Edom.

31. And Iacob said, Sell me this day thy birthright.

32. And Esau said, Behold, I am at the point to die: and what profit shall this birthright doe to me?

33. And Iacob said, Sweare to mee this day: and he sware to him: and he sold his birthright unto Iacob.

34. Then Iacob gave Esau bread and pottage of lentiles; and he did eate and drinke, and rose up, and went his way: thus Esau despised his birthright.

(27) *cunning* SKILFUL
      plaine possibly ORDINARY, NOT HAVING ANY SPECIAL SKILL, thus contrasting with Esau in ability (although cf. NEB: BUT JACOB LED A SETTLED LIFE AND STAYED AMONG THE TENTS)

(29) *sod*: past tense of *seethe* BOIL; cf. OE strong Class II *sēoþan*, *sīeþþ* (3rd present singular), *sēaþ* (3rd preterite singular) *sudon* (preterite plural), *soden* (past participle)
      pottage SOUP, esp. THICK SOUP; ?STEW

(8) From E.K.'s Preface to Spenser's *Shepheardes Calender* (1579)

Text (8) is from the preface to Edmund Spenser's *The Shepheardes Calender* (printed 1579). The preface was not written by Spenser, but by a friend 'E.K.' (probably Edward Kirke). Spenser was the most celebrated archaiser of his day (see p. 153 above), and E.K.'s essay is a defence of the resources of the English language to express heightened sentiment.

The text is taken directly from the sixteenth-century edition, with a few modifications of layout and the introduction of sentence-numbering.

Interpretative notes appear at the end of the passage; the words and phrases they refer to are underlined.

(1) <u>Vncouthe vnkiste</u>, Sayde the olde famous Poete Chaucer: vvhom for his excellencie and vvonderfull skil in <u>making</u>, his scholler <u>Lidgate</u>, a vvorthy scholler of so excellent a maister, calleth the <u>Loadestarre</u> of our Language; and whom our Colin clout in his Æglogue calleth Tityrus the God of shepheards, comparing hym to the worthines of the Roman Tityrus Virgile. (2) VVhich prouerbe, myne owne good friend Ma. Haruey, as in that good old Poete it serued vvell <u>Pandares purpose</u>, for the bolstering of his <u>baudy brocage</u>, so very vvell taketh place in this our nevv Poete,

vvho for that he is vncouthe (as said Chaucer) is vnkist, and vnknown to most men, is regarded but of fevv. (3) But I dout not, so soone as his name shall come into the knovvledg of men, and his vvorthines be sounded in the tromp of fame, but that he shall be not onely kiste, but also beloued of all, embraced of the most, and vvondred at of the best. (4) No lesse I thinke, deserueth his vvittinesse in deuising, his pithinesse in vvtering, his complaints of loue so louely, his discourses of pleasure so pleasantly, his pastorall rudenesse, his morrall vvisenesse, his devve obseruing of Decorum euerye vvhere, in personages, in seasons, in matter, in speach, and generally in al seemely simplycitie of handeling his matter, and framing his vvords: the vvhich of many thinges which in him be straunge, I knovv vvill seeme the straungest, the vvords them selues being so auncient, the knitting of them so short and intricate, and the vvhole Periode & compasse of speache so delightsome for the roundnesse, and so graue for the straungenesse. (5) And firste of the vvordes to speake, I graunt they be something hard, and of most men vnused, yet both English, and also vsed of most excellent Authors and most famous Poetes. (6) In vvhom vvhenas this our Poet hath bene much traueiled and throughly redd, hovv could it be, (as that vvorthy Oratour sayde, but that vvalking in the sonne although for other cause he vvalked, yet needes he mought be sunburnt; and hauing the sound of those auncient Poetes still ringing in his eares, he mought needes in singing hit out some of theyr tunes. (7) But whether he vseth them by such casualtye an custome, or of set purpose and choyse, as thinking them fittest for such rusticall rudenesse of shepheards, eyther for that theyr rough sounde vvould make his rymes more ragged and rustical, or els because such olde and obsolete wordes are most vsed of country folke, sure I think, and think I think not amisse, that they bring great grace and as one vvould say, auctoritie to the verse.

(1) *Vncouthe vnkist* UNKNOWN (and therefore) UNKISSED
making POETICAL COMPOSITION
Lidgate John Lydgate, fifteenth-century poet and disciple of Chaucer
Loadestarre MAGNETIC STAR

(2) *Pandares purpose* i.e. Pandarus' intentions (Pandarus, a character in Chaucer's *Troilus and Criseyde*, was the archetypal procurer of sexual favours)
baudy brocage LEWD PIMPING

(4) *vvittinesse* INTELLIGENCE
     rudenesse SIMPLICITY
     roundnesse i.e. fullness or careful finish of language
     straungenesse FRESHNESS

(9) From John Milton's *Areopagitica* (1644)

Text (9) is a passage, perhaps the best known, from John Milton's great
denunciation of censorship, the *Areopagitica* of 1644. Milton's writing shows
the impact of an intensely classical education, and, as well as being considerably later than E.K.'s preface, represents a distinct kind of argumentative
prose. A useful text of the *Areopagitica* is printed in the Columbia edition of
Milton's *Works*, Volume IV (F.A. Patterson gen. ed., New York: Columbia
University Press, 1931).

   Interpretative notes appear at the end of the passage; the words and
phrases they refer to are underlined.

(1) Lords and Commons of England, consider what Nation it is
wherof ye are, and wherof ye are the governours: a Nation not slow
and dull, but of a quick, ingenious, and piercing spirit, acute to
invent, suttle and sinewy to discours, not beneath the reach of any
point the highest that human capacity can soar to. (2) Therefore
the studies of learning in her deepest Sciences have bin so ancient,
and so eminent among us, that Writers of good antiquity, and
ablest judgement have bin perswaded that ev'n the school of
Pythagoras, and the *Persian* wisdom took beginning from the old
Philosophy of this Iland. (3) And that wise and civill Roman, *Julius
Agricola*, who govern'd once here for *Cæsar*, preferr'd the naturall
wits of Britain, before the labour'd studies of the French. (4) Nor
is it for nothing that the grave and frugal *Transilvanian* sends out
yearly from as farre as the mountanous borders of *Russia*, and
beyond the *Hercynian* wildernes, not their youth, but their stay'd
men, to learn our language, and our *theologic* arts. (5) Yet that
which is above all this, the favour and the love of heav'n we have
great argument to think in a peculiar manner propitious and
propending towards us. (6) Why else was this Nation chos'n before
any other, that out of her as out of *Sion* should be proclam'd and
sounded forth the first tidings and trumpet of Reformation to all
Europ. (7) And had it not bin the obstinat perversnes of our Prelats
against the divine and admirable spirit of Wicklef, to suppresse him
as a schismatic and *innovator*, perhaps neither the *Bohemian Husse*
and *Jerom*, no nor the name of *Luther*, or of *Calvin* had bin

ever known: the glory of reforming all our neighbours had bin compleatly ours. (8) But now, as our obdurat Clergy have with violence demean'd the matter, we are become hitherto the latest and the backwardest Schollers, of whom God offer'd to have made us the teachers. (9) Now once again by all concurrence of signs, and by the generall instinct of holy and devout men, as they daily and solemnly expresse their thoughts, God is decreeing to begin some new and great period in his Church, ev'n to the reforming of Reformation it self: what does he then but reveal Himself to his servants, and as his manner is, first to his English-men; I say as his manner is, first to us, though we mark not the method of his counsels, and are unworthy.

(1) *quick* LIVING

(4) *stay'd men* ESTABLISHED MEN

(7) *Wicklef* John Wycliffe, fourteenth-century English Church reformer

(10) From John Dryden, *All for Love or, the World Well Lost* (1677/1678)

Arguably Dryden's greatest play, *All for Love* was first performed in 1677 and seems to have displaced in popularity its model, Shakespeare's *Antony and Cleopatra*, throughout the eighteenth century. Whatever its merits as drama, the language of Dryden's 'classical' tragedy presents a useful set of forms for comparison with those of the earlier play.

The passage following, the opening of *All for Love*, has been taken directly from the First Quarto of the text, published by Henry Herringman in 1678. A useful edition, though in modern spelling, is by D.M. Vieth (London: Arnold, 1972). The three characters are Serapion and Myris, priests of Isis, and Alexas the Eunuch, Cleopatra's servant.

Interpretative notes appear at the end of the passage; the words and phrases they refer to are underlined.

Act I, Scene [1], *The Temple of* Isis.

Enter Serapion, Myris, *Priests of* Isis.

Serap. Portents and Prodigies are grown so frequent,

That they have lost their Name. Our fruitful *Nile*

Flow'd e're the wonted Season, with a Torrent

So unexpected, and so wondrous fierce,

That the wild Deluge overtook the haste,

Ev'n of the Hinds that watch'd it: Men and Beasts

Were born above the tops of Trees, that grew
On th'utmost Margin of the Water-mark.
Then, with so swift an Ebb, the Floud drove backward
It slipt from underneath the Scaly Herd: 10
Here monstrous <u>Phocae</u> panted on the Shore;
Forsaken *Dolphins* there, with their broad Tails,
Lay lashing the departing Waves: Hard by 'em,
<u>Sea-Horses</u> floundring in the slimy Mud,
Toss'd up their heads, and dash'd the ooze about 'em.
Enter Alexas *behind them.*
Myr. Avert these Omens, Heav'n.
Serap. Last night, between the hours of Twelve and One,
In a lone Isle o'th'Temple, while I walk'd,
A Whirl-wind rose, that, with a violent blast,
Shook all the *Dome*: the Doors around me clap,   20
The Iron <u>Wicket</u> that defends the Vault,
Where the Long Race of *Ptolemies* is lay'd,
Burst open, and disclos'd the mighty dead.
From out each Monument, in order plac'd,
An Armed Ghost start up: the Boy-King last
Rear'd his inglorious head. A peal of groans
Then follow'd, and a Lamentable Voice
Cry'd, *Egypt* is no more. My blood ran back,
My shaking Knees against each other knock'd;
On the cold Pavement, down I fell intranc'd,   30
And so unfinish'd left the horrid Scene.
Alexas shewing himself. And, Dream'd you of this? or, Did invent
the Story?
To frighten our *Egyptian* Boys withal,
And train 'em up betimes in fear of Priesthood.
Serap. My Lord, I saw you not,
Nor meant my words should reach your Ears; but what
I utter'd was most true.
Alex. A foolish Dream,
Bred from the fumes of indigested Feasts,   40
And holy <u>Luxury.</u>
Serap. I know my duty:
This goes no farther.
Alex. 'Tis not fit it should.
Nor would the times now bear it, were it true.

All Southern, from yon Hills, the *Roman* Camp
Hangs o'er us black and threatning, like a Storm
Just breaking on our Heads.
Serap. Our faint *Ægyptians* pray for *Antony;*
But in their Servile Hearts they own *Octavius.*   50

(11)   *Phocae* SEALS

(14)   *Sea-Horses* HIPPOPOTAMI

(21)   *Wicket* GATE

(41)   *Luxury* WANTONNESS

(11) From *The Letters of Lady Brilliana Harley* (1642)

This portion of a letter from Lady Harley to her son Edward is offered as an example of informal prose from the middle of the seventeenth century. Lady Brilliana (*c.*1600–1643) was the third wife of the distinguished politician Sir Robert Harley. The family supported Parliament against King in the English Civil War. At the time of writing, Lady Harley was herself besieged by Royalists in her home, Brampton Bryan Castle near Ludlow; although the siege was lifted after six weeks, Lady Harley died of *a very greate coold* the following year.

Lady Harley's usage shows that fixed spelling had not yet been fully adopted even in the fairly sophisticated and literate circles in which she moved. A convenient text appears in C. Davies, *English Pronunciation from the Fifteenth to the Eighteenth Century* (London: Dent, 1934); the following text has been checked against the print made by the Camden Society (1854). Interpretative notes appear at the end of the passage. Other letters by Lady Harley, with very useful annotation, appear in Burnley (1992: 255–259).

Interpretative notes appear at the end of the passage; the words and phrases they refer to are underlined.

14th Feb. 1642

(1) My deare Ned – I am confident you longe to heare from me, and I hope this will come to your hand, though it may it will be long first. (2) We are still threatned and iiniured as much as my enimyes can poscibell. (3) Theare is non that beares part with me but Mr. Jams, whoo has shouwed himsellfe very honnest; (4) none will looke towards Brompton, but such as truely fears God; (5) but our God still takes care of vs, and has exceedingly sheawed His power in presaruing vs...

(6) Now they say, they will starue me out of my howes; (7) they haue taken away all your fathers rents, and they say they will

driue away the cattell, and then I shall haue nothing to liue vpon;
(8) for all theare ame is to enfors me to let thos men I haue goo,
that then they might seas vpon my howes and cute our <u>throughts</u>
by a feawe rooges, and then say, they knewe not whoo did it; (9)
for so they say, they knew not whoo <u>draeue</u> away the 6 coolts, but
Mr. Conigsby keepes them, though I haue rwite to him for them.
(10) They haue vsed all means to leaue me haue no man in my
howes, and tell me, that then I shall be safe; (11) but I haue no caus
to trust them. (12) I thanke God we are all well. (13) I long to see
my cosen <u>Hackellt</u>. (14) I pray God blles you.

(15) Your most affectinat mother,
BRILLIANA HARLEY.

(3) *Jams* JAMES

(6) *they* The Royalists in the area

(8) *throughts* THROATS

(9) *draeue* DROVE

(13) *Hackellt* HAKLUYT

Part three

Bibliography, Glossary and Thematic Index

Annotated Bibliography

This is a list of full-length books which may be used to accompany or to follow on from the materials presented here. No claims of special fullness are made; these works are simply some of those I have found useful in teaching Early English. I have classified each book on a scale of difficulty/sophistication, rising from (1) (Basic) to (3) (Advanced).

Some of the works referred to here have also been discussed in an earlier, more advanced Annotated Bibliography in Smith 1996.

C.L. Barber, *Early Modern English* (London: Deutsch, 1976) (2). An outstanding survey, which complements and is not replaced by Görlach 1991. Full of textual data, with many quotations from, in particular, the works of Shakespeare; the material is presented extremely clearly without being in any way simplistic. The best kind of philological work; I have graded it as (2) because its expression is so clear, but it is full of suggestions for advanced work.

C.L. Barber, *The English Language: a Historical Introduction* (Cambridge: Cambridge University Press, 1993) (1). An updated and considerably rewritten version of the author's *The Story of Language* (1964). A clear and useful single-volume account, perhaps the best now available for the beginning student.

A.C. Baugh and T. Cable, *A History of the English Language* (London: Routledge, 1993) (1). Probably the most widely used single-volume history, this book contains a mass of useful material. Particularly good on 'external history' issues; less strong on those requiring theoretical orientation.

J.A.W. Bennett and G.V. Smithers eds, *Early Middle English Verse and Prose*, with a Glossary by N. Davis (Oxford: Clarendon Press, 1974 edition) (3). A superb scholarly collection of texts from the Early Middle English period. Good commentaries, both literary and linguistic, but demanding a high degree of philological sophistication. The Glossary is masterly.

N.F. Blake, *A History of the English Language* (Basingstoke: Macmillan, 1996) (2). An interesting recent account from a novel perspective, focusing on the evolution of standard varieties. Not a book for beginners, but there are several insights reflecting the author's experience as a teacher of the subject and as editor of Vol. II in the *Cambridge History of the English Language* (see Hogg 1992 – below for further details).

G. Bourcier (trans. and rev. C. Clark), *An Introduction to the History of the English Language* (Cheltenham: Stanley Thornes, 1981) (2). A useful single-volume account, with good bibliography to the year of publication.

K. Brunner (trans. G. Johnston), *An Outline of Middle English Grammar* (Oxford: Blackwell, 1963) (2). A handy single-volume survey of Middle English sounds and morphology; nothing much on syntax, though.

J.D. Burnley, *A Guide to Chaucer's Language* (Basingstoke: Macmillan, 1983) (2). A valuable account of Chaucerian usage which complements Sandved 1985. Its orientation is literary and stylistic, but there is good material on the linguistic situation in late Middle English.

J.D. Burnley, *The History of the English Language: A Source-Book* (London: Longman, 1992) (2). A very useful collection of texts illustrating the history of the language, with brief linguistic apparatus. This book makes a good follow-up to the materials presented here.

J. Burrow and T. Turville-Petre, *A Book of Middle English* (Oxford: Blackwell, 1997 edition) (2). This book was designed as a companion to Mitchell and Robinson 1995 (q.v.), but has learned from the earlier volume. The skew of the book is clearly literary, but the linguistic apparatus is admirably clear and well presented, although it does demand close attention on the reader's part. Traditional grammatical knowledge is assumed. The selection of texts is for the most part excellent, with very good commentaries.

E. Ekwall (trans. A. Ward), *A History of Modern English Sounds and Morphology* (Oxford: Blackwell, 1974) (2). The title is self-explanatory. A good, concise introduction to Early Modern English, with some material from after that date.

A.C. Gimson (rev. S. Ramsaram), *An Introduction to the Pronunciation of English* (London: Edward Arnold, 1989) (2). Perhaps the standard phonetics textbook, with some historical material. MacMahon 1997 makes a very useful prequel.

M. Görlach, *Introduction to Early Modern English* (Cambridge: Cambridge University Press, 1991) (3). Görlach's book falls into two main parts: descriptive and illustrative. The former, in many respects excellent and certainly of great value for the advanced student, demands considerable linguistic sophistication on the part of the reader. Perhaps more immediately useful is the second part, which contains a huge selection of Early Modern English texts from a wide variety of genres.

M. Görlach, *The Linguistic History of English: An Introduction* (Basingstoke: Macmillan, 1997) (3). A challenging and thought-provoking book which advanced students will find of considerable value. The author treats his readers as research colleagues; this makes for an invigorating experience, and (despite its subtitle) the book is not an easy read. Research questions are posed frequently throughout.

D. Graddol, D. Leith and J. Swann, *English: History, Diversity and Change* (London: Routledge, 1997) (1). A good introductory textbook: stimulating, thoughtful, intelligently organised around particular topics in the history of English. Originally designed for the Open University, it is perhaps best approached not in a linear way but as a source-book for seminar discussion.

S. Greenbaum and R. Quirk, *A Student's Grammar of the English Language* (London: Longman, 1990) (2). Perhaps the standard one-volume grammar for student use. Beginners will find it handy, however, to approach the book through the medium of something more introductory, e.g. Leech *et al.* 1982.

R. Hogg gen. ed., *The Cambridge History of the English Language* (Cambridge: Cambridge University Press, 1992–) (3). A multi-volume work, still in progress. The *Cambridge History* is designed as an authoritative account at a high level of sophistication, and there is an immense amount of information and insight contained in it. It is not a book for beginners. One of its strengths – openness to varying points of view – is of course also a weakness, in that individual authors have developed their own orientations which do not necessarily cohere as a whole. It is perhaps also a little weak on what is traditionally termed the 'external history' of the language. Nevertheless it is a massive achievement. The volumes on Old and Middle English have now been issued; the volume on Early Modern English is in press (1998).

S.S. Hussey, *The Literary Language of Shakespeare* (London: Longman, 1982) (1). An eminently sensible survey of Early Modern English which links linguistic concerns to a humane literary sensibility. Recommended for its insights into Shakespeare's dramatic meaning as well as for its discussions of Elizabethan and Jacobean English.

R. Lass, *The Shape of English* (London: Edward Arnold, 1987) (3). An important and highly stimulating historical account, though its orientation remains controversial. See further Smith 1996 below.

G. Leech, M. Deuchar and R. Hoogenraad, *English Grammar for Today* (Macmillan: Basingstoke, 1982) (1). A clearly written and well organised outline of the principles of modern English grammar, designed for the beginning student. This book serves as a good introduction to more advanced works, such as Greenbaum and Quirk 1990.

M.K.C. MacMahon, *Basic Phonetics* (Glasgow: Department of English Language, 1997) (1). There are many introductions to phonetics, but in my opinion this textbook, by an experienced teacher of the subject, is one of the best. It is a prequel to larger and more ambitious works, e.g. Gimson 1989. Copies are currently available from the author at the Department of English Language, University of Glasgow, GLASGOW G12 8QQ, Scotland.

C. Millward, *A Biography of the English Language* (Fort Worth: Holt, Rinehart and Winston, 1989) (1). Perhaps the best single-volume history to emerge in the United States. Highly readable and full of anecdote; some useful theoretical orientation. A limitation for the European reader is that, like many American works, it does not use consistently the notations of the International Phonetic Association. A useful accompanying workbook is also available.

B. Mitchell, *An Invitation to Old English and to Anglo-Saxon England* (Oxford: Blackwell, 1995) (1). Designed as a prequel to Mitchell and Robinson 1995, this book contains a mass of information about Old English language, literature, society and culture. An invaluable reference point for Anglo-Saxon studies in general, although the linguistic material remains pretty challenging.

B. Mitchell and F. Robinson, *A Guide to Old English* (Oxford: Blackwell, 1995 edition) (2). This book is probably the most widely used textbook on Old English for Anglophone readers. It is a mine of useful materials, and the accompanying reader is excellently produced. The linguistic material makes quite heavy demands on the beginner, though, and in my experience the book requires a fair bit of teachers' explication before its (considerable) virtues become clear.

O. Robinson, *Old English and its Closest Relatives* (London: Routledge, 1992) (2). Unaccountably omitted from the Annotated Bibliography in Smith 1996, this survey is clear, beautifully laid out and illustrated, and includes bibliographies for all aspects of Germanic linguistics.

A.O. Sandved, *Introduction to Chaucerian English* (Cambridge: Brewer, 1985) (2). A fairly traditional and very clear introduction to Chaucerian phonology and morphology. An authoritative account.

J.M.Y. Simpson, *A First Course in Linguistics* (Edinburgh: Edinburgh University Press, 1979) (2). A new edition is in preparation. A very thorough survey of the subject by an experienced teacher.

J.M.Y. Simpson, *Making Sense of Traditional Terms in Grammar* (Dundee: Lochee Publications, 1985) (1). A clear and concise descriptive account. Invaluable not only for students of English but also for anyone attempting to teach or learn a foreign language.

J.J. Smith, *An Historical Study of English: Function, Form and Change* (London: Routledge, 1996) (3). This book is designed as a bridge between basic philological work and a broader understanding of the kinds of research question with which English historical linguistics deals.

B.M.H. Strang, *A History of English* (London: Routledge, 1970) (2). Still in some ways the leading single-volume history of English although now in need of updating. Sophisticated and informative; its organisational principle (working back from Present-Day English to Germanic) can be confusing but has considerable intellectual justification.

H. Sweet, rev. N. Davis, *Sweet's Anglo-Saxon Primer* (Oxford: Clarendon Press, 1953 edition) (2). Henry Sweet was the leading British philologist of the nineteenth century and the founder of many branches of modern linguistics and phonetics. *Sweet's Primer* was the standard introduction to Old English (in British universities at least) for many years. The book has many virtues: authority, clarity, accuracy and handiness; and its approach to illustrative texts is somewhat similar to that adopted in this book. However, it makes many demands upon modern students. It assumes a knowledge of the classical languages and a clear grasp of traditional grammatical categories, and Davis's revision, although a superb piece of precise scholarship, actually increased the difficulty somewhat in comparison with Sweet's original edition of 1882.

Old English Glossary

This Glossary lists and glosses the OE forms which occur in Part I, Chapter 3 and in Part II, Section A. Unless the paradigmatic relationship between forms is clear (e.g. *lufodon* is not given, but *lufian* is), all the OE vocabulary used in this book is given.

NOTE: *æ* is listed with *a* and *ā*; *þ/ð* between *t* and *u*. All long vowels are listed with their equivalent short forms. All words beginning with *ge-* appear in the order of the letter following, e.g. *gebindan* appears in the *b-* section.

Abbreviations: The following abbreviations have been adopted: acc = accusative, Aj = adjective, Av = adverb, cj = conjunction, d = determiner, dat = dative, e = enumerator (numeral), Fem = feminine, gen = genitive, ij = interjection, infin = infinitive, Irreg = irregular, Masc = masculine, N = noun, Neut = neuter, nom = nominative, p = preposition, pl = plural, pn = pronoun, pres = present, pret = preterite, prop = proper (noun), sg = singular, St = strong, subj = subjunctive, V = verb, Wk = weak; 1, 2, 3 = first, second and third persons respectively; + = followed by (case).

Transitive verbs all govern the accusative, unless otherwise indicated.

ā Av ALWAYS
Ābel N Masc prop ABEL
Abrahām N Masc prop ABRAHAM
ac cj BUT, AND
ācwellan V Wk KILL
ādlig Aj SICK
ādwǣscan V Wk EXTINGUISH, END
ǣdre Av QUICKLY
ǣfre Av EVER

æfter p (+ dat) AFTER
æfter Av AFTER(WARDS)
æfter (þan þe) cj AFTER
æftergenga N Masc SUCCESSOR
Æglesþrep N Masc prop AYLESFORD
ælmihtig Aj ALMIGHTY
ænig Aj ANY
ǣr Av FORMERLY
ǣr (þan þe) cj BEFORE
ǣrdæg N Masc DAWN, EARLY MORNING; in pl FORMER DAYS
ǣrest Av FIRST
ætgædere Av TOGETHER
æþele Aj NOBLE
æþeling N Masc PRINCE
āfyllan V Wk FELL
āgan V Irreg OWN
āhēawan V St CUT DOWN
āhebban V St RAISE, LIFT UP
āhōf (1, 3 pret sg): see āhebban
āhreddan V Wk SET FREE, RESCUE
āhrēosan V St FALL, FALL DOWN
āhruron (pret pl): see āhrēosan
ālecgan V Wk DEFEAT
ālēdon (pret pl): see ālecgan
ālēh (1, 3 pret sg): see ālēogan
ālēogan V St LEAVE UNFULFILLED, FAIL TO PERFORM
ān e ONE
and cj AND
andbīdian V Wk WAIT FOR
andswarian V Wk ANSWER
andswaru N Fem ANSWER
Angel N Neut prop ANGELN (in Schleswig, North Germany)
ānmōd Aj UNANIMOUS
ānmōdlīce Av UNANIMOUSLY
ārās (1, 3 pret sg): see ārīsan
ārǣran V Wk, RAISE, BUILD (UP)
ārīsan V St ARISE
arodlīce Av QUICKLY, READILY; BOLDLY
āscian V Wk, ASK
āscofen (past participle): see āscūfan
āscūfan V St THRUST
āsettan V Wk, SET, PLACE
assa N Masc ASS, DONKEY
āstyrian V Wk, (RE)MOVE
ātēah (1, 3 pret sg): see ātēon
ātēon V Irreg (contracted) DRAW, TAKE OUT
āþumswēoras N Masc pl SON- AND FATHER-IN-LAW; āþumswēoran = dat
    pl (Irreg)
Augustīnus N Masc prop AUGUSTINE
āwacian V Wk AWAKE
āwācian V Wk WEAKEN
āweorpan V St THROW, CAST OUT, REJECT

āwurpon (pret pl): see *āweorpan*

Babilōniscan N Masc prop pl BABYLONIANS
bæcere N Masc BAKER
bær (1, 3 pret sg): see *beran*
bæron (pret pl): see *beran*
bān N Neut BONE
band (1, 3 pret sg): see *bindan*
gebannan V Wk (+ dat of person, acc of thing) BID, ORDER
bāt N Fem BOAT
bēacen N Neut SYMBOL, SIGN, STANDARD
bēag N Masc RING, BRACELET
bēam N Masc (PART OF) TREE; RAY OF LIGHT
bearn N Neut SON, CHILD
be-arn (3 pret sg): see *be-irnan*
bebūgan V St SURROUND
becōm (1, 3 pret sg): see *becuman*
becuman V St COME
gebed N Neut PRAYER
Bēda N Masc prop BEDE
bedǣlan V Wk DEPRIVE OF
bedd N Neut BED
beorn N Masc MAN, WARRIOR
bēorþegu N Fem BEER-RECEIVING
begēotan V St SPRINKLE, POUR OUT, SHED
beginnan V St BEGIN
begoten (past participle): see *begēotan*
behealdan V St BEHOLD
behēoldon (pret pl): see *behealdan*
be-irnan V St RUN INTO, COME INTO
Bēl N Masc prop BAAL
belīefan V Wk BELIEVE
bēodan V St OFFER, COMMAND
bēon/wesan V Irreg BE
beorg N Masc MOUND, HILL
beorht(ost) Aj BRIGHT(EST)
bēorþegu N Fem BEER-DRINKING
bēot N Neut BOAST, PROMISE
beran V St BEAR
berstan V St BREAK, BURST
beseah (1, 3 pret sg): see *besēon*
besēon V Irreg (contracted) LOOK, LOOK INTO/AROUND
bestēman V Wk MAKE WET
bet(e)ra Aj (comparative of *gōd*)
betst Aj (superlative of *gōd*)
betwix p (+ dat/acc) BETWEEN
beweaxan V St OVERGROW
bewindan V St WRAP, WIND AROUND
bewunden (past participle): see *bewindan*
biddan V St ASK FOR, PRAY, BID
biernan V St BURN
bifian V Wk TREMBLE

bindan V St BIND
binnan p (+ dat) INSIDE, WITHIN
biscop N Masc BISHOP
blāwan V St BLOW
blēowon (pret pl): see *blāwan*
blīþemōd Aj GLAD, CHEERFUL
blōd N Neut BLOOD
bōc N Fem BOOK
bod N Neut COMMAND, MESSAGE
brecan V St BREAK
bregdan V St PULL
brēmel N Masc BUSH, BRAMBLE
Breten N Fem PROP BRITAIN
Brettas N Masc prop pl BRITONS (= Celts)
(ge)brocian V Wk AFFLICT
brōþor N Masc BROTHER
brūcan V St ENJOY
būgan V St BEND, BOW DOWN
gebū(g)an V Wk DWELL, SETTLE IN
(ge)bunden (past participle): see *bindan*
burg N Fem FORTIFIED PLACE, STRONGHOLD
būton p (+ dat) WITHOUT
būtū Aj BOTH
bysmerian V Wk MOCK, INSULT

Cāin N Masc PROP CAIN
ceafl N Masc JAW
cealf N Masc/Neut CALF
ceaster N Fem CASTLE, FORT
Cedwalla N Masc prop CEDWALLA
cēnlīce Av BRAVELY
Centland N Neut prop KENT
cēosan V St CHOOSE
(ge)ciegan V Wk CALL, NAME
gecīged (past participle): see *(ge)cīegan*
cild N Neut CHILD
cildhād N Masc CHILDHOOD
cirice N Fem CHURCH
cleric N Masc CLERK (i.e. ECCLESIASTIC)
clipian V Wk CALL, SUMMON
clypode (1, 3 pret sg): see *clipian*
cnapa N Masc BOY, SERVANT
cnāwan V St KNOW
cniht N Masc YOUTH
cōm (1, 3 pret sg): see *cuman*
cōmon (pret pl): see *cuman*
crēopan V St CREEP
cuman V St COME
cunnan V Irreg CAN
cūðon: see *cunnan*
cwæþ (1, 3 pret sg): see *cweþan*
cwealm: N Masc DEATH, KILLING

cwēn N Fem QUEEN
cweþan V St SAY, SPEAK, NAME, CALL
cwic Aj LIVING
cynincg: see *cyning*
cyning N Masc KING
cynn N Neut, RACE, FAMILY, KIND
cyrce: see *cirice*
cyst N Fem BEST EXAMPLE

daga, dagas, dagum: see *dæg*
dǣd N Fem DEED
dæg N Masc DAY (*nb.* vowel in stem varies between *æ* and *a*)
dǣlan V Wk SHARE OUT
Daniēl N Masc prop DANIEL
delfan V St DIG
dēman V Wk JUDGE
dēmon N ?Masc DEMON
dēofolgield N Neut IDOL
deorc Aj DARK
disc N Masc DISH, PLATE
dōgor N Neut DAY
dohtor N Fem, DAUGHTER
dolg N Neut WOUND
dōn V Irreg DO
dorste (1, 3 pret sg): see *durran*
draca N Masc DRAGON
drēam N Masc JOY, BLISS, MIRTH, REJOICING
gedriht N Fem COMPANY
Drihten: see *Dryhten*
drihtguma N Masc RETAINER
drincan V St DRINK
drȳ N Masc MAGICIAN, SORCERER, WIZARD
Dryhten N Masc LORD (often LORD GOD)
dūn N Fem HILL, DOWN
durran V Irreg DARE
duru N Fem, DOOR
dydon (pret pl): see *dōn*
dysig Aj FOOLISH

ēac Av ALSO, MOREOVER
ēadig Aj BLESSED
ēadiglīce Av BLESSEDLY
ēage N Neut EYE
eald Aj OLD
Ealdseaxe N Masc prop pl OLD SAXONS
ealgearo Aj ENTIRELY READY
eall Aj ALL
Eallwealdend N Masc RULER OF ALL (i.e. GOD)
ēam N Masc (MATERNAL) UNCLE
eard N Masc LAND, HOME, REGION, DWELLING
ēare N Neut EAR
earfoðlīce Av WRETCHEDLY, PAINFULLY

earm N Masc ARM
geearnung N Fem MERIT
eaxl N Fem SHOULDER
eaxlgespann N Neut INTERSECTION (OF A CROSS)
ēce Aj ETERNAL
ecg N Fem EDGE, POINT, WEAPON, SWORD
ecghete N Masc VIOLENCE ('EDGE-HATE')
ēcnyss N Fem ETERNITY
ef(e)stan V Wk HURRY, HASTEN
eft Av AFTERWARDS, AGAIN
ege N Masc FEAR
ēhtere N Masc PERSECUTOR
ellen N Masc STRENGTH, COURAGE, ZEAL (*nb.* stem becomes *eln*- in certain inflexions)
ellengǣst N Masc POWERFUL DEMON
elne (dat sg): see *ellen*
ende N Masc END
engel N Masc ANGEL
engeldryht N Fem ANGEL-MULTITUDE
Engle N Masc prop PL ANGLES
Englisc Aj ENGLISH
ēode, ēodon (pret): see *gān*
eorþe N Fem EARTH
eoten N Masc GIANT
ēow pn pl YOU
etan V St EAT

far (imperative): see *faran*
fæder N Masc FATHER
fæger Aj FAIR, BEAUTIFUL
fǣhð N Fem FEUD, HOSTILITY
fæste Av FIRMLY, SECURELY
fæsten N Masc STRONGHOLD, FASTNESS
(ge)fæstnian V Wk FASTEN, MAKE SECURE
faran V St GO
gefeah (1, 3 pret sg): see *gefēon*
feallan V St FALL; FALL (IN ADORATION)
fela Aj MANY (followed by gen of modified noun)
fen(n) N Neut FEN, MARSH
fēng (1, 3 pret sg): see *fōn*
gefeoht N Neut FIGHT, BATTLE
feohtan V St FIGHT
fēoll (1, 3 pret sg): see *feallan*
gefēon V St (+ gen) REJOICE
fēond N Masc ENEMY, FIEND
feorh N Masc/Neut LIFE (nb. inflected forms drop -*h*-, e.g. *fēorum* dat pl)
feorran Av FROM AFAR
fēower e FOUR
fēran V Wk GO, TRAVEL
gefēra N Masc COMPANION
gefetian V Wk FETCH
fette (1, 3 pret sg): see *(ge)fetian*

(ge)fierd N Fem ARMY
fīfelcynn N Neut RACE OF MONSTERS
fīras N Masc pl LIVING BEINGS, MEN (poetical)
flēogan V St FLY
flēon V Irreg (contracted) FLEE
flōd N Masc/Neut FLOOD
flugon (pret pl): see *flēon*
folc N Neut PEOPLE
folcscaru N Fem PUBLIC LAND
folcstede N Masc DWELLING-PLACE
folde N Fem EARTH, GROUND
fōn V St (contracted) TAKE, SEIZE, etc.
fordīlgian V Wk DESTROY
fordōn V Irreg DESTROY
foresǣdan: see *foresecgan*
forescēawian V Wk PROVIDE
foresecgan V Wk MENTION BEFORE
forgeald (1, 3 pret sg): see *forgieldan*
forgieldan V St PAY FOR
forlǣtan V St LEAVE, ABANDON
forlēton (pret pl): see *forlǣtan*
forma e FIRST
forscrīfan V St CONDEMN (+ dat)
forstandan V St PROTECT, DEFEND
for þǣm (*þe*) cj BECAUSE
forþearle Av VERY GRIEVOUSLY
forþgesceaft N Fem CREATION
forþon...forþon... cj and Av BECAUSE/THEREFORE ... THEREFORE/
    BECAUSE
forwrecan V St BANISH, DRIVE AWAY
fōt N Masc FOOT
fracod Aj WICKED
gefrægn (1, 3 pret sg): see *(ge)frignan*
(ge)frignan V St LEARN
frætwan V Wk ADORN
fram p (+ dat) FROM
Frēa N Masc LORD
fremman V Wk PERFORM, DO
frēond N Masc FRIEND
frumsceaft N Fem CREATION, ORIGINS
gefrūnon (pret pl): see *(ge)frignan*
fuhton (pret pl): see *feohtan*
(ge)fullian V Wk FULFIL; BAPTISE
fultum N Masc HELP, TROOPS
fyll N Masc FALL (IN BATTLE)
(ge)fyllan V Wk FILL
gefylsta N Masc HELPER
fȳnd = *fīend* (pl); see *fēond*
fȳr N Neut FIRE
fyren N Fem CRIME, SIN, WICKED DEED
fyrst N Masc TIME; SPACE OF TIME

gaderian V Wk GATHER
gān V Irreg GO
gāst N Masc SPIRIT
gǣst N Masc SPIRIT, SOUL
geaf (1, 3 pret sg): see *giefan*
gealga N Masc GALLOWS
gēar N Neut YEAR
geāra Av LONG AGO; *geāra iū* VERY LONG AGO
gearo Aj READY
gēn Av STILL, FURTHER, YET
geogoð N Fem YOUTH
geond p (+ acc) THROUGH(OUT), ALONG, OVER
geong Aj YOUNG
georne Av EAGERLY
Germānia N Fem prop GERMANY
gesceaft N Fem CREATION
giefan V St GIVE (+ dat of person and acc of thing)
giefu N Fem GIFT
gieldan V St PAY
gif cj IF
gīgant N Masc GIANT
gimm N Masc GEM
gingest Aj (superlative of *geong*)
gingra Aj (comparative of *geong*)
glōf N Fem GLOVE
God, god N Masc GOD
gōd Aj GOOD
gold N Neut GOLD
gōs N Fem GOOSE
grǣdig Aj GREEDY
Grendel N Masc prop GRENDEL
grim(m) Aj GRIM, FIERCE, ANGRY
guma N Masc MAN
gyfan = *giefan*
gȳta Av YET, STILL

habban V Wk HAVE
hæfdon (pret pl): see *habban*
(ge)hǣlan V Wk HEAL
hæleþ N Masc MAN, HERO
hālig Aj HOLY
hām N Masc HOME, DWELLING
hātan V St COMMAND
hē pn HE
hēah Aj HIGH
healǣrn N Neut HALL-BUILDING
healdan V St HOLD
heall N Fem HALL
healreced N Neut HALL-BUILDING
hēanne (acc sg): see *hēah*
hearpe N Fem HARP
heaðowylm N Masc HOSTILE FLAME

hebban V St LIFT UP
hell N Fem HELL
helpan (+ gen/dat) V St HELP
Hengest N Masc prop HENGEST
heofon N Masc HEAVEN
Heofonfeld N Masc prop 'HEAVENFIELD'
heofonrīce N Neut HEAVENLY KINGDOM
heora pn = *hiera*
Heorot, *Heort* N Masc prop HEOROT
heorte N Fem HEART
hēr Av HERE; IN THIS YEAR
here N Masc (RAIDING) ARMY
herespēd N Fem SUCCESS IN WAR
herian V Wk PRAISE
hēt (1, 3 pret sg): see *hātan*
hēton (pret pl): see *hātan*
hīe pn THEY, THEM (acc); also HER (acc)
hīehst Aj (superlative of *hēah*)
hīerra Aj (comparative of *hēah*)
him pn HIM, IT, THEM (all dat)
hine pn HIM (acc)
hīred N Masc FAMILY, HOUSEHOLD, COURT
his pn HIS, ITS (gen)
hlāf N Masc LOAF, BREAD
hlāford N Masc LORD
hlǣfdīge N Fem LADY
hlīfade (1,3 pret sg): see *hlīfian*
hlīfian V Wk STAND HIGH, TOWER
hlūd Aj LOUD
holt N Masc *or* neut FOREST, WOOD
hond N Fem HAND, SIDE
horngēap Aj WIDE-GABLED
Horsa N Masc prop HORSA
hrēmig Aj EXULTING
Hring-Dene N Masc pl prop CORSLET-DANES
hrōf N Masc ROOF
Hrōðgār N Masc prop HROTHGAR
hryre N Masc FALL
hund e HUNDRED
hūru Av INDEED, CERTAINLY, HOWEVER
hūs N Neut HOUSE
hūð N Fem BOOTY, SPOIL
(ge)hwā pn WHO (interrogative)
hwǣr Av WHERE; also in *swā hwǣr swā* WHERESOEVER
(ge)hwā pn EACH, EVERYONE, EVERYTHING
(ge)hwæs pn (gen): see *(ge)hwā*
(ge)hwām pn (dat): see *(ge)hwā*
hwæt (1) ij LO, BEHOLD; (2) pn WHAT, WHICH
(ge)hwæþ(e)re cj HOWEVER, BUT, NEVERTHELESS
hwīl N Fem WHILE (= SPACE OF TIME)
gehwylc pn WHICH
hwyrfan V Wk TURN, CHANGE, RETURN

hycgan V Wk THINK
hyldan V Wk BOW DOWN, BEND
(ge)hȳran V Wk HEAR (+ acc); LISTEN TO (+ dat)

ic pn I
ieldest Aj (superlative of *eald*)
ieldra Aj (comparative of *eald*); as N, ANCESTOR, ELDER
inn Av IN(SIDE)
inwidhlemm N Masc MALICIOUS WOUND
is V Irreg (3 PRES SG): see *bēon/wesan*
Īotan N Masc prop pl JUTES
Isaāc N Masc ISAAC
īs N Neut ICE
iū: see *geāra*
iugoþ: see *geogoð*

lǣdan V Wk LEAD, CARRY, BRING, TAKE
lǣg (1, 3 pret sg): see *licgan*
lǣssa Aj (comparative of *lȳtel*, i.e. LESS)
lǣst Aj (superlative of *lȳtel*, i.e. LEAST)
land N Masc LAND
landbūend N Masc INHABITANT
lang Aj LONG
lār N Fem TEACHING
lāð Aj HOSTILE, HATEFUL
(ge)laþian V Wk INVITE
lēaf N Neut LEAF
gelēafa N Masc FAITH, BELIEF
lēan N Neut REWARD, REQUITAL
lenge Aj ?AT HAND
lengest Aj (superlative of *lang*)
lengra Aj (comparative of *lang*)
lēo N Masc *or* Fem LION
lēode N Fem pl PEOPLE
lēof Aj BELOVED, DEAR
lēoht N Neut LIGHT
lēoma N Masc LIGHT
lēon, lēona, lēom (Irreg nom/acc pl, gen pl, dat pl): see *lēo*
libban V Wk LIVE
licgan V St LIE (as in LIE DOWN)
(ge)līefan V Wk BELIEVE (+ gen/dat)
līf N Neut LIFE
lifdon (pret pl): see *libban*
līg N Masc FLAME
gelimpan V St HAPPEN
lofgeorn Aj EAGER FOR PRAISE
lomb N Neut LAMB
gelomp (1, 3rd pret sg): see *gelimpan*
lufian V Wk LOVE
Lundenbyrig N Fem prop LONDON
lūs N Fem LOUSE
gelȳfed: see *(ge)līefan*

lyft N Masc *or* Fem *or* Neut AIR
lȳsan V Wk REDEEM
lȳtel Aj LITTLE

mæg (1, 3 pres sg): see *magan*
mǣg N Masc KINSMAN (*māgas, māga, māgum* pl)
mǣgþ N Fem TRIBE, NATION, FAMILY, GENERATION
mǣre Aj GLORIOUS
mǣst Aj (superlative of *micel*, i.e. MOST)
(ge)mǣtan V Wk DREAM (used impersonally)
(ge)mǣtte (3 pret sg): see *(ge)mǣtan*
magan V Irreg BE ABLE TO
magodriht N Fem BAND OF YOUNG RETAINERS
man pn ONE
(ge)man (1, 3 pret sg): see *(ge)munan*
mān N Neut CRIME, WICKEDNESS
mancynn N Neut MANKIND
manig Aj MANY
mann N Masc MAN (*menn* nom, acc pl)
māra Aj (comparative of *micel*, i.e. MORE)
mē pn ME (acc, dat)
mearcstapa N Masc WANDERER IN THE BORDERLAND
medoærn N Neut BEER-HALL
menn: see *mann*
mēos N Masc/Neut MOSS
mergen: see *morgen*
Metod N Masc GOD
micel Aj BIG, LARGE, GREAT
mid p (+ dat) WITH
mid Aj MIDDLE; in *tō midre nihte* IN THE MIDDLE OF THE NIGHT
middangeard N Masc WORLD
miht N Fem MIGHT, POWER
mihte (1, 3 pret sg) V Irreg MIGHT
mīn pn MY, MINE
mōd N Neut MIND, HEART
mōdgeþanc N Masc THOUGHT, UNDERSTANDING, MIND, CONCEPTION
mōdig Aj BRAVE, COURAGEOUS; PROUD
mōdor N Fem MOTHER
mōna N Masc MOON
mōr N Masc MOOR, MARSH, WASTELAND
morgen, mergen N Masc MORNING; MORROW
mōtan V Irreg BE ALLOWED
(ge)munan V Irreg REMEMBER
mūs N Fem MOUSE

nægl N Masc NAIL
nama N Masc NAME
(ge)nāmon (pret pl): see *(ge)niman*
ne Av NOT
(ge)nemnan V Wk NAME
nēosan, nēosian V Wk (+ gen) SEEK OUT, VISIT, ATTACK, GO TO, INSPECT
niht N Fem NIGHT

nim (imperative): see *(ge)niman*
(ge)niman V St TAKE, SEIZE
nis = ne + is
(ge)nōg Aj ENOUGH, MANY
Norþhymbre Aj NORTHUMBRIAN
nosu N Fem NOSE
nyllan V Irreg NOT WANT TO
nȳten N Neut BEAST, ANIMAL

ofer p (+ acc) OVER, UPON, THROUGHOUT, AGAINST, MORE THAN
(ge)offrian V Wk OFFER, SACRIFICE
offrung N Fem OFFERING
ofslēan V Irreg SLAY, KILL
ofslōg (1, 3 pret sg): see *ofslēan*
on p (+ dat/acc) ON, IN, INTO, AGAINST
ond: see *and*
onfēngon (pret pl): see *onfōn*
onfōn V Irreg (contracted) RECEIVE
ongēan p (+ dat/acc) TOWARDS, AGAINST
ongyrede (1, 3 pret sg): see *ongyrwan*
ongyrwan V Wk STRIP, DISROBE, UNDRESS
onmiddan p (+ dat) IN THE MIDST OF
onsendan V Wk SEND FORTH, GIVE UP
onstealde (1, 3 pret sg): see *onstellan*
onstellan V Wk CREATE, ESTABLISH, ORIGINATE
onwæcnan V St ARISE, BE BORN
onwōcon (pret pl): see *onwæcnan*
open Aj OPEN
ōr N Neut BEGINNING, ORIGIN
orcnēas N Masc PL MONSTERS, EVIL SPIRITS
Ōswold N Masc prop OSWALD
ōþer (1) e SECOND (2) Aj OTHER
oþ (þæt) cj UNTIL
oðð þæt: see *oþ þæt*
oþþe cj OR

Peohtas N Masc prop pl PICTS
pīnung N Fem TORMENT, PUNISHMENT

ræst N Fem REST, RESTING-PLACE
ramm N Masc RAM
reccan V Wk RELATE, GIVE AN ACCOUNT OF
rēhte (1, 3 pret sg): see *reccan*
rēoc Aj FIERCE, SAVAGE
reordberend N Masc SPEECHBEARER (= HUMAN)
rest N Fem REST, RESTING-PLACE
rēþe Aj VIOLENT, FIERCE
rīce N Neut KINGDOM
rīcsian V Wk REIGN, GOVERN
rīdan V St RIDE
ridon (pret pl): see *rīdan*
rihtlīce Av RIGHTEOUSLY

rīnan V Wk RAIN
rīnde (3 pret sg): see *rīnan*
rōd N Fem CROSS
Rōmanisc Aj ROMAN; *þā Rōmaniscan* THE ROMANS

sacan V St QUARREL
samod Av TOGETHER, ALSO, AS WELL
sandceosol N Masc SAND
sang N Masc SONG
(ge)sāwe (pret subj sg): see *(ge)sēon*
sāwol N Fem SOUL
(ge)sāwon (pret pl): see *(ge)sēon*
scacan V St SHAKE
sceal (1, 3 pres sg): see *sculan*
sceamu N Fem SHAME
scēap N Neut SHEEP
scēatas N Masc PL CORNERS, SURFACES
scēotan V St SHOOT
sceþþan V St HARM, INJURE
scieppan V St CREATE
Scieppend N Masc CREATOR
scieran V St CUT
scīnan V St SHINE
scip N Neut SHIP
sciprāp N Masc CABLE
scolde V Irreg (1, 3 pret sg) HAD TO
scoldon V Irreg (pret pl) HAD TO
scop N Masc POET, SINGER
scōp (1, 3 pret sg): see *scieppan*
Scotland on sǣ N Neut prop 'SCOTLAND ON SEA', i.e. the Irish Kingdom of
     Dalriada
scræf N Neut CAVE
scūfan V St PUSH
sculan V Irreg MUST, HAVE TO
sculon (pres pl): see *sculan*
Scyppend: see *Scieppend*
se, sē d THE, THAT (see further p. 73–4 above)
(ge)seah (1, 3 pret sg): see *(ge)sēon*
sealde (1, 3 pret sg): see *sellan*
sēaþ N Masc PIT, WELL
(ge)sēcan V Wk SEEK
secgan V Wk SAY
sele N Masc HALL
sēlest Aj (superlative of *gōd*)
self pn SELF
sellan V Wk GIVE (+ dat of person and acc of thing)
sēlra Aj (comparative of *gōd*)
sendan V Wk SEND
seofon e SEVEN
seofoþa e SEVENTH
(ge)sēon V St (contracted) SEE
sēoþan V St BOIL

gesettan V Wk SET, ESTABLISH
sīde N Fem SIDE
(ge)sīene Aj VISIBLE
sige N Masc VICTORY
sigehrēþig Aj VICTOR
simle Av CONTINUALLY
sinc N Neut TREASURE, ORNAMENT
sind(on) V Irreg (pres pl) ARE (see *bēon/wesan*)
singan V St SING
sittan V St SIT, SETTLE, STAY
sīþian V Wk GO, JOURNEY
siþþan Av AFTERWARDS, SINCE, THEN; cj AFTER, WHEN
(ge)slægen (past participle): see *(ge)slēan*
slǣp N Masc SLEEP
slǣpan V St SLEEP
(ge)slēan V St (contracted) KILL, SLAY
slege N Masc SLAYING
slōh (1, 3 pret sg): see *(ge)slēan*
(ge)sōhton (pret pl): see *(ge)sēcan*
sōna Av AT ONCE
sorg N Fem SORROW
sōþlīce Av TRULY
sprecan V St SPEAK
(ge)stāh (1, 3 pret sg): see *(ge)stīgan*
stān N Masc STONE
standan V St STAND
stede N Masc PLACE
stefn N Fem (1) VOICE
stefn N Masc (2) TRUNK, ROOT
stelan V St STEAL
(ge)stīgan V St MOUNT, ASCEND
stīþmōd Aj RESOLUTE, COURAGEOUS
stōd (1, 3 pret sg): see *standan*
stōdon (pret pl): see *standan*
stōw N Fem PLACE
strǣt N Fem ROAD
strang Aj STRONG
strengest Aj (superlative of *strang*)
strengra Aj (comparative of *strang*)
(ge)sundfull Aj HEALTHY
sunne N Fem SUN
sunu N Masc SON
swā Av SO, AS
swā swā cj AS, LIKE
swefan V St SLEEP
swefn N Neut DREAM, VISION
swēg N Masc SOUND, MUSIC
sweord N Neut SWORD
sweostor N Fem SISTER
swerian V St SWEAR
swilce Av LIKEWISE
swīþe Av VERY (MUCH)

swutol Aj CLEAR, MANIFEST
swȳþe: see *swīþe*
(ge)syhþ N Fem SIGHT, VISION
sylf: see *self*
syllic Aj WONDROUS, MARVELLOUS, WONDERFUL, UNUSUAL
symbel N Neut FEAST, BANQUET; *sym(b)le* = dat sg

talu N Fem TALE
tēode (1, 3 pret sg): see *tēon*
tēon V St (contracted) ADORN, CREATE
teran V St TEAR
(ge)timbrian V Wk BUILD
tō p (+ dat) TO
tōbærst (1, 3 pret sg): see *tōberstan*
tōberstan V St BREAK
torr N Masc TOWER
tōtǣron (pret pl): see *tōteran*
tōteran V St TEAR TO PIECES
tōwearp (1, 3 pret sg): see *tōweorpan*
tōweorpan V St OVERTHROW, DESTROY
tredan V St TREAD
trēow N Neut TREE, WOOD
getrymman V Wk STRENGTHEN, CONFIRM
tūcian V Wk ILL-TREAT
tūn N Masc 'TOWN', SETTLEMENT, etc
tunge N Fem TONGUE
twā e TWO

þā (1) Av THEN; (2) cj WHEN
þā þā cj WHEN
þā . . . þā . . . correlative cj THEN . . . WHEN . . .
þǣr Av THERE
þǣrrihte Av STRAIGHTAWAY
þæt cj THAT; also d
þanon Av THENCE, FROM THERE
þe pn WHO, WHICH, etc
þēah (þe) cj ALTHOUGH
þeg(e)n N Masc THANE, NOBLEMAN
þēos d THIS
þēow N Masc SERVANT
þīn pn YOUR(S)
þing N Masc THING
geþolian V Wk SUFFER, ENDURE
þrāg N Fem TIME
þrēo e THREE
þridda e THIRD
þū pn YOU (sg)
þūhte (3 pret sg): in *þūhte mē* IT SEEMED TO ME; see *þyncan*
þurfan V Irreg NEED
þurh p (+ acc) THROUGH, BY
þurhdrīfan V St DRIVE THROUGH, PIERCE
þurhdrifon (pret pl): see *þurhdrīfan*

þus Av THUS
þūsend e THOUSAND
þȳ instrumental form of *se* etc
þȳ lǣs (*þe*) cj LEST, UNLESS
þyncan V Wk SEEM
þȳstru N Fem DARKNESS

unc, uncer pn US TWO, OF US TWO
unfriþ N Masc STRIFE (lit. 'UN-PEACE')
unhǣlo N Fem EVIL, DESTRUCTION
unnan V Irreg (+ dat/gen), GRANT, ALLOW
untrum Aj WEAK, INFIRM
untȳdre N Masc EVIL PROGENY, EVIL BROOD
uppan p (+ dat) ON, UPON
ūrne pn OUR
ūs pn US
uton ij LET US
ūþe (1, 3 pret sg): see *unnan*

wæcnan V St WAKEN, ARISE, SPRING, BE BORN
wæfersȳn N Fem SHOW, SPECTACLE
wælfyllo N Fem FILL OF SLAUGHTER
wælhrēow Aj SAVAGE, CRUEL
wælnīð N Masc HOSTILITY, DEADLY HATE
wælsliht N Masc SLAUGHTER
wǣpen N Neut WEAPON
wǣron (pret pl): see *bēon/wesan*
wæs (1, 3 pret sg): see *bēon/wesan*
wæter N Neut WATER
wang N Masc PLAIN, FIELD, COUNTRY, PLACE
geweald N Neut POWER
weall N Masc WALL
Weard N Masc GUARDIAN
weardian V Wk GUARD, OCCUPY
(ge)weaxan V St GROW, INCREASE
wēnan V Wk (+ gen/acc) IMAGINE, BELIEVE
wendan V Wk TURN, GO
wendon (pret pl): see *wendan*
wēndon (pret pl): see *wēnan*
wēofod N Neut ALTAR
weorc N Neut WORK, DEED
weorpan V St THROW
weorþan V St BECOME
weorþian V Wk HONOUR
weorþmynd N Masc/Fem HONOUR
gewēox (1, 3 pret sg): see *(ge)weaxan*
wēpan V St WEEP
wer N Masc MAN
werg N Masc OUTLAW, CRIMINAL
werian V Wk DEFEND
werod N Neut TROOP, HOST
wesan: see *bēon/wesan*

wīc N Neut DWELLING-PLACE, ABODE
wīdcūþ Aj WIDELY KNOWN
wīde Av WIDELY
wīdsǣ N Masc/fem OPEN SEA
wier(re)st Aj (superlative of *yfel*)
wiersa Aj (comparative of *yfel*)
wīf N Neut WOMAN
wīg N Neut WAR, BATTLE
wiht N Fem CREATURE
wile: see *wille*
willan V Irreg WANT TO
wille V Irreg (1, 3 pres sg) WANT TO
wine N Masc FRIEND
winemǣg N Masc DEAR KINSMAN
winemāgas (pl): see *winemǣg*
gewinn N Neut STRIFE, BATTLE
winnan V St FIGHT
winter N Masc/Neut WINTER; in reckoning time, YEAR
wīs Aj WISE
wīsdōm N Masc WISDOM
wīse N Fem MANNER, WAY
witan V Irreg KNOW
wīte N Neut PUNISHMENT
wītega N Masc PROPHET
wiþ p (+ dat/acc) AGAINST
wiþstandan V St (+ DAT) WITHSTAND, RESIST
wlitebeorht Aj BEAUTIFUL
wolde V Irreg (1, 3 pret sg) WANTED TO
woldon V Irreg (pret pl) WANTED TO
wonsǣli(g) Aj UNHAPPY
wonsceaft N Fem MISERY
word N Neut WORD, SENTENCE, SPEECH
worhtan (pret pl, *sic*): see *(ge)wyrcan*
(ge)worhton (pret pl): see *(ge)wyrcan*
gewrǣc (1, 3 pret sg): see *wrecan*
wrecan V St AVENGE
wrēgan V Wk PERSECUTE
wrēon V St (contracted) COVER, HIDE
(ge)writ N Neut WRITING, LETTER
wrītan V St WRITE
wudu N Masc WOOD
Wuldorfæder N Masc GLORIOUS FATHER
wundor N Neut WONDER, MIRACLE
wunian V Wk LIVE, DWELL
wurdon (pret pl): see *weorþan*
wurþmynt N Masc/Fem HONOUR; see also *weorþmynd*
wylle V Irreg (1, 3 pres sg) WANT TO
wynn N Fem JOY
(ge)wyrcan V Wk MAKE
gewyrcean (infin): see *(ge)wyrcan*
Wyrtgeorn N Masc prop VORTIGERN

yfel Aj EVIL
yfelnyss N Fem EVIL-DOING, WICKEDNESS
ylca Aj SAME
yldo N Fem AGE, OLD AGE
ylfe N Masc PL ELVES
ymbclyppan V Wk CLASP, EMBRACE
Ypwines-flēot N Masc prop EBDSFLEET

Thematic Index

This index is not exhaustive. It is designed to give readers access to initial definitions of linguistic terms, and cross-refer them to the use of those terms in the descriptions of the various language-states. Thus the references are to definitions and to principal discussions of the category in question. References are given to Part I only.

The following abbreviations are commonly used here and elsewhere in this book: acc.: accusative; dat.: dative; EModE: Early Modern English; gen.: genitive; ME: Middle English; nom.: nominative; OE: Old English; PDE: Present-Day English; pl.: plural; sg.: singular